D1520494

DEMOCRACY AND AUTHORITARIANISM IN INDONESIA AND MALAYSIA

Democracy and Authoritarianism in Indonesia and Malaysia

The Rise of the Post-Colonial State

Syed Farid Alatas
Lecturer, Department of Sociology
National University of Singapore
Singapore

First published in Great Britain 1997 by
MACMILLAN PRESS LTD
Houndmills, Basingstoke, Hampshire RG21 6XS and London
Companies and representatives throughout the world

A catalogue record for this book is available from the British Library.

ISBN 0–333–71105–X

 First published in the United States of America 1997 by
ST. MARTIN'S PRESS, INC.,
Scholarly and Reference Division,
175 Fifth Avenue, New York, N.Y. 10010

ISBN 0–312–17661–9

Library of Congress Cataloging-in-Publication Data
Alatas, Farid, Syed.
Democracy and authoritarianism in Indonesia and Malaysia : the
rise of the post-colonial state / Syed Farid Alatas.
p.   cm.
Includes bibliographical references and index.
ISBN 0–312–17661–9 (cloth)
1. Indonesia—Politics and government—1950–1966.   2. Indonesia–
–Politics and government—1966–   3. Indonesia—Colonial influence.
4. Authoritarianism—Indonesia.   5. Malaysia—Politics and
government.   6. Malaysia—Colonial influence.   7. Democracy–
–Malaysia.   I. Title.
JQ776.A43 1997
320.9595'09'045—dc21   97–17009
                                                                                                    CIP

This book is printed on paper suitable for recycling and made from fully managed and
sustained forest sources.

10   9   8   7   6   5   4   3   2   1
06   05   04   03   02   01   00   99   98   97

Printed in Great Britain by
The Ipswich Book Company Ltd
Ipswich, Suffolk

To my parents
Syed Hussein Alatas and S. Zaharah Alatas
who give me much love, encouragement and support

Contents

List of Tables

Preface

This work on democratic and authoritarian post-colonial states is based on an historical study of the emergence of the dominant forces that shaped the types of regimes found in Malaysia and Indonesia. Both emerged as democratic post-colonial states. However, in Indonesia the democratic process was suspended altogether and after about a decade of independence, an authoritarian state emerged. Meanwhile, Malaysia still retains, comparatively speaking, a functioning democratic system. The contrast between Indonesia and Malaysia, then, is an opportunity to study the conditions under which democracy can be sustained in post-colonial states.

The study provides an empirical field on which to examine the origins of the post-colonial state. The Indonesian and Malaysian cases exemplify two paths that led to authoritarian and democratic states respectively. These cases offer two very different origins of post-colonial states upon which theoretical issues generated by the literature can be brought to bear. The reason for their selection is that the region consisting of what is today known as Indonesia and Malaysia was historically a cultural entity with similar notions of statecraft, religions and language. I will attempt to show that factors such as the level of economic development and modes of colonial administration, must be ruled out as explanations of different post-colonial state forms in these two countries.

This study, in searching for an alternative explanation, looks at how the interplay of three factors, that is, the elite cohesion, internal state strength and armed resistance, led to two different outcomes, that is, authoritarian and democratic post-colonial states.

Three conditions under which democracy can survive in post-colonial states, based on the experience of Malaysia and Indonesia, are (1) the absence of armed resistance against the state, (2) the presence of an internally strong state, and (3) a high degree of elite cohesion.

The imposition of colonialism upon the pre-capitalist societies of Malaysia and Indonesia left several classes and groups with competing interests in these countries upon formal independence. It is against this historical backdrop that the above factors are examined. It is held that the absence of armed resistance, the presence of an internally strong state and a high degree of elite cohesion led to democratic outcomes, as in Malaysia, while armed resistance in the context of a weak state and elite factionalism led to authoritarian outcomes, as in Indonesia. In this way, two different paths to state forms can be, as it were, mapped.

The theoretical perspective of this study, therefore, focuses on the class composition of the state and the dominant elite. Given that both Malaysia and Indonesia emerged as democratic post-colonial states, the reasons for the struggling persistence of democracy in one and its failure in the other have mainly to do with a relatively stronger state and a higher degree of elite cohesion in Malaysia as compared to Indonesia. In addition to regional instability and communist insurgency, the greatest opposition and obstacle to parliamentary democracy came from the elite itself in Indonesia. Democracy was introduced to Indonesia and Malaysia by the Europeans. In such circumstances, democracy can survive only if certain conditions are fulfilled. All three of the above conditions were fulfilled in Malaysia and Indonesia during and immediately following formal independence. However, in Indonesia a decade after independence, the internally weak state took its toll on democracy. The democratic phase of the Indonesian state failed to solve pressing economic problems and state elites were divided as to the course that should be taken. This culminated in the rise to power of anti-democratic forces. In Malaysia, the political elite were never divided to the extent that the democratic nature of the state was undermined for the long term.

The significance of this study lies in the fact that there has not been any comparative work done on the state in Malaysia and Indonesia. Furthermore, the few works on the state in the two countries tend to focus on issues not directly related to the question of the origins of the post-colonial state. Democracy in post-colonial states was introduced from without. What needs explanation is how and why democracy persisted in some post-colonial states and gave way to authoritarianism in others. This study is an effort in this direction.

Acknowledgements

An earlier version of this work took the form of a Ph.D. dissertation which was submitted in 1991 to the Department of Sociology, The Johns Hopkins University. I would like to express my gratitude to my doctoral committee consisting of Professors Christopher Chase-Dunn and Stephen Bunker for their comments, suggestions and criticisms. Professor Chase-Dunn as chairman was extremely helpful and encouraging during the various stages of this work.

I would also like to thank Professor Alejandro Portes who offered useful comments during an early stage of the project and Professor Andy Cherlin who was kind enough to advise me when I began postgraduate training at the Johns Hopkins University. Not to be forgotten are the non-academic staff of the University's Department of Sociology, Binnie, Shirley and Pam who provided much technical and moral support while I was at Hopkins.

The dissertation took its final form after I had joined the University of Malaya as a lecturer in 1989, where I was fortunate to have been able to discuss some points with Professors J. Kathirithamby-Wells and Lim Teck Ghee. I also wish to thank Professor K. S. Jomo who made the computer facilities of the Institute of Advanced Studies at the University available to me, and the staff of the Main Library at the University, for their very kind assistance. I would also like to thank Mr Julio Andrews, Asia Foundation, Kuala Lumpur, for a travel grant that enabled me to spend a couple of weeks on a field trip in Jakarta in June 1991.

The Department of Sociology, National University of Singapore, provided a conducive working environment while the dissertation was being turned into this book. Also, of great help to me was Ms Dahlia Shamsuddin at the Reference and Information Services, as well as other library staff at the Central Library, National University of Singapore.

I owe a special debt of gratitude to my parents and to Babsy for their enthusiasm and many forms of support throughout my period of study and after.

Finally, I wish to thank my wife Mojgan, who provided much encouragement over many years, and whose love and optimism has sustained me through the years. The arrival of our children, Imad and Afra, has only enhanced the atmosphere of delight and joy in which I work.

SYED FARID ALATAS

1 Post-colonial Discourse on the State in Indonesia and Malaysia

THE STATE IN INDONESIA AND MALAYSIA

The fact that the Malaysian state has managed to maintain a relatively democratic regime, while an authoritarian regime came to power in Indonesia has never been the focus of historical and comparative analysis despite certain cultural, social, and historical affinities between these two countries. This work explains this difference in terms of contrasting class structures and alliances and also examines differences in political challenges to the Indonesian and Malaysian states from popular forces.

The state has been defined in narrow as well as in broad terms. On the one hand, it has been defined in terms of specific institutions such as the judiciary or the executive of the government. On the other hand, the state has been referred to as consisting of the various institutional aspects of a political system without any concrete structures identified. This study employs a definition that adopts the middle ground between these two extremes. A broader understanding of the state is combined with the specification of concrete structures. The state, then, is understood as an established organization which exercises coercive authority over the members of society. The management and control of society by the state includes the creation of laws or legislation, the administering of law by the judiciary, and the managing of external and internal security, welfare and justice by the government. Therefore, the state has its legislative, judicial and executive branches which take on different forms in different states. In this study, the state is also understood in terms of its relationship vis-à-vis the means of production which includes control, domination, and ownership.

The democratic state is defined as one in which (1) the posts of the executive are elective, (2) political parties are prominent and their members can be elected to representative bodies such as parliament, (3) there is genuine competition among opposing political parties for votes, (4) elections are honestly conducted, (5) it is civilians which are prominent in the political process, and (6) there is a separation of powers

1

such that the executive of the state is itself subject to the law. In a democratic state, it should be possible for the majority of the people to change their government through the electoral system should they so desire.

The authoritarian state is defined, first negatively, as one in which the above traits of democracy are absent, or if they are present, are shams. In the modern world there are several types of authoritarian states that include fascist, totalitarian, and military states and dictatorships. The kind of authoritarian state that concerns us here is what various scholars have referred to as the bureaucratic polity, bureaucratic–authoritarian, and bureaucratic–capitalist state, which is dominated by both civilian and military bureaucrats and in which democratic procedures are purely formal or non-existent.[1] In other words, if the majority of the people wish to change their government they could not do so except by force.

The Malaysian and Indonesian post-colonial states as they exist today are examples of democratic and authoritarian states respectively. Objections are likely to be raised to the characterization of the Malaysian state as democratic. As we shall see below, some have referred to the state in Malaysia as being authoritarian or neither democratic nor authoritarian. As a result, some questions may be raised concerning the comparability of the two cases of Indonesia and Malaysia. The justification for comparison in the present study arises from the fact that while democratically-elected government existed in the early post-colonial period in both countries, the transition to an institutionalized, consolidated democratic regime[2] did not take place in Indonesia. This, of course, raises the question as to whether such a transition took place in Malaysia to warrant our attempt at comparison. A meaningful comparative analysis can be made only if, amidst the overall similarities between the two cases, crucial differences can be identified that may explain differences in the outcome of regime types. But such a method is valid only if it is accepted that the outcomes are different, that is, there are differences in the phenomenon to be explained to begin with. If one takes the view that both Indonesia and Malaysia are authoritarian states, the historical comparative method resorted to would be very different from the one attempted in this study. Therefore, it is necessary to justify the designation of Malaysia as a democratic state.

While it can be conceded that the Malaysian state does not live up to the standards of Western liberal democracies, nor does it aspire to, it is a system in which democratic procedures and institutions distinguish it qualitatively from the regime in Indonesia. Here Aron's discussion on the nature of democracies is insightful. All regimes whether democratic or authoritarian are oligarchic in nature. The essence of politics is such that decisions are taken for and not by the community. Popular sovereignty should not be taken to mean that the people are directly involved in decision making.[3] If every regime masks an oligarchy, how are democracies distinguished from authoritarian regimes? Important distinctions lie in the manner in which power is wielded, the rules according to which the dominant minority governs, and the extent to which the ruling minority is open, and the means by which they are selected. The political system is more democratic to the extent that the ruling minorities of the regime are open for entry by way of democratic procedures. Along these lines of argument it is fair to say that Malaysia, in comparison to liberal democracies, is corrupted by too much oligarchy, which is not to say that it is an authoritarian state. Instead, relatively free elections give power to representatives of privileged minorities.

While it may be true that democratic procedures would only be adhered to as long as the ruling elite maintain their positions of power and continue to advance their ideal and material interests,[4] the conditions under which this is so must be explained and this is to be done in comparison to the Indonesian case. At this point, a brief note on the political structures of Indonesia and Malaysia would be in order.

The Malaysian form of state is a federated constitutional monarchy, with an executive consisting of a prime minister and a cabinet. The national legislature consists of a bicameral federal parliament. The Senate (Dewan Negara) has 68 members, of whom 26 are elected from the state legislatures and 42 are appointed by the king. The House of Representatives (Dewan Rakyat) has 180 members who are directly elected. The Dewan Negara has a six-year term of office while the Dewan Rakyat has a five-year term. There are also 13 state governments with their own State Councils or cabinets and legislatures.

Since independence in 1957 general elections have been held regularly, the first being in August 1959. Subsequently, elections were held in 1964, 1969, 1974, 1978, 1982, 1986, 1990 and 1995. The post-independence of Malaysia has seen three consecutive changes of heads of government and eight general elections.[5] Throughout this period civilian authority in the state has been the rule. Nevertheless, the democratic nature of the state must be understood with certain qualifications, to be discussed in the next section. What exists in Malaysia is more than the mere form of democracy. It differs qualitatively from authoritarian states, Indonesia included. Opposition as well as government parties exist at the national as well as regional levels.

Apart from an almost two-year period of 'suspended democracy' following racial riots after the 1969 elections, parliamentary democracy has functioned continuously. Whatever the causes of the suspension of democracy were (to be discussed in Chapter 6) they did not operate sufficiently long enough nor were they severe enough to result in the appearance of a non-democratic state.

Apart from the existence of opposition parties and the frequency of general elections (in the 1970s and in 1990 there were cases of opposition parties winning elections and forming state governments in some states of Malaysia), another aspect of democracy in Malaysia has been the separation of powers, by which is meant the independence of the judiciary from the government. Some examples can be cited. There have been several important court cases that have gone against the government. In February 1987 the court granted a writ of habeas corpus to an Internal Security Act (ISA) detainee which was upheld by the Supreme Court in November. In September the Home Ministry was ordered by the court to allow the social protest group, Aliran, to publish their periodical in the Malay language (they had already been publishing in English). Yet another example is the ruling of the High Court and Supreme Court in favour of the plaintiff, Lim Kit Siang (leader of a major opposition party, the Democratic Action Party), 'in granting an injunction against United Engineers Malaysia signing a lucrative contract with the government to build and operate a long stretch of the north-south highway'.[6] In February 1988 UMNO (United Malays National Organization – the dominant party of the ruling coalition) was declared illegal by the High Court due to certain irregularities surrounding the UMNO party elections in April of the previous year. These are just some examples among many.

The compromise of the independence of the judiciary by the suspension of the Lord President Tun Mohamed Salleh Abas as well as the dismissal of three Supreme Court judges is certainly a chapter in the decline of democracy in Malaysia.[7] Nevertheless, there are also numerous examples which indicate a slow expansion of civil society. For example, since the formation of the National Advisory Council for the Integration of Women in Development (NACIWD) in 1976 and the establishment of the Women's Secretariat (HAWA) in 1983, several non-governmental organizations (NGOs) have been set up in Malaysia. These NGOs are all concerned with improving the status of women in Malaysia but express this concern in different ways. Some are involved in the exchange and dissemination of information and research materials on various problems such as health, reproductive rights, and domestic violence. Others are more active in raising public awareness of issues concerning women. Yet others are more practice-oriented and provide counselling, training and shelter for women.

It should be obvious that the Malaysian state has a number of features which set it apart from Third World authoritarian regimes which tend to be totalitarian, military-dominated, one-party systems, or bureaucratic authoritarian. The regularity of general elections, universal suffrage, and the legal existence of opposition parties coexist with a powerful state which derives legitimacy from the functioning of democratic institutions but which continues to play a dominant role in structuring politics and social life.[8] The quasi-, semi- or statist democratic nature of the Malaysian state should not allow one to labour under the impression that democracy is merely a facade. Furthermore, it is not being argued here that the Malaysian state is a liberal democracy, simply that it is more democratic than Indonesia.

Turning to Indonesia, the situation there can be seen to be quite different. The form of state is a presidential government. The national legislature, the Majlis Permusyawaratan Rakyat (MPR) consists of all 500 members of the House of People's Representatives (Dewan Perwakilan Rakyat, DPR) and 500 appointed members. The MPR meets every five years to elect the president and vice-president. Four hundred members of the DPR are elected while 100 are appointed by the president as representatives of the armed forces.[9]

Sovereignty was transferred from the Dutch to the Indonesians in 1949. The general view is that there was a period of parliamentary democracy lasting from 1949 till 1957. However, following Goh,[10] if we exclude those periods of nominated parliaments and cabinets, the liberal democracy period consisted of just 13 months of elected government (March 1956 – April 1957). From 1949 to 1957, there was a constant change of cabinets and government coalitions.[11] By 1952, under the Wilopo cabinet, severe criticisms from the enemies of Wilopo and the use by politicians of military officers to undermine the Minister of Defence led to a petition from military leaders with the permission of the cabinet asking for the dissolution of parliament and new elections. This was refused by President Sukarno and led to open mutiny in three of seven army divisions against army headquarters. Wilopo finally resigned in July 1953 after a vote of no confidence.[12] In September 1955 Indonesia's first parliamentary elections were held. However, in 1956, the Ali cabinet faced a military conspiracy in West Java as well as a series of revolts in Sumatra, Kalimantan and Sulawesi. In the face of regional revolts and hostile government coalition partners the Ali cabinet resigned in March 1957.

The Ali cabinet was the first and last Indonesian cabinet to be set up on the basis of free elections. 1957 saw the beginning of the era of Guided Democracy in which the president and the army played active and prominent roles. Under this system Masyumi (Majlis Syura Muslimin Indonesia – a progressive Muslim Party) and the PSI (Indonesian Socialist Party) were outlawed due to their support for democracy. Furthermore, the monopoly of political parties in political representation was broken. Half the seats in parliament were allocated to functional groups (*golongan karya*) which were formed on the basis of occupation and special status. The military occupied seats in legislative assemblies as one of the functional groups. Sukarno was elected president-for-life.[13]

As the Indonesian economy collapsed in the early 1960s, a series of events including armed rebellions culminated in the rise to power of General Suharto who set up an anti-communist cabinet and placed Sukarno under house arrest.

Under Suharto's New Order (Orde Baru), which commenced in 1967 and continues to this day, functional groups and parties were merged under one government party, Golkar. Only two opposition parties were allowed – the Development Unity Party (PPP) which was formed from the merger of four Muslim parties, and the Indonesian Democratic Party (PDI) formed from the merger of three secular parties and two Christian parties.[14] The 1971 elections were the first to be held since 1955 after which there were five more in 1977, 1982, 1987, 1992 and 1997.[15] The last presidential elections were held in 1993 with Suharto currently serving his sixth presidential term. Genuine political contestation was checked by the government's management and control of the electoral system. Suharto himself had said that the country did not need opposition party politics as Indonesian politics was based upon consultation and consensus, both of which were provided for in the constitution and the pancasila.[16] Laws pertaining to the electoral process and political parties favour Golkar. For example, criticizing government policies during the election campaigns is prohibited.[17] In addition to this, from the early 1980s the Indonesian government required all parties and social organizations, including those in the opposition to adopt the Indonesian state doctrine, *pancasila,* as the 'sole principle' (*asas tunggal*).[18]

Most important of all is the People's Consultative Assembly (MPR – Majlis Permusyawaratan Rakyat), the highest constitutional body in the country. According to Indonesian law the 500 seats in the MPR are awarded partly by government appointment and partly according to the results of the last general election. Nevertheless, all members must be approved by the government regardless of whether they were elected or not.[19] Golkar has always been able to obtain more than 60 per cent of the vote in the last six general elections.[20] In addition to this its allies in the armed forces and government appointed regional representatives must be taken into account.[21] As mentioned above, the MPR is responsible for the selection of the president and vice-president for a five-year term.

Apart from the severe curtailment of the electoral process and the dominance of the MPR over politics by law, the independence of the judiciary is also restricted. While the minister of justice is a civilian, the attorney general is an army general, and it is he who decides whether someone is prosecuted or detained without trial. Generally, political crimes are seen to endanger national security and if such cases are brought to trial they are handled by a military tribunal.[22] The military, therefore, is not only conspicuous in the executive and legislative branches of government but also in the judiciary. The prominence of the military in government may impose limits on the growth of civil society if the military mentality dominates government as well. The military mind is dogmatic and emphasizes group conformity, discipline, and the blind acceptance of authority. The discussion of issues by the public, the consideration of policy alternatives, and reflection are hallmarks of democratic societies but are at odds with organizations run along military lines.[23]

A quick overview of democratic and authoritarian tendencies in Southeast Asia may serve to underline the significance of the current study on Indonesia and Malaysia. Democratic forms of rule do not automatically accompany the development of capitalism. This is particularly true of the Third World where various forms of authoritarianism are prevalent.

THE PRECARIOUS NATURE OF DEMOCRACY IN SOUTHEAST ASIA

There has been much discussion on democratization in some of the developing nations of Southeast Asia. During the last 25 years or so some 30 countries around the world made transitions from authoritarian to democratic governments. What are the prospects for such transitions in the region?

The initial period of Filipino democracy lasted from independence from the United States in 1946 to 1972 when martial law was declared by the late President Marcos, ostensibly to enable the government to embark uninterruptedly on a course of development planning. Democracy was re-established in the Philippines as a result of the toppling of Marcos. Nevertheless, democracy in the Philippines is seen to be fragile. As noted by former President Corazon Aquino, traditional political institutions are alone insufficient to preserve democracy. In 1972, Congress and the courts could not save democracy (*source*: Straits Times, 21 June 1993).

Democracy in Malaysia has been in place since independence from the British in 1957. Some have referred to the political system in Malaysia as a quasi- or semi-democracy because of the presence of certain anti-democratic elements such as the abolishment of local-level polls and the Internal Security Act (ISA). Nevertheless, apart from a brief interregnum of non-democratic rule from 1969 to 1971 after racial rioting broke out, Malaysia has enjoyed eight general elections, changes in heads of government, and a certain degree of freedom of expression. A good example of the latter is the presence of opposition party newspapers that are fairly critical of the government.

Thailand is a state that seems to oscillate between democracy and authoritarianism. In 1932, the King of Thailand became a constitutional monarch and the government came under the effective control of military and civilian bureaucrats. In 1973 the Thais began to experiment with democracy. But this experiment was terminated by a military coup in 1976. The first elected government in Thailand after this period was that of Prime Minister Chatichai Choonhavan who came to office in 1988. But conflicts between politicians and the military led to another coup in February 1991. After the elections of March 1992, the Thai public expected the leader of the party with the most votes to assume the office of Prime Minister. What happened instead was that the military was able to manipulate the situation and install General Suchinda Kraprayoon as the new Prime Minister. Such a violation of democratic norms led to mass protests and a bloody crackdown on pro-democracy demonstrators by the military. These pro-democracy forces were eventually to topple the Suchinda government in May 1992. The government of Chuan Leekpai remained in power till the elections and the democratically-elected government of the caretaker Prime Minister, Banharn Silpa-archa, was installed in July 1995.

Indonesia had practised parliamentary democracy for about a decade since independence from the Dutch in 1949. The imposition by Sukarno of 'Guided Democracy' in 1957 marked the beginning of the decline of party politics. Amidst regional separatism and Dutch neo-colonialism Sukarno and the army operated under martial law. In 1965, the confrontation between the Communist Party of Indonesia (PKI) and the army led to the destruction of the PKI, the massacre of thousands of PKI supporters by the army, and the eroding of Sukarno's powers. In March 1966 Sukarno handed over authority to the commander of the army, General Suharto, who was eventually proclaimed President of the 'New Order' state in 1968.

In both Indonesia and Thailand, politics has tended to be dominated by military and civilian bureaucrats rather than political parties and other interest groups. There is also a close business relationship between the military–civilian bureaucracy on the one hand and the private sector on the other. For example, a leading bureaucrat may become a director in a certain corporation, thereby assuring this corporation of obtaining official licences, contracts, and other business opportunities. The military in these countries are also involved in business due to the need for 'unconventional financing'. Senior military officers would be placed in positions of control of giant corporations to raise funds on behalf of the military, while official military budgets were kept very small. Thailand also has secret army funds which possibly originate from business relations with the private sector.

THE PROCESS OF DEMOCRATIZATION

There has been much talk of democratization in Southeast Asia. Many observers speak of change away from states controlled by military and civilian bureaucrats to states led by democratically-elected political parties, with certain levels of freedom of expression and the public accountability of governments. What we actually see in some countries of the region is not democratization in terms of the implantation of Westminster-style parliamentary democracies, but rather the triumph of elements of democracy and some expansion of civil society.

During the 1970s and 1980s, the developing countries that made the transition to democratic forms of government were overwhelmingly Catholic. This group of countries includes several Latin American countries as well as the Philippines.

In the last few years, both Thai and Filipino politics have witnessed an expansion of civil society in terms of the rise of the importance of pressure groups that are so important for the consolidation of democracy. Pressure groups in a democracy seek to influence public policy and the political process through lobbying legislators. While lobbying has not become entrenched in the politics of these countries, recent events have shown that forces that lie outside of the government do have an effect on government. In Thailand, people from various NGOs, the business community, and academic institutions banded together to form an electoral watch organization to oversee the elections of March 22nd, 1992. In the Philippines, NGOs played similar roles in the 1986 and 1992 elections. What the participation of these groups shows is not only the commitment of citizens to democracy but also the presence of restraining influences on anti-democratic tendencies in government.

Another important element of democracy concerns the independence and authority of the judicial system. In Indonesia, questions have been raised in public regarding the position of the law in society. In December 1992, Supreme Court Judge H. Purwoto S. Gandasubrata lamented in his opening address at a law seminar that the authority of and obedience to the law is far from a reality in Indonesia, adding that the law has come to be an object of play. This is not the first time that this issue has been raised, but it is significant that it was raised most recently by Purwoto, who is head of the Supreme Court. Even more interesting is the reversing of the 1994 ban on *Tempo* magazine. In a landmark judgement, the Jakarta Administrative Court ruled that the revoking of *Tempo*'s licence by Information Minister Harmoko contradicted several Indonesian laws. The Administrative Court had been recently set up with the task of protecting the Indonesian public from the arbitrary exercise of power.

Some observers said that prospects for the expansion of democracy in Malaysia had become bright after 1993 with the agreement of the Malay Rulers to endorse amendments to the constitution which seek to remove their personal immunity. In the media, various individuals and groups had raised the point that it is not only the Rulers that are to be held accountable for their actions but also the executive branch of the state. The move to strip the Rulers of their immunity is seen to ensure the preservation of the monarchy. Apart from this, it has consequences that extend beyond the question of the Rulers themselves. It serves to highlight the issues of the abuse of the law by any public servant and the idea that nobody occupies a position higher than that of the Constitution.

LEADERSHIP SUCCESSION

What are the prospects for more meaningful transitions from authoritarian to democratic governments in the region?

The upheavals of the second half of the 1980s and leading into the 1990s in Eastern Europe and the former Soviet Union gave rise to the now familiar terms of *glasnost* and *perestroika*. More importantly, these events had the world thinking that a wave of democracy was sweeping our planet. A notable example of the transition to democracy is in South Africa where efforts had been underway not only to completely dismantle apartheid but also to create a non-racial democratic system. Closer to home is the granting of more civil liberties in South Korea by the country's first civilian head of state since 1961, Mr Kim Young Sam, who in 1994 granted amnesty to more than 40 000 dissidents or prisoners. In the region itself the Philippines made the transition to democracy in 1986 upon ousting the late Ferdinand Marcos. There has been much talk of democratization in Indonesia and Thailand, two states in which the military have prominent roles in the political process.

Closely related to the issue of the transition to democracy and the growth of civil society is that of leadership succession. The way in which political leaders succeed each other in office is vital to the existence of a functioning democracy. In highly authoritarian regimes political leaders seem to be unremovable from office except through violent means. What distinguishes democratic from authoritarian leaders are the norms that determine how the former come to power. As far as the future of democracy and civil society in Southeast Asia are concerned two points must be mentioned. One is that many cases of political succession come about as a result of force or violence. Secondly, such violence typically involves military participation and take-overs. Let us consider each of these two points.

The means of political succession in Brunei, Malaysia and Singapore are well defined and clear-cut. In Brunei there has been only one instance of succession where the present Sultan succeeded his father to the throne. In Malaysia and Singapore constitutional provisions for elections have consistently determined the manner of succession. Filipinos experienced 15 years of authoritarian rule under Marcos before they revolted in February 1986 and established a functioning democracy. In the first presidential elections of the post-Marcos era held in 1992, Corazon Aquino was succeeded by Fidel Ramos. But the orderly succession of leaders via elections is not the norm in other countries of the region.

In Thailand succession often came about as a result of coups, while in Indonesia, leadership succession took place only once. President Sukarno, the man who proclaimed Indonesia's independence in 1945, was overthrown in 1965. Power passed into the hands of the army commander of the time, General Suharto. Since then the People's Consultative Assembly (MPR), with a strong army representation, has continuously endorsed Suharto as president, the most recent occasion being in March 1993.

Although Myanmar obtained independence in 1948 it was not until 1962 that the armed forces took over the state machinery by means of a coup d'état. In 1974 the military handed over power to civilian leaders who were in fact ex-military high-ranking officers who consolidated a one-party socialist system. In September 1988, amidst an economic crisis and mass malcontent the military stepped in and resumed state power.

In the cases of Thailand, Indonesia and Myanmar political succession must be seen in the context of the domination of government by the military. In these states civilians share political power with military bureaucrats. Political power and decision making is located in the bureaucracy that comprises the military, the police, and the civil administration. There is much less of a role played by political parties and civil society organizations. Bureaucrats participate extensively in economic activities and enter into various forms of partnership with the private sector. The military as well as individual military personnel have shares in both state-run and private concerns and are therefore major players in the accumulation of capital. Military bureaucrats are also very prominent in administration. In Indonesia, for example, many governmental departments, provinces and districts are headed by military men.

The role of the military in political succession and their subsequent control over the machinery of government serves to counter any democratic tendencies that may be felt in such countries. Democratization in Southeast Asia, therefore, will be limited to the extent that the military mentality is dominant in our lives. And we can be confident that it will continue to be dominant in the region for some time to come. Political succession has often brought military regimes to power both in countries oriented to capitalism and private enterprise such as Thailand and Indonesia as well as the socialist developing nations of the region such as Vietnam and Myanmar. Even Thailand, which is currently in its democratic phase after the ousting of General Suchinda in 1992, must remain aware of the threat of the return of the military to power at the expense of democracy. In Myanmar the National Convention had been discussing a new charter that would convert Myanmar into a democratic state. But this new charter is said to give the *tatmadaw* (military) a prominent role in politics. Myanmar's powerful military intelligence chief, Lieutenant-General Khin Nyunt, is also the First Secretary of the ruling State Law and Order Restoration Council (SLORC). It would be interesting to observe how the military in Myanmar is going to have a leadership role in politics in the context of a multi-party democratic system. A boost to the democratic movement in Myanmar was received with the release of Burmese activist and Nobel Peace Prize winner Aung San Suu Kyi in July 1995.

Thus, there is no clear future for democracy and civil society in Southeast Asia. A complete transition to democracy as found in advanced industrialized nations is unlikely. This would require fundamental changes in the political cultures, economies, and politics of these countries. What we are witnessing in the region, however, are tendencies that create enclaves of democracy which may help to socialize men and women to life in a society that is more tolerant of differences and, therefore, freer.

The predominance of authoritarian military-dominated regimes in the region suggests that there is a need to explain the conditions under which democracies can emerge and attain a degree of stability and identify the forces of democratization.

THE STATE IN INDONESIAN AND MALAYSIAN STUDIES

Studies of the state in Indonesia and Malaysia in particular, and the Third World in general, can be divided into at least four aspects.

The first concerns the issue of democratization in the post-colonial period,[24] as opposed to the question of the origins and rise of the post-colonial state. In these studies, the prospects for democracy are discussed. An increasing number of such works began to appear after the fall of communism in the former Soviet Union and Eastern Europe. Democratization has received far greater attention in Indonesia and is carried out at a more empirical and concrete level than in Malaysia. For example, there have been discussions looking at the broad and theoretical issue of the relationship between democracy and civil society in Malaysia or the attempt to understand democratization in Malaysia in terms of a Foucauldian approach.[25] This is not to say that there are no discussions on democratization in Malaysia of a more empirical nature.[26] Nevertheless, there are very few works that address the issue of democratization in Malaysia when compared to Indonesia. Works on democratization in Indonesia are both of a general and specific nature.

There are writings discussing general trends in democratization.[27] There are also works discussing the specifics of democratization with respect to the military, grassroots organizations, parliament, the government party Golkar, and so on.[28]

The second aspect of the state that has been the object of attention in Indonesian and Malaysian studies is that of its role in the process of development and the relationship between the state on the one hand, and capital and labour on the other.[29] The state in developing societies is an important determinant of what men and women wish to and can achieve. This is no less true when it comes to the management of economic development. While many are uninterested in the activities of the state, nobody remains unaffected by it. State power is unceasingly wielded in the name of economic development and there are various roles that the state plays in this area, which can be listed as follows: (1) provision of infrastructure, (2) transfer of income, (3) research and development, (4) regulation of the economy, (5) formation of state-owned enterprises, and (6) advancement of the private interests of state officials.

The provision of social and economic infrastructure such as electricity, water, sanitation, roads and communications helps to facilitate economic activities and is a basic function of any state. The state may step in to redress the problem of income inequality through the instrumentality of transfer payments which include subsidies, grants and welfare payments. The state may also fund basic scientific and technological research.

But beyond these, the state can play a more involved role in the process of economic development through the regulation of the economy by means of various monetary and fiscal policies as well as a host of other development policies that involve exchange rate and wage controls, industrial licensing, investment incentives and immigration quotas.

For a variety of reasons the state may find it necessary to be directly involved in capital accumulation through the formation of state-owned enterprises which are public corporations owned and operated by the government.[30]

Beyond the above-mentioned roles there is also what we may refer to as the corrupt role of the state in the process of economic development. This refers to the role that state officials play in advancing their private material interests which takes its toll on economic development.[31]

Most of the works on the role of the state in the process of development in Indonesia and Malaysia discuss the regulation of the economy, the formation of state-owned enterprises, and the advancement of the private interests of state officials.

The third aspect of the state that is discussed in works on Indonesia and Malaysia and the Third World in general is the nature of democracy and authoritarianism. The various theoretical perspectives that attempt to understand the characteristics and workings of the state in the Third World can be divided into three broad categories, that is, those dealing with (1) types of democracies, (2) types of authoritarian states, and (3) transystemic types.

The variety of democratic systems that have been noted in the literature include consociational democracy, liberal corporatism and communitarian democracy.[32] The types of authoritarian systems discussed include the state capitalist regimes of dependent economies,[33] the bureaucratic polity[34] and the bureaucratic–authoritarian state.[35] Finally, there are works on transystemic systems, that is, systems which are found in both democracies and authoritarian states. This includes the theory of relative autonomy associated with Alavi and others who write on post-colonial states and the theory of kleptocracy.[36]

In the case of Indonesia, what is commonly discussed is the nature of pancasila democracy. These works are generally concerned with the genesis and various meanings attached to the term.[37] Another set of writings is on the nature of the military–bureaucratic regime which seek to conceptualize and describe the workings of the military–bureaucratic political machinery in Indonesia.[38] Afan Gaffar understands the nature of the New Order Indonesian state in terms of the notion of the hegemonic party system which is characterized by a repressive security apparatus, the depoliticization of the masses, the emasculation of political parties, and the implementation of electoral laws that guarantee victory for the government party, Golkar.[39]

While the authoritarian nature of the Indonesian state is not a controversial subject, there is some disagreement over the nature of the Malaysian state. According to von Vorys, Malaysian democracy lacks a 'broad normative consensus found in Western democracies' but is founded on consensus at the elite level which he terms a constitutional contract among command groups.[40]

The presence of traditional authoritarian elements as well as certain anti-democratic features such as the Internal Security Act, and the abolishment of local-level polls in 1971 have led some to characterize the Malaysian state as a 'quasi-democracy' that has only been partially successful in applying Western democratic standards.[41] For Hua, bourgeois democracy was limited and juridical equality compromised for various reasons including the opposition of the Malay Rulers and the need to contain non-Malay dissent.[42]

Crouch, on the other hand, prefers to think of the Malaysian state in terms of modified authoritarianism rather than modified democracy due to post-1969 authoritarian features such as the use of the ISA, laws restricting the scope of public debate such as the Seditions Act, the lack of democratic values in the judiciary, and the control of the press. While it cannot be denied that these restrictions are in place, I would say that Crouch's argument that 'Malaysia's democratic institutions have been little more than a facade disguising effective authoritarian rule'[43] is rather exaggerated in light of the fact that, especially between 1957 and 1969, opposition party newspapers, a relatively open media, some degree of political contestation, some trade union freedom, and academic freedom, have all served to distinguish Malaysia from Indonesia. Elsewhere, Crouch has characterized the Malaysian state as neither democratic nor authoritarian but as having both democratic and authoritarian elements.[44] It would be more fruitful to bring in the concept of oligarchy to qualify our understanding of democracy in Malaysia, as was attempted above.

The fourth aspect of the state that is discussed in post-colonial Indonesian and Malaysian studies, which is also the focus of this work, is the formation and stability of democratic and authoritarian post-colonial states. There are very few works of this nature. Furthermore, they tend not to be theoretically informed by the literature on peripheral states and post-colonial state formation and are generally descriptive. Those few attempts to explain the rise of the post-colonial state in these two countries are referred to in the next chapter on theories of post-colonial and peripheral state formation as well as in later chapters.

POST-COLONIAL STATE FORMATION: INDONESIA AND MALAYSIA

In the theoretical perspective that I have adopted, I focus on variations in elite cohesion, the internal strength of the state, and armed resistance against the state on post-colonial state forms.

The theoretical perspective of this study focuses on the class composition of the state and the dominant elite. It looks at how the interplay of three factors, that is, elite cohesion, the internal strength of the state, and armed resistance against the state, led to two different outcomes, that is, authoritarian and democratic post-colonial states. The historical background is presented by way of an introduction to the different ways in which pre-capitalist systems and colonial domination

The State in Indonesia and Malaysia 17

interacted in British Malaya and the Netherlands East Indies. In other words, understanding the differential impact of colonialism on pre-capitalist society in these two colonies provides some insight into the origins and nature of their respective post-colonial state structures, class make-ups, and the bases for urban and rural resistance against the state. In this way, two different paths to state forms can be, as it were, mapped.

Given that both Malaysia and Indonesia emerged as democratic post-colonial states, the reasons for the failure of democracy in one and its persistence in the other have mainly to do with the greater degree of cohesion of the Malaysian elite as opposed to that of the Indonesian. In addition to regional instability and communist insurgency, the greatest opposition and obstacle to parliamentary democracy came from within the state itself in Indonesia. Democracy was implanted in Indonesia and Malaysia from without. In such circumstances, democracy can survive only if certain conditions are fulfilled. There should be little or no armed and mass resistance to the democratic programme and the state, the state should be internally strong, and there should be a high degree of elite cohesion. All three of these conditions were fulfilled in Malaysia and Indonesia during and immediately following formal independence. However, in Indonesia a decade after independence, the internally weakened state proved to be detrimental for democracy. In its democratic phase the Indonesian state was unable to adequately deal with economic problems and state elites were divided over policy. This resulted in anti-democratic forces gaining control over the state. In Malaysia, while there were also economic problems encountered by the state, the ruling elites were not divided to the extent that the democratic nature of the state was threatened and the dominant class continued to support the state.

This study proceeds as follows. Chapter 1 has introduced the subject matter of the study, discussing the definitions of democratic and authoritarian states and how they apply to the cases of Indonesia and Malaysia. There has also been a discussion of the state in Indonesian and Malaysian studies. In Chapter 2, theoretical perspectives on state formation are discussed, some of which are specifically directed to the issues of authoritarianism and democracy in Indonesia and Malaysia. In this chapter the theoretical perspective employed in this study is introduced. Chapter 3 begins with a brief discussion on the Malay–Indonesian Archipelago as a Muslim cultural entity which contained similar world-views, and notions of power and authority. This is followed by an overview of the economy and society in the pre-independence

Malay–Indonesian world covering the regions that today comprise Malaysia and Indonesia. It is divided into two parts. The first deals with pre-capitalist modes of production. The second part deals with colonial economy and society. This chapter provides an historical backdrop to the study of the role of the peasantry and the dominant classes in post-colonial state formation. Chapter 4 is about peasants and mass movements and discusses the degree to which Malay and Indonesian peasants were actors in the anti-colonial movements and in the post-colonial state. Indonesia differs from Malaysia with respect to the far greater incidences of armed rebellions and separatist movements. Chapter 5 goes on to discuss the development of the nationalist impulse in British Malaya and the Netherlands Indies and its culmination in democracy in Malaya and Indonesia. Highlighted are the differences in the internal strength of the state between Malaya and Indonesia. Chapter 6 turns to the post-independence period and addresses the issue of why democracy persisted in Malaysia but gave way to authoritarianism in Indonesia, stressing differences in elite cohesion. This is done within the context of discussions of the role of the state in the mobilization of private domestic as well as state capital. Finally, the last chapter summarizes the main conclusions and discusses various theoretical implications.

2 Theories of Democratic and Authoritarian State Formation

APPROACHES TO THE STUDY OF DEMOCRACY AND AUTHORITARIANISM

For the purposes of reviewing works on post-colonial state formation in general, it would be convenient to adopt a taxonomy that divides the study of the state in terms of three analytic approaches, the psychological, cultural, and structural. In the course of discussing these perspectives some remarks will also be made on attempts to explain democracy and authoritarianism in Indonesia and Malaysia.

The psychological approach draws attention to aspects of human personality, attitudes, emotions, perception and motivation and their relationship with regime types. This approach looks at democracy and authoritarianism as ways of life which include specific behaviour and personality types. Theories of the state which come under the cultural approach are concerned with the role of values and norms in state formation. The structural approach looks at the functional and structural requisites necessary for different regime types. The key variables of this approach include stratification, the distribution of goods and services and the allocation of power and responsibility. While it is not to be denied that the psychological and cultural aspects of democracy and authoritarianism may be as crucial as structural determinants, the approach employed in this study tends to be structural.[1] Before discussing this approach, however, I would like to make some remarks on cultural theories of democracy and authoritarianism as they are of immediate relevance to the cases of Indonesia and Malaysia.

Cultural theories of state formation focus on the interaction between state formation on the one hand and ideologies, values and norms on the other regardless of whether the latter are the dependent, independent or intervening variables. For example, Huntington explained the failure of transition to democracy in terms of the presence of authoritarian elements in the culture of a society.[2] Cultural arguments have been made with respect to the question of democracy and authoritarianism in Malaysia and Indonesia. For example, democracy in Malaysia is seen to be partly the result of a level of social and cultural pluralism that leads to religious tolerance and social harmony and, therefore, some degree of democratic orientation and behaviour.[3]

A cultural theory with a similar focus but different argument is based on the assumption that shared values are a prerequisite to democracy. Divisive value conflicts obstruct compromise, bargaining and consensus, all of which are vital for the functioning of a democracy.[4] Ethnically, linguistically and religiously plural societies would tend to be less democratic than culturally homogeneous societies.[5] Scholars such as Dahl and Lipset claim that these cultural differences cause conflict and inhibit the establishment of coalitions and compromise across various cultural groups. To this extent, these differences obstruct the development of multiple, cross-cutting group memberships that are held to be essential to the development of democratic institutions.[6] This being the case, cultural pluralism should be associated with lower levels of democracy. This is certainly one argument that has been made for the case of Indonesia.[7]

The theory that linguistic, religious and ethnic pluralism is associated with lower levels of democracy can be tested for the cases of Indonesia and Malaysia by examining the numbers of people in distinctive linguistic, ethnic and religious groups for the period around formal independence. A measure of this, known as the index of ethnolinguistic fractionalization is available for the period 1960–5.[8]

Ethnolinguistic fractionalization in Malaysia has been scored at 0.72 and in Indonesia at 0.76 for the period 1960–5.[9] Since the difference is slight it is tempting to conclude that this is not an important explanatory variable for regime type formation.[10]

Ethnic and linguistic pluralism, or to be more general, cultural pluralism, involves vertical forms of association based on linguistic, religious and ethnic differences. These forms of association clash with other forms which cut across cultural groups that are essential to the workings of democratic institutions. Cultural differences create conflict between different religious, linguistic and ethnic groups and obstruct the process of coalition formation across cultural groups. According to Rabushka and Shepsle, democracy 'cannot be sustained under conditions of intense, salient preferences because outcomes are valued more than procedural norms. The plural society, constrained by the preferences of its citizens, does not provide fertile soil for democratic values or stability'.[11]

According to this reading of the effects of cultural pluralism on the formation of democracy, we would expect little variation between Malaysia and Indonesia. Even though Indonesia's ethnolinguistic fractionalization score is slightly higher than that of Malaysia, in another sense, ethnic diversity in Malaysia is greater. Indonesia consists of several linguistic groupings, the majority of which belong to the Islamic religion. There is, therefore, a form of affiliation that transcends ethnic and linguistic boundaries and would arguably tend to lower the degree of ethnic conflict relative to Malaysia. In Malaysia, on the other hand, the most serious ethnic conflicts are between the Malays and Chinese that belong to two very distinct civilizations, let alone ethnic or linguistic groups. In spite of the comparatively high degree of ethnic pluralism, Malaysia has managed to maintain democratic institutions, while Indonesia has not. This is not to say that ethnolinguistic or cultural pluralism, then, is not a factor that explains the different outcomes in post-colonial state forms in Malaysia and Indonesia. As will be discussed in Chapter 4, cultural factors played an important role in Indonesia in the form of regional armed rebellions.

In the case of Indonesia, another cultural approach, that of 'cultural politics' has also been taken to explain the forces behind the New Order regime in some studies of the country.[12] These works look at the dominance of the Javanese cultural perspective and world-view as factors in the consolidation of Javanese political power. There is also the question of the politics of Islam and regional variations in religious identification. To be sure, such cultural factors cannot be discounted when attempting to account for state formation. Nevertheless, although culture is not irrelevant to the workings of the political systems in these countries, not all of these factors will be taken into account in this work.[13]

Turning to the structural tradition, pre-war studies of state formation tended to focus on legal and administrative institutions. The propensity to democracy was seen in terms of the ability of nationalist leaders to work successfully at the development of democratic institutions such as legislative councils and local authority systems.[14] One attempt has been to distinguish between former British colonies, on the one hand, and those of Belgium, France, the Netherlands, Portugal and Spain, on the other. The argument is that British colonial policy resulted in the successful transference of democratic institutions to the colonies that allowed for a peaceful and orderly transition to independence.[15] This claim has also been made for Indonesia and Malaysia. It is said that the British introduced British concepts of law and government that eventually led to representative government in Malaysia.[16]

In Indonesia, on the other hand, the Dutch did not attempt to introduce Western law, but relied more on traditional institutions.[17] As a result 'Indonesians seem more unsure of what their standards of political behavior should be than most Southeast Asians'.[18] Butwell suggested that the failure of democracy in Indonesia was partly due to inexperience with self-rule. This is in contrast to Malaysia where the British assisted in the establishment of democracy. For example, a national election for an all-indigenous parliament was held in 1955, two years before independence.[19]

If it is true that there is a difference in Dutch and British modes of colonial administration that led to different post-colonial state forms, then this difference should be readily observed through the study of these administrative systems. While it is certainly true that there were differences in Dutch and British administrative systems, it is by no means clear that these differences led to the establishment of democratic ideals and institutions in one country, and to the lack of such ideals and institutions in the other.

There are several comparative studies on British and Dutch colonial rule as well as works delineating the colonial administrative structures in Malaya and Indonesia. From these studies it is possible to ascertain if British and Dutch colonial administrations had differential impacts on the development of democratic institutions in the region.[20]

In fact it turns out that this is not the case. Various councils had been introduced in Malaya and the Netherlands Indies and ostensibly involved the indigenous peoples in decision making along democratic lines. In reality they did not always do this. However, the workings of these councils had exposed the indigenous elites to the idea of representation through democratic institutions. What is more important, if these councils were not really democratic, this was true for both Malaya and the Netherlands Indies.

In the Netherlands Indies, the *vergadering* (gathering) was a regular meeting between the Resident, Regent or subdistrict officer and village headmen and administrative officers. The vergadering was democratic in nature where the presiding officer was able to get a sense of the views of the representatives of the people.[21] There was also the Regency Council. The Regency Council Ordinance of 1924 placed the Council above the Regent. The Regency Council had the power to criticize the Regent and have him execute policies against his will.[22] The *Volksraad* (People's Council) was established in 1918 and it consisted of both elected and appointed members. In 1931, it had 30 Indonesians, 5 Dutch, 4 Chinese, and 1 Arab member.[23] Despite problems faced by the Volksraad, it had the power to initiate and amend legislation as well as the right of petition.[24]

In British Malaya, State Councils were created for legislative purposes although their real effect on legislation was negligible. The Council met only seven times a year but it was the means by which public opinion on proposed legislation could be voiced. With the establishment of the Federated Malay States, the Federal Council was set up in 1909.

The elite of both British Malaya and the Netherlands Indies had experience with democratic institutions and many of them had been educated in British and Dutch schools and had, in fact, been nurtured in democratic ideals while they had not necessarily experienced democracy. The difference between Dutch and British forms of colonial administration, as far as the inculcation of democratic ideals is concerned, was not a factor leading to different post-colonial state outcomes in Malaysia and Indonesia.

The structural approach does not only examine concrete institutional factors. There are theoretical perspectives within the approach which examine analytic structures, which are characteristics or properties abstracted from the behaviour of concrete structures such as class consciousness, bureaucratic accountability and elite cohesion. Structural–functionalist, Marxist, and neo-Marxist theories are examples of analytic structural approaches. Before outlining the specific analytic approach of the present study, it would be useful to skim over some of the other structural approaches in the analytic mode, for the purpose of contrast.

THEORIES OF THE CAPITALIST STATE

The classic Marxist perspective on the development of political democracy stresses the fact that the bourgeoisie, by virtue of the economic resources it controls, wields tremendous political power. To quote a famous expression, 'the executive of the modern state is but a committee for managing the common affairs of the whole bourgeoisie'.[25] This comes about because the state is dependent on the commercial credit which the bourgeoisie extends to it via the stock exchange, taxation and so on.[26] This view of the state has come to be known as the instrumentalist conception where the state is seen to act for and on behalf of the bourgeoisie as a result of its dependence on the bourgeoisie.

A Marxist work that sees not one path to Western democracy but three distinct paths to the modern world is that of Barrington Moore,

Jr. In discussing England, France, America, Germany, Japan, Russia and China, Moore sees three routes from pre-industrial to modern societies. In England, France and America, the bourgeoisie was successful in drawing the aristocracy and peasantry into the modern economy, where the surplus from agriculture was invested in industry. In these cases, the bourgeoisie was economically dominant and was able to remove the 'obstacles to a democratic version of capitalism that have been inherited from the past'.[27] In Germany and Japan, however, a bourgeois revolution was either unsuccessful or never took place. Instead, industrialization was carried out from above through an aristocratic–bourgeoisie coalition in which the bourgeoisie was the weaker partner. The result was a right-wing authoritarian state.[28] Finally, in the Russian and Chinese cases, the bourgeoisie was too weak to 'constitute even a junior partner' in modernization.[29] A huge peasantry provided the revolutionary force that overthrew the old order and led to communist rule.[30] Chase-Dunn makes the point that Moore's approach complements the view of Marx who recognizes that, as the working class expands through industrialization and establishes autonomous political organizations such as political parties and unions, it is able to pressure the state into granting citizenship and welfare rights.[31] Marx also said that such pressures forced the bourgeoisie 'into democratic conditions, which at every moment help the hostile classes to victory and jeopardize the very foundations of bourgeois society'.[32] To put it in more general terms, Marx and Moore's approaches have in common the focus on relationships among different classes of society, and the economic interests controlling political power.[33]

While the presence of a strong bourgeoisie and working class for the existence of stable democracies as underlined by Moore is a notion that is drawn upon in the present study, it must be understood in its proper historical context. The link between parliamentary democracy and the capitalist mode of production is historical and nothing more. There is nothing inherent in capitalism that causes it to yield democratic forms of government as is evident from the cases of the advanced peripheral capitalist societies of Latin America and East Asia. While the growth of the middle and working classes had placed persistent demands on non-democratic leaders for the extension of political rights in the nineteenth and early twentieth centuries in Europe and North America, the same demands today cause governments to act oppressively in post-colonial societies.

While Marxist and neo-Marxist theories of the state emphasize the role of classes in modern capitalist societies, various elite theories of the state focus attention on other types of elite which are seen as significant actors in their own right, the analysis of which is not reduced to class. Classical formulations of elite theory[34] form the background of contemporary elite perspectives such as that of Mills. Mills identified three types of elites which we may term the executive, military and corporate elites, that is, those who occupy the top posts in the executive branch of government, the military, and the private sector. The coincidence of political, military and class interests bind the three together in a power elite. Elite theories have been used to explain the historical emergence or breakdown of democracies in the West and stress the importance of elite cohesion, consensus or integration for democratic stability.[35] Elite cohesion is yet another idea that is important to the argument of this study.

Structural approaches, however, are not limited to class and elite analyses. Modernization theory, which encompasses the psychological, cultural, as well as structural approaches focuses attention on the legal and administrative institutions of political democracy, and the necessary psychological and cultural traits needed to make these work. Modernization theory, or the modernization paradigm as it is commonly referred to, takes an evolutionary perspective and views the process of development in the Third World as an imitative one in which the economic structures, social and political institutions, and human attitudes of the industrialized West gradually become implanted in underdeveloped areas.[36] Contributions to modernization theory have come from sociology, economics and political science, and are all based on the distinction between tradition and modernity so central to the social sciences.[37] In sociology, Hoselitz applied Parson's pattern variables of particularism, characterizing modernization as a process in which particularism, ascription and diffuseness were replaced by universalism, achievement and specificity.[38] The contribution to modernization theory from economics came in the work of Rostow, who understood development as a universal process that unfolded in five stages. Rostow's economic stages are (1) traditional society, (2) the preconditions for takeoff, (3) takeoff, (4) the drive to maturity and (5) the age of high mass consumption.[39]

Of more relevance to us, however is the contribution from political science. The modernization perspective within political science conceived of political development in terms of the presidential or parliamentary democracies of the United States or Britain and is strongly influenced by structural–functionalism. The pioneer in this line of thinking was Almond. Political development as an aspect of modernization was understood in terms of structural differentiation, subsystem autonomy and cultural secularization and he understood political systems as evolving through stages of development in the direction of greater rationality, with the pattern variables of specificity, universalism, achievement and affective neutrality becoming dominant.[40] Furthermore, it was believed that Anglo–American political culture was the ideal against which political development in the Third World could be studied and appraised.[41]

Another structural–functionalist approach to the study of political modernization, is that of Apter who makes a distinction between secular–libertarian and sacred–collectivity systems. The former are modern reconciliation systems based on bargaining, compromise, and diversified power and leadership and are exemplified by liberal democracies. The latter are modern mobilization systems based on charismatic leadership and represent transitional points between traditional and modern societies.[42]

The work of Organski, modelled after Rostow's *Stages of Economic Growth,* examines the role of government in terms of four stages of development, that is, (1) primitive national unification, (2) industrialization, (3) national welfare and (4) abundance, and understands development in terms of democracy, capitalism and mass consumption.[43]

The failure of the democratic experiment which became apparent in the 1960s, was addressed by Huntington who, while accepting the basic premises of modernization theory, argued that the management of development in Third World societies could best be achieved in an authoritarian state in order that chaos, disorder and revolution could be avoided. Nevertheless, Huntington believed that authoritarianism would not persist and that an emerging middle class would play a central role in the transition to democracy.[44]

Most works on political development within the modernization paradigm have in common a number of features which are open to objection. One is that modernization in theory and practice was hardly differentiated from Westernization, that is, the wholesale imitation of Western institutions, practices and attitudes. Secondly, backwardness and underdevelopment are seen to be caused by internal rather than external factors. Change, therefore, can only come about as a result of internal changes with the help of external aids from the West. Finally, although there was a focus on internal factors, modernization theory failed to draw attention to underlying forces that relate class to political power and the concomitant effects on state forms.

Marxist theories had attempted to do just this, the point of departure being the orthodox Marxist theory of the capitalist state. It was recognized that the instrumentalist conception of the state is not the only conception of the state to be found in Marx's works. There is another view which emerged from Marx's observations of Bonapartism. The coup d'état of Bonaparte led to an independent state.[45] According to Marx, Bonaparte saw himself as a representative of both the bourgeoisie and the peasantry.[46]

> But above all, Bonaparte looks on himself as the chief of the society of December 10, as the representative of the *lumpenproletariat* to which he himself, his *entourage,* his government and his army belong . . . This contradictory task of the man explains the contradictions of his government, the confused grouping about which seeks now to win, now to humiliate first one class and then another and arrays all of them uniformly against him . . . [emphasis Marx's].[47]

By representing all classes, by breaking their political power too, through an enormous bureaucratic and military organization, the state remained independent of the wishes of any one class.[48]

THEORETICAL PERSPECTIVES ON THE STATE IN THE THIRD WORLD

In the Marxist tradition, various theoretical perspectives have developed from the critique of the instrumentalist conception of the state. It is not my intention here to enter into an extended discussion of these theories. Nevertheless, some remarks on a few of the more prominent perspectives would be in order as the theoretical framework adopted in this study either draws upon other theories or is a reaction to them. Most works on the state in the Third World are concerned with the state's role in development and, more recently, the question of democratization, rather than with the nature of authoritarianism and democracy or the issue of Third World state formation. The various theoretical perspectives that address the question of the rise of authoritarian and democratic Third World states can be listed as follows:

(1) the economic theory of democracy,
(2) dependency/world system theory,
(3) the bureaucratic authoritarian state model,
(4) elite theories of the state,
(5) post-colonial state theory,
(6) the non-capitalist path of development.

Table 2.1   Gross domestic product per capita ($US)

	Indonesia	Malaysia
1950	48	–
1955	69	208[a]
1960	82	226
1965	82	272

[a] for 1957

Source: Arthur S. Banks, *Cross-Polity Time Series Data*, Cambridge MA, The MIT Press, 1971, pp. 260, 262.

There are several classic studies on the development of democracies in that part of the Third World which experienced decolonization after the Second World War. Most of these studies concentrate on economic determinants of democracy in the sense that, as the economic sources of a society are transferred to the bourgeoisie and modern labour force, the state is pressured into granting political rights and liberties.[49] Greater degrees of industrialization, urbanization, growth of literacy rates, improved communications and greater social mobilization are all associated with economic development. Therefore, we would expect that countries that have high scores on the various indicators of economic development would also have high levels of democracy.

If we look at the level of economic development indicated by GDP per capita in Malaysia and Indonesia and compare them over time it will be seen that Malaysia has enjoyed higher levels from independence (Table 2.1). In comparison with other states, Malaysian per capita income falls in higher deciles in the world distribution than Indonesian. During the 1970–80 decade, Malaysian per capita income moved up from the 5th to the 6th decile while that of Indonesia moved up only from the 2nd to the 3rd decile.[50] However to say that the greater level of economic development in Malaysia led to democracy while the lower level of economic development in Indonesia led to authoritarianism begs the question of the form of the relationship between economic development and regime type. In other words, what is there about greater economic development that leads to democracy? Conversely, what is there about economic underdevelopment that leads to less democracy or authoritarian state forms? Some possible answers of a general nature can be found in the dependency and world-systems perspectives which, having brought attention to international determinants of economic and political developments, offer the possibility of richer theoretical statements on the relationship between economic development and regime type.

There have been studies in the dependency and world-systems tradition of analysis that have recognized the correlation between the levels of economic development and the degree of democratization.[51] Those countries which have low scores on indicators of development would tend to be less democratic or undemocratic. The view that economic development is a determinant of democracy can be tested for the cases of Malaysia and Indonesia.

The relationship between economic development and democratization has received a great deal of attention from scholars both in the modernization and world-systems/dependency traditions. That the level of economic development has a profound effect on democracy is generally not disputed and is consistent with theoretical explanations. In a cross-national design that looks at both economic and non-economic determinants of democracy Bollen and Jackman found that the dominant explanatory variable was GNP. When various non-economic factors were included the effect of GNP on democracy remained very high.[52]

When we speak of economic development in underdeveloped countries, we refer not simply to GNP per capita but to various other indicators that measure a country's overall position in the hierarchy of the capitalist world economy. Therefore, what is relevant is not just economic development but economic dependency as well. The comparison between Malaysia and Indonesia in terms of the economic determinants of regime types must consider economic dependency as an aspect of economic determinants of democracy.

A study conducted by Bollen found that different levels of integration into the world economy are associated with different levels of democracy. Furthermore, peripheral position has a greater negative effect on democracy than does semi-peripheral position.[53] The independent variables that he employs to determine the effects on democracy of position in the world-system pertain to world-system positions. He did not break down this general variable into the various aspects of economic dependency such as has been done in studies by Chase-Dunn, Bornschier and Rubinson.[54] These studies have shown that investment and debt dependence have negative effects on economic development. Since there is a definite relationship between economic development and democracy, it would be reasonable to suggest that economic dependency has a retarding effect on the level of democracy as well. This conclusion was drawn by Timberlake and Williams.[55] Also of interest is Rubinson's study on the effect of economic dependence on

Table 2.2   Debits on investment income per capita (million $US)

	Indonesia	Malaysia
1955	1.37	–
1960	0.81	13.04
1965	0.89	16.86
1970	1.13	5.88
1979	8.89	24.61

Source: Compiled from International Monetary Fund, *Balance of Payments Yearbook*, vols. 9, 13, 21, 28, Washington DC, and International Bank for Reconstruction and Development, *World Tables*, 2nd edn., Baltimore & London, Johns Hopkins University Press, 1980.

Table 2.3   External public debt per capita (millions current $US)

	Indonesia	Malaysia
1967	18.60	26.26
1970	24.78	33.90
1973	39.90	56.10

Source: Compiled from Volker Bornschier & Peter Heintz, eds, *Compendium of Data for World-System Analysis: A Sourcebook Based on the Study of MNCs, Economic Policy and National Development*, Zurich: Soziologisches Institut der Universitat Zurich, n.d., and International Bank for Reconstruction and Development, *World Tables*.

state strength.[56] The conclusions drawn from these various studies can be the basis of a simple model of the determinants of democracy for the purpose of comparing Malaysia and Indonesia. According to this model, economic dependency has a negative effect on both the level of democracy and state strength. Looking at the pertinent variables for Indonesia and Malaysia respectively, we see that this model does not hold[57] (Tables 2.2; 2.3).

Of course it can be argued that the differences between Indonesia and Malaysia over these scores on debt dependence may not be significant when compared to the larger distribution of scores among other countries. Looking at foreign property as a percentage of GDP, we see that not only does Malaysia have higher scores than Indonesia, but in comparison with other states the difference in scores between the two countries is significant, as can be seen from the deciles reported in Table 2.4.

On the other hand, looking at export partner concentration, we find that Indonesia is more dependent than Malaysia (Table 2.5). The scores

Table 2.4   Foreign property as a percentage of GDP

Country	Year	%	Decile
Indonesia	1971	9.6	6
	1975	11.5	8
	1978	11.2	8
Malaysia	1971	20.7	9
	1975	24.7	10
	1978	17.6	9

Source: Georg P. Muller (with the collaboration of Volker Bornschier), *Comparative World Data: A Statistical Handbook for the Social Sciences*, Baltimore & London: The Johns Hopkins University Press, 1988.

Table 2.5   Export partner concentration

Country	Year	%	Decile
Indonesia	1970	33.3	6
	1975	43.9	9
	1980	49.3	9
Malaysia	1970	21.6	4
	1975	20.3	4
	1980	22.8	5

Source: Muller, *Comparative World Data*.

for the two countries are significantly different from each other as is evident from the deciles reported.

In terms of debt and foreign property as a percentage of GDP, the above figures show that Malaysia is more dependent than Indonesia. For export partner concentration the reverse is true. Nevertheless, if we were not willing to state that overall Malaysia is more dependent than Indonesia we certainly could not claim that the reverse is true. Even if it is said that Indonesia and Malaysia do vary in terms of economic dependency, we may still rule out economic dependency as a cause of the difference between Indonesian and Malaysian regime types. Table 2.6 shows that the Malaysian state has greater economic power than Indonesia. A possible explanation as to why the Malaysian state is democratic in spite of greater economic dependency might be that its greater economic power has enabled it to retain the dominant class support of both Chinese and Malay capital (Table 2.6). In fact, in Chapter 6, I argue that the failure of democracy in Indonesia was

Table 2.6   Government revenue as a percentage of GDP (current $US)

	Indonesia	Malaysia
1960	12.7	–
1965	3.9	20.6
1970	10.3	24.4
1973	14.8	24.0

Source: Bornschier & Heintz, *Compendium of Data.*

due to the fragmentation of the dominant classes and ruling elite, a cause of which is a relative lack of economic power.

Thus, the economic determinants of democracy, specified in terms of the effects of economic development, economic dependency, and the economic power of the state, must be complemented by in-depth case studies to illuminate the means by which state elites and dominant classes coped with economic problems and the type of regimes that resulted from attempts to solve these problems. Economic dependency is ruled out as a cause of the different outcomes in regime types in Malaysia and Indonesia because the relationships between economic dependency and democracy are not as expected in these two cases. At the same time it makes little sense to suggest that greater economic dependency leads to democracy while lesser economic dependency leads to authoritarianism. Reasons for different outcomes in regime types have to be searched for elsewhere. The link between dependency and democracy which is found in cross-national studies is not present for the case of Indonesia and Malaysia. This means that there are other variables accounting for the difference in regime type that were strong enough to overcome the link between democracy and dependency that has been established in cross-national comparisons. In other words, what has to be addressed is why Malaysia achieved democracy in spite of being relatively more dependent, and why Indonesia, not withstanding lesser economic dependence, could not maintain parliamentary democracy? Economic dependency is ruled out as a cause of variance.

While the dependency and world-systems perspectives may not be useful in explaining the different regime types in Indonesia and Malaysia, they are still of theoretical value at another level.

First of all, they are a welcome corrective to works that tend to stress the role of internal factors as the determinants of post-colonial state forms, to the neglect of the international political economy. According to many dependency and world-system theorists, the usual political concomitant of economic development that obtained in the industrialized nations of the core, do not exist in many peripheral and semi-peripheral societies because of their disadvantaged positions in the hierarchy of the world capitalist system.

Secondly, these perspectives raise the very important issue of state strength, an issue of direct relevance to this study. As capitalism expands to peripheral and semi-peripheral areas in search of cheap raw materials and labour, international capital requires the cooperation of some elements in these areas. A commonality of interests between the landed classes, merchant capital and core capital cause elites in the periphery and semi-periphery to 'constantly attempt to use their local state structures to secure and advance their economic advantages'.[58] In return, economic, political and military aid are extended to them by the core. The help that the core extends to peripheral and semi-peripheral elites hinders the development of democratic institutions. In this regard, there are generally two perspectives in dependency theory.[59]

According to one perspective the bourgeoisie in the periphery and semi-periphery is too weak to be the basis of a democratic state and enters into alliance with the landed and merchant classes. This alliance promotes an economy based on the export of raw materials and the import of manufactures and consequently undermines the power of domestic capital.[60]

The second perspective suggests that domestic capital is not relatively weak but is active itself in supporting an authoritarian state.[61] To be sure, both perspectives are correct and apply to different societies, depending on whether a strong domestic bourgeoisie is present or not.

Related to the issue of the relationship between economic dependency and political democracy is that of internal state strength. This refers (1) to the ability of the state to control various types of resources – as opposed to other organizations and groups outside of the state apparatus,[62] (2) 'the degree to which state managers and state agencies support each others' actions',[63] and (3) the amount of support the state receives from powerful classes. But there is no simple correspondence between regime type (democratic or authoritarian) and state strength. Both democratic and authoritarian states may be internally weak or strong.[64] But democratic states are more likely to be internally stronger than authoritarian states.[65] This makes theoretical sense, as only a state which is unable to command sufficient resources would have to resort to militarism, which is a sign of weakness.[66]

Another prominent theory on the rise of authoritarian states, with specific attention to Latin America is O'Donnell's theory of the bureaucratic–authoritarian state. The bureaucratic–authoritarian state emerged in the midst of economic crisis. The failure of the democratic government to bring the crisis to an end, amidst the failure of import substitution industrialization and the opposition faced by the populist sector, leads to the reactive formation of an authoritarian regime in which the military's role is paramount.[67]

Elite theories that have been applied to Third World polities argue that democratic stability arises from the ability of elites to reduce political fragmentation by successfully negotiating political pacts. Stability originates in elites' settlements or pacts in which conflicting groups negotiate compromises on their fundamental disputes, thus paving the way for a successful transition to democracy.[68]

Post-colonial state theory refers to the works associated with Hamza Alavi, Colin Leys, John Saul and Issa Shivji. These works deal with Asian and African post-colonial states. The works of Alavi will be discussed at some length in the next section.

The last perspective is represented by East European and Soviet theorists on the non-capitalist path of development,[69] but is of little relevance to this study.

THE POST-COLONIAL STATE

Among the different approaches mentioned above to the study of the Third World state, it is only those of Hamza Alavi and his critics which specifically address the issue of the formation of the post-colonial state, although he takes a perspective very different from that of this study.

Following is a brief account of Alavi's theory of the origin of the post-colonial state.

Hamza Alavi's contribution to the literature on the state in peripheral societies has been to elaborate on the concept of the relative autonomy, or independence of the state and apply it to the case of peripheral societies. The triumph of capitalism over feudalism leaves two fundamental classes in contradiction, the bourgeoisie and the proletariat, and the state is established by the bourgeoisie. This is not the case in peripheral societies. Here, the class bases are much more complex. After the colonial period, the post-colonial state was left with three propertied classes each with competing interests. In view of this, the state cannot be considered the instrument of a single class.[70] Rather, it is 'relatively autonomous and it mediates between the competing interests of the three propertied classes, namely the metropolitan bourgeoisies, the indigenous bourgeoisie and the landed classes'.[71] The state as an element of the superstructure is not seen as being determined in a mechanical manner by the economy but has some autonomy. This autonomy in post-colonial societies derives from the fact that the state has to mediate the rival interests of the three dominant classes. By virtue of this, it enjoys a relative autonomy from each class.[72] This, then is supposed to explain the relative power of the post-colonial state with respect to each class in its society.

In dealing with the origins of the post-colonial state, Alavi was required to consider the dominant classes of post-colonial societies, the interests between which the state mediates. Further, it was necessary for him to understand the manner in which these classes and their interrelations had emerged during the colonial period. Briefly, Alavi's point has been to assert that colonialism brought into being a new mode of production that had some of the attributes of capitalism, but nevertheless lacked the dynamic of core capitalism. This form of peripheral capitalism that Alavi found in the colonies, he termed the colonial mode of production.[73] A correct understanding of the colonial mode of production in turn required a consideration of the pre-capitalist mode of production, for it was the interaction between the pre-capitalist mode of production and colonial domination that determined the nature of the colonial mode of production, its class structure and relations.

The positive aspects of Alavi's theory is that he departs from the instrumentalist version of the state and that he arrives at this point by considering the class make-up of post-colonial societies as the outcome of the interaction between pre-capitalist modes of production and colonial domination.

In spite of these positive aspects of Alavi's theory of the post-colonial state, there are three major problems that have yet to be resolved. These are discussed in what follows.

The first problem concerns the form of the post-colonial state. In his discussion on the relative autonomy of the post-colonial state, Alavi discusses both states dominated by the bureaucratic–military oligarchy as well as democratic forms of the state.[74] Based on his reflections on developments in Pakistan and Bangladesh, he intended to bring out the essential features of the post-colonial state, particularly the special role of the bureaucratic–military oligarchy or the military and state bureaucracy.[75] He refers to the bureaucratic–military oligarchy as being the apparatus of the relatively autonomous state but immediately takes note of the post-colonial state where politicians and political parties have formal authority over the bureaucratic–military oligarchy. He refers to this as a democratic form of government.[76] Thus, there is a clear reference to democratic forms of the post-colonial state, in which politicians and political parties exercise authority over the bureaucracy and military. What is not clear is the form of the state that is dominated by the bureaucracy and the military. Is such a state an authoritarian state, a dictatorship, a fascist state, or a totalitarian state? Although Alavi does not provide a definition of the state dominated by the bureaucracy and the military, it does appear that what he has in mind is similar to O'Donnell's bureaucratic–authoritarian state. Such states are those which are excluding and non-democratic, dominated by military and civilian technocrats, and allied with foreign capital.[77] I believe that this fits Alavi's description of the post-colonial state dominated by the military and bureaucracy. Given that there are two such forms of post-colonial states, that is, democratic and authoritarian, Alavi's account on the origin and bases of the post-colonial state are presented at a level too general to account for the differences between these two forms of state. It is true that all post-colonial states are relatively autonomous in the way Alavi describes the term. Even his description of relative autonomy lying in the need and ability of the state to mediate between the contending interests of the metropolitan bourgeoisies, indigenous bourgeoisies, and the landed classes, apply with qualification to many, if not all, post-colonial states. For the most part, it is possible to substitute any post-colonial state for Pakistan and Bangladesh in Alavi's work without invalidating the conclusions.

After all this, the question of why certain post-colonial states took on authoritarian forms and certain others took on democratic forms remains unanswered. This stems from the level of generality at which Alavi presents his theory of the origins of the post-colonial state. His theory usefully orients the study of the post-colonial state, but in order to deal with such questions as the one posed above, it would have to be more specific without losing its theoretical status.

The second problem with Alavi's theory concerns the specification of the various classes that the emerging post-colonial state has to mediate between. He says that the convergence of interests between the indigenous bourgeoisie, the metropolitan neo-colonialist bourgeoisies and the landed classes allows a bureaucratic–military oligarchy to mediate their competing interests and demands.[78] This provides a rather simplistic picture of the emerging post-colonial class structure.

To be sure, there are the neo-colonial metropolitan bourgeoisies that the emerging post-colonial state has to deal with. But (1) as far as the local bourgeoisie was concerned, they were not necessarily indigenous. This was particularly true of many of the post-colonial societies of

Africa and Asia, where an indigenous bourgeoisie was virtually non-existent. Instead there were immigrant, ethnic minority bourgeoisies. (2) In Alavi's work there is no discussion on the merchant classes in post-colonial societies. Again, these classes may be both indigenous as well as immigrant, ethnic minorities. (3) As far as the landed classes are concerned, Alavi does not discuss the fact that in many colonial societies, these classes were converted to salaried officials and thereby separated from ownership of the means of production.

The third problem with Alavi's theory is that it focuses primarily on the dominant classes. There is not enough discussion of the producer classes (peasants and workers). Although Alavi departs from the orthodox Marxist view of the peasantry as a minor revolutionary force,[79] he does not discuss the producer classes in general and the peasantry in particular in terms of how they relate to the three dominant classes in the emerging post-colonial state. In other words, there is little systematic discussion of anti-colonial rural and urban movements, and their struggles against the dominant classes.

Furthermore, there is a problem with the idea of the relative autonomy of the state. Alavi discusses this concept which is relevant to our purpose. There are two bases of the relative autonomy of the post-colonial state that are important.[80]

First of all, the relative autonomy of the state derives from the fractionalization of the various classes in society. According to Poulantzas' reading of Marx, the capitalist state can 'truly serve the ruling class in so far as it is relatively autonomous from the diverse fractions of this class, precisely in order to organize the hegemony of the whole of this class'.[81] To Alavi, this does not apply to the post-colonial state. The issue is not the diverse fractions within a single class, but three different propertied classes with competing interests.[82] Alavi seems to assert that the difference between the capitalist and post-colonial state is that the fractionalized class exists only in the former. In this respect, Thomas' criticism is fundamental. According to him, Alavi fails to see that in both capitalist and post-colonial societies, the ruling classes would be fractionalized.[83] Thus, the diverse fractions exist within each of the three propertied classes that Alavi speaks of. The fractionalization of classes, therefore, is a basis of the relative autonomy of the state that capitalist and post-colonial states share.

The second basis of the relative autonomy of the post-colonial state is that the state is overdeveloped. This refers to the situation in which the 'colonial state is equipped with a powerful bureaucratic–military apparatus and mechanisms of government which enable it, through its routine operations, to subordinate the native social classes'.[84] The post-colonial state inherits this overdeveloped bureaucratic–military apparatus through which it controls the indigenous classes.[85] There are several objections to the 'overdeveloped' state idea. Colin Leys, in responding to John Saul's assertion about the need for an 'overdeveloped' state in Tanzania to subdue the pre-capitalist classes in the colonial period,[86] questions the necessity of this if there are no strong indigenous classes to begin with.[87] Leys also makes the point that even if it is true that a larger than necessary colonial state was deployed to subdue native classes, it is not necessarily the case that by the time of independence the force at the disposal of the inherited state would be larger than necessary.[88]

The discussion on the emergence of the post-colonial state and its relative autonomy applies to a host of countries such as Bangladesh, India, Indonesia, Malaysia, Pakistan and Sri Lanka, not to mention several African states. But then, Alavi's theory of the post-colonial state is more of a general statement applicable to the experience of several post-colonial states rather than a theoretical framework enabling us to conceptualize certain issues. For example, while the account of relative autonomy applies to both Malaysia and Indonesia, it can tell us nothing of the crucial differences between the two states, of which three stand out. Firstly the Indonesian state was created by a revolution while the Malaysian state emerged peacefully. Secondly Indonesia is a military state while Malaysia is a constitutional democracy. And thirdly the early formative period of the Malaysian state saw a close working relationship with capital while this was not the case in Indonesia.

In view of the fact that the theory of the post-colonial state, as elaborated by Alavi, turns out to be deficient in several respects, we need to look elsewhere as well.

THE THEORETICAL PERSPECTIVE OF THIS STUDY

The alternative explanations of state formation briefly described above do not hold for Indonesia and Malaysia. Looking at the formative period of the post-colonial state, my theoretical perspective focuses on the class composition of the state and the dominant elite. I argue, given that both Indonesia and Malaysia emerged as democratic post-colonial states, the reasons for the failure of democracy in one and its persistence in the other have largely to do with the greater degree of elite cohesion among the Malaysian elite as opposed to that of the Indonesian. In Indonesia, not only was there armed resistance to the emerging post-colonial state, but in the context of an internally weak state, serious opposition and obstacles to parliamentary democracy came from within the state itself. Democracy was implanted in Indonesia and Malaysia from without. In such circumstances, democracy can survive if (1) there is no mass resistance to the democratic programme and the state, (2) if the state is internally strong, and (3) the ruling elite is homogeneous, that is, its members have similar class backgrounds and ideologies.[89] All three of these conditions obtained in Malaysia during and immediately following formal independence. The absence of any one of these conditions may result in authoritarian tendencies or trans-formations. This was the case in Indonesia. The state was not inter-nally strong. The democratic phase of the Indonesian state failed to solve severe economic problems and state elites were divided as to the course that should be taken. Anti-democratic forces won the struggle eventually. In Malaysia, while there were also economic problems en-countered by the state, the ruling elites were not divided to the extent that the democratic nature of the state was threatened and the domi-nant class continued to support the state.

The method that is employed, in formal terms, is that of historical comparison.[90] The logic behind this method is that potential sources of variation are ruled out as explanatory factors. These potential sources of variation are known or suspected to influence a dependent variable, but in the present study are held not to vary. In this study, the depen-dent variable is post-colonial state forms. The potential sources of variation are derived from the various alternative views on the origins of democratic and authoritarian post-colonial state forms that stress economic development, cultural pluralism and modes of colonial ad-ministration. Another potential source of variation is culture. I show that either these factors do not vary for the cases of Indonesia and Malaysia, or if they do vary, they are insufficient by themselves to explain differential post-colonial state outcomes. If it can be shown that in terms of economic development, cultural pluralism and modes of colonial administration, British Malaya and the Netherlands Indies have much in common, it will be possible either to rule out these factors, or at least minimize their importance in explaining the different outcomes in the two countries, or understand their workings in a different context of theoretical explanation. As a result, the search for factors leading to particular state forms in these two countries can be directed to other conditions in which the two societies differ. It is my conten-tion that such conditions pertain to three factors, namely, the homoge-neity of the ruling elite, the internal strength of the state, and mass resistance against the state. In other words, the variation in post-colonial state forms is explained in terms of variations in these factors.

The historical comparative method is advantageous where quantitative cross-national research is inadequate. For example, although a high correlation between various indicators of development and levels of democracy may be established, the nature of the relationship between economic performance and state forms can be discerned only by way of qualitative and historical comparative research. In addition, historical comparative research may shed light on exceptions to general trends revealed by cross-national studies. Historical comparative studies provide more in-depth analysis even if the research agenda was suggested by cross-national work to begin with.

The preceding discussion on theories of the state reveals certain principles that attend the formation and maintenance of democratic and authoritarian post-colonial states.

The historical circumstances under which post-colonial state formation took place must be borne in mind. While these societies were inextricably tied into the world capitalist system by the time of formal independence, for the most part both capitalism and democracy were imposed from without, by the colonial powers. The indigenous elite, through which the colonial powers ruled the colonies by the method of indirect rule, were educated in the Western tradition and took up positions in the colonial administration. They strived for the democratic ideals in which they were nurtured and, in the struggle against colonialism, used the language of the oppressors. Because of these circumstances, the democratic system was the one they knew best and, in a sense, was what post-colonial states found themselves under upon independence. In many cases, the new democracies were genuine, but failed to achieve stability and eventually declined only to be replaced by authoritarian forms. Given that many post-colonial states achieved formal independence as democracies, what were the conditions under which genuine democracy can be maintained? To my mind, they are the following:

(1) *Absence of armed resistance.* The extent to which armed and mass resistance in the countryside or in the urban sector threatens the interests of the state elite and the dominant classes determines the stability of the democratic state. History is replete with examples of mass resistance either leading to the reactive establishment of authoritarian regimes or supporting and being mobilized by authoritarian forces.

(2) *An internally strong state.* Especially important are the resources that a state can mobilize in situations when its power is challenged.[91] Another indication of internal state strength is the support it receives from the dominant classes whether industrial or merchant capital, or the landed classes. If a democratic state is internally strong it can withstand opposition without having to respond by suspending the democratic process altogether. Moore referred to the strong bourgeois impulse as a requirement for democracy. What is important is the general principle behind this, that is, strong class backing for the democratic state.

(3) *A high degree of elite cohesion.* By this is meant that there is a convergence of material and ideological interests among the members of the ruling elite, that is, those of the ruling class that actually make up the various state institutions. If this condition is satisfied, the state will not be plagued by intra-state conflicts and opposition that could potentially lead to reactive responses in authoritarian state forms. Relevant here is one of the bases of the relative autonomy of the state. The state has autonomy by virtue of the fact that not only are there competing propertied classes, but each one of these classes is fractionalized. But this status of relative autonomy turns out to be only a potential source of autonomy because class fractionalization translates into effective state autonomy, power, and strength only when the state itself is internally united. Such a democratic state is stable.

Also of some importance is foreign power support. Such support may be economic, political, or military and has often been crucial in the maintenance of many regimes, whether democratic or authoritarian. However, in this study, I will focus on the three internal factors defined above.

I will argue, using the cases of Malaysia and Indonesia, that these conditions prevailed in the former and not in the latter. The experiences of the two countries vary in that there were more armed rebellions and secessionist movements in Indonesia than in Malaysia, and there are great contrasts between the two in terms of elite cohesion and state strength.

First of all, Indonesia was plagued by a series of armed rebellions and secessionist movements which was in part responsible for the prominent role of the military in political life. This contrasts sharply with the Malaysian case which faced relatively little armed resistance to the state.

Secondly, the Malaysian state faced, and was supported by, the only economically dominant class, that is, predominantly Chinese capitalists. On the other hand, the Indonesian state was confronted since formal independence by several classes and class fractions with conflicting ideologies and interests. The struggle between different ideologies and political forces eventually led to the triumph of domestic capital which actively supported the reactive authoritarian regime. These were Chinese industrial capital and indigenous merchant and industrial capital.

Thirdly, the Malaysian ruling elite was relatively homogeneous ideologically and there was a greater degree of elite cohesion in Malaysia than in Indonesia. In the former, the ruling elite consisted of members of the old aristocracy while in the latter they consisted of members of the indigenous aristocracy, the merchant class and the traditional religious elite. The ideological unity that characterized the Malaysian state never existed in Indonesia.

The differences in these three factors of armed resistance against the state, internal state strength and elite cohesion in Indonesia and Malaysia are held to have led to the different post-colonial state outcomes in these two countries. This study will concentrate on the internal factors while foreign power support will be referred to as well.

3 Economy and Society in the Pre-independence Malay–Indonesian World: An Overview

ISLAMIZATION AND THE CREATION OF A MUSLIM CULTURAL ENTITY

The period of the rapid Islamization of the Malay–Indonesian Archipelago, approximately between the thirteenth and sixteenth centuries, was a distinctive period which implanted a Muslim civilization in the area during these centuries.

In Southeast Asia three major cultural areas can be discerned in the pre-Islamic period before the thirteenth century. These are the Indianized, Sinicized and the Philippines cultural areas.[1] The result of the process of Islamization in Southeast Asia was the appearance of another cultural area that, after the thirteenth century, overlapped the previously Philippines and Indianized cultural areas. The Islamization of the Indianized cultural area resulted in a Malay–Indonesian cultural entity into which part of the Philippines cultural area, Sulu and Mindanao, was drawn. Other parts of the Indianized cultural areas such as Angkor were excluded from this new area as they were not Islamized. The Malay–Indonesian Archipelago, then, as a Muslim cultural entity after the thirteenth century consisted of what is today known as Malaysia, Indonesia and the Muslim areas of Southern Thailand and the Philippines. This cultural entity is not simply defined by the number of its inhabitants professing Islam. There are both cultural and material criteria which delineate this region as a Muslim one. They can also be considered as possible criteria for a Muslim period.

In the cultural sphere, the Islamization of the Malay–Indonesian Archipelago resulted in the establishment of a common language, Malay, throughout the archipelago, and the consolidation of a Muslim world-view through the medium of Islamic philosophical literature via the Malay language.

Contemporaneous with the Islamization of the archipelago was the development of Malay as the lingua franca of the region. The importance

43

of the Malay language is no doubt partly due to Malay dominance in shipping, to Malay influence in the coastal trading ports, and to some extent to the political and economic strength of the Malays,[2] but certainly not least to the role this language played after the coming of Islam.[3] The use of Malay as the literary and philosophical language of Islam gave it the status of a literary language and enabled it to displace the hegemony of Javanese as the language of Malay–Indonesian literature.[4]

> The 9th/16th and 10th/17th centuries witnessed the unrivalled prolificness of Malay writing on philosophical mysticism and rational theology. The first Malay translation of the Quran with commentary based on al-Baydawi's famous Commentary, and translations, commentaries and original works on philosophical mysticism and rational theology also appeared during this period which marked the rise of rationalism and intellectualism not manifested anywhere before in the Archipelago.[5]

As far as Muslim statecraft was concerned, ideological elements from Islam contributed to Malay–Indonesian notions of kingship. Although the roots of Malay–Indonesian kingship in the pre-Islamic past are not to be denied, various Islamic concepts did make their way into kingship notions. An example is the mystical concept of *al-insan al-kamil* (the perfect man).[6]

The discussion on language, literature and statecraft has been brief because their relevance to the Islamization process has been dealt with by others, in the works cited above. Here, it has been necessary to show that the Malay–Indonesian world can be understood in terms of a cultural entity. This is very important when it comes to the historical and comparative study of Malaysia and Indonesia. In trying to understand the different impact of colonialism on the peasantry in Indonesia and Malaysia, or the different post-colonial state forms in Malaysia and Indonesia, a potential source of variation is culture. If the region can be understood in terms of a single cultural entity defined by Islam (which is not to say that there are no regional variations in the degree of the Hindu–Buddhist and other influences) it would be possible to gain some control over cultural factors that are usually held to be a major source of variation.

PRE-CAPITALIST MODES OF PRODUCTION

The colonial impact on pre-capitalist Malay–Indonesian economy and society can only be appreciated after the pre-capitalist modes of production are understood. It is best to begin by making the distinction, as van Leur and others have done, between the highly bureaucratized inland states found mainly in Java, and the coastal maritime states found in Sumatra, the Malay Peninsula, Borneo, Sulawesi and the other islands.[7] Consistent with this distinction is that made by Bronson and Hall, between riverine and rice plain exchange networks. The former were found along the coastal areas of the archipelago and involved the 'control of a drainage basin opening to the sea by a center located at or near the mouth of that basin's major river'.[8] Examples of states which were at the centre of a riverine system were Malacca, Brunei, Jambi, Palembang, Aceh and Banjarmasin. Each of these centres controlled a hinterland from which originated the goods that were marketed to various international destinations through the riverine centre.[9] For the most part these states were dependent on the acquisition of surpluses from maritime trade and tended to have less centralized bureaucratic state structures.

On the other hand, the rice plain regions, the most important being in Java, depended on agriculture for the acquisition of the economic surplus. Clusters of villages in the rice plain economy provided agrarian products that ultimately made their way to ports, major cities and royal centres through the intermediary of small and large-scale merchants.[10] These were not small port-city states but empires whose centres were located in the interior regions of the realm and were characterized by more complex and centralized bureaucratic structures.

In order to briefly discuss the modes of production that adequately conceptualize the riverine and rice plain exchange networks it is necessary to begin with the concept of the mode of production itself. An oft-quoted statement of Marx reads:

> In the social production of their existence, men inevitably enter into definite relations, which are independent of their will, namely relations of production appropriate to a given stage in the development of their material forces of production.[11]

The mode of production, then, consists of the relations and forces of production. The relations of production refer to the mode of acquisition of the economic surplus and the economic ownership of the forces of production that correspond to that mode of acquisition.[12] The forces of production are the means of production and the labour process. It refers to the labour process involved in the transformation of the raw material of nature into products by means of the tools, skills, organization and knowledge of the worker.[13] For example, in the capitalist mode of production the economic surplus is acquired in the form of surplus value by a class of non-producers, the capitalists, which owns the means of production. Workers are forced to sell their labour-power for wages in order to buy commodities for personal consumption, as they do not own the means of production. Every mode of production has a determinant form of the relations of production and the forces of production. Thus, in order to identify a particular mode of production it is necessary to specify both the relations and forces of production. Three pre-capitalist modes of production relevant to the Malay–Indonesian Archipelago are discussed later in this chapter.

In the Malay–Indonesian Archipelago of pre-capitalist times the main areas of surplus acquisition were agriculture, trade, mining and the craft industry, with the former two being the most important. The following account of the sources and recipients of the economic surplus is largely based on historical data from states of the Malay Peninsula and Java, the former being representative of the maritime economies of the riverine exchange networks and the latter of the agrarian empires of the rice plain exchange networks. These examples are held to be fair representations of these two types of economic systems although variations in detail and terminology do exist.

In the Malay Peninsula the largest political unit was the *negeri* (state).[14] In the nineteenth century, before the establishment of British colonial rule, eight negeri existed in the Malay Peninsula, each with its own ruler referred to as the *yang di pertuan besar* (he who is made lord) or the *sultan*.[15] Each negeri was divided into *jajahan* or districts.[16]

The territory comprising a state was determined by the geographical structure of the peninsula as well as by the use of rivers as the lines of communications and trade.[17]

> A state was typically the basin of a large river or (less often) of a group of adjacent rivers, forming a block of land extending from the coast inland to the central watershed. The capital of the state was the point at which the main river ran into the sea. At this point the ruler of the state could control the movement of all persons who entered or left his state, he could defend it from external attack and he could levy taxes on its imports and exports.[18]

Since these states were to be found in river valleys, the political boundary was the central watershed. There was a wide variation in the size of states. For example, Perak was about 7980 square miles while Negri Sembilan was 2550 square miles.

The ruler of a district was known as the *datuk* (district chief) whose lineage usually had historical connections with the district.[19] The subject class were peasants known individually or collectively as *rakyat*. They resided in the smallest political unit, the *kampung* (village).[20] Each village had a headman known as the *penghulu*.[21]

Land was owned nominally by the ruler but real power over the land was wielded by the district chiefs and peasants generally had access to land on the basis of usufruct. There were several categories of labour, freeman (*orang merdeka*), corvée labour (*kerah*), debt-bondsmen (*orang berhutang*), and slaves (*abdi*).[22] Some of the freemen were the followers of the district chief who also had his own personal army.[23]

The district chief was responsible for the collection of taxes in his district and was supposed to remit a portion of this to the sultan, although it was not often that a sultan received all the taxes that were part of the royal dues.[24] It was mainly trade goods that were taxed by the district chief as these goods made their way from district to district. The sultan had to rely mainly on import and export taxes in the district over which he presided. The power of the sultan, then, derived from his control over, not the whole negeri, but his district.[25] If the sultan's district was an important trading centre, such as was the case with Malacca in the fifteenth century, then the sultan benefited more from taxes on trade. In addition to his role as a district chief and the local power that he commanded, the sultan was important in symbolizing and preserving the unity of the state through the institution of the sultanate. The opposition of the various district chiefs to each other tended to neutralize the overall opposition to the sultan. Furthermore, the need for defence, and law and order over an area wider than the district legitimized the role of the sultan. As Gullick observes, while district chiefs intrigued to put one claimant on the throne as opposed to another, they had never sought to destroy the sultanate.[26]

Mining was another area of the acquisition of economic surplus. In large mining centres in the latter part of the nineteenth century such as at Larut and Kuala Lumpur, Chinese miners paid taxes to the district chiefs only when the tin had to pass through the district on its way to the coastal port.[27] The mining industry had attracted Chinese labour especially during the latter half of the nineteenth century when there was a great increase in demand for tin during the rise of British capitalism. In the Malay Peninsula, the influx of Chinese workers took place even before the British established colonial rule there. The owners of the tin mines were both Malay chiefs and Chinese entrepreneurs.[28] Labour was provided by both Malays and Chinese and remuneration was through wages as well as profit-sharing.[29]

Craft industry was relatively undeveloped compared with India, China and the Ottoman Empire. Whatever full-time craftsmen there were, were mainly under the employ of the sultan and chiefs and very few villages had even minor industry.[30] An urban surplus derived from taxes and duties on craft industry, therefore, was virtually non-existent.

The Malay negeris of the peninsula were representative of the maritime economies of the archipelago that were to be found throughout the region and not only in the peninsula. We now turn to the agrarian empires of the rice plain exchange networks, using the example of Java.

The largest political unit was the *nagara* (state). One such nagara was the empire of Mataram that existed from the sixteenth to the nineteenth centuries. The nagara ruled by the *raja,* sultan or *ratu,*[31] consisted of various regencies, each headed by a regent (*bupati*). The empire was administered in terms of the distinction between the core regions (*nagaragung*) the surrounding regions (*mancanegara*) and the coastal provinces (*pasisir*).[32] The administration of the realm was entrusted to officials (*punggawas*) who were recruited mainly from the *priyayi* class which consisted of the families and descendants of the punggawas.[33] The sultan and various regional powers awarded *lungguh* (appanages) and *bengkok*[34] (salary-fields) as sources of remuneration to their officials. Lungguh were assigned regions from which the assignee had the right to gain profit. The assignee, however, had no right on the land itself. The bengkok was an area of arable land belonging to the sultan that was assigned to an official. It was tilled by levy-service for the benefit of the official to whom it was granted.[35] While it is not clear what all the differences between the lungguh and the bengkok were, one certainly was that the former consisted of vast territorial expanses while the latter consisted of plots of land. The subject class was composed of peasants known collectively as *wong cilik*[36] who resided in the smallest political unit, the village (*desa*).

As in the maritime societies, land in Java was nominally owned by the sultan but effective power was in the hands of the various regional officials who derived power from the holding of appanages or from their positions as regional chiefs. Land was farmed communally by the village.[37] The several categories of labour were the communal land shareholder (*kuli kenceng*), slaves (*kawula*) and convicts.[38]

The produce of the land accrued to the tiller of the soil, to the village head, the bupati, the bupati's officials, the sultan, and to his treasury.[39] The peasant who worked the land usually received 40 to 50 per cent of the yield, while the village chief received about 20 per cent. The remainder went to the sultan. Of the sultan's portion, three-fifths went to his treasury and the rest to his officials.[40] Taxation in kind applied to the nagaragung of the empire where the appanage system was in effect as well as in the mancanegara. The sultan, thus, shared the income of the land with lungguh-holders in the nagaragung and with the regional chiefs in the mancanegara as well as with officials and peasants. There were two types of land, however, that were not subject to this form of taxation. One was the so-called freeholds (*dharma lepas*) which were distributed by the sultan to religious communities in return for the performance of religious services.[41] The other were crown lands (*narawita*) and tax territories (*siti pamajegan dalem*) which were under the direct management of the sultan, and its produce, revenue and labour services were entirely for his benefit.[42]

While Java was basically an agrarian society, agriculture was not the only important source of surplus acquisition. Taxes and duties were imposed on goods entering Javanese ports and numerous toll houses were set up on rivers and along the main roads.[43] As was the case with the maritime economies, craft industry was relatively undeveloped and its surplus insignificant.

The distinction between the maritime, coastal economies of the archipelago and the inland agrarian empires has been made. Whether these two types of economies correspond to two different modes of production is another issue. In the case of the coastal areas of the archipelago that have been described in terms of riverine or maritime economies, the concept of the feudal mode of production has been applied. There was a debate that was begun a century ago by British colonialists over the nature of the Malay mode of production.[44] The British colonial officer, Maxwell characterized pre-colonial Malaya as feudal because he saw surplus from the land being extracted in the form of what he saw as a species of feudal rent.[45] This is based on his belief in the existence of evidence of the extraction of a tenth of agricultural produce by the ruler as a feudal rent. Another British colonial officer, Swettenham, denied the existence of such evidence of any system of land rent for that matter, suggesting instead that the appropriation of surplus by the rulers was an arbitrary and unsystematic affair.[46] The debate was continued by Malaysian scholars such as Jomo Kwame Sundaram, Lim Teck Ghee and David Wong.[47] Generally, the definition of feudalism had not been presented in a thorough manner. Nor has there been any systematic attempt to assess the relevance of the concept for the Malay–Indonesian Archipelago. It is insufficient to look at the juridical status of a rent to determine if a certain mode of production is feudal or not. The discussion must be carried beyond the legal expressions of material relations.

The concept of feudal mode of production can be applied to parts of the archipelago with certain qualifications. Before stating these qualifications, however, it will be necessary to define the feudal mode of production.

Feudalism is a mode of production in which land is the dominant means of production. The fragmented nature of sovereignty is due to the independence of the landed nobility and the urban crafts from the state, that is, there is private property in both landed and urban manufactories. The central feature of the feudal mode of production as it was found in Europe was the fief. The fief was granted by the lord to a vassal in return for military services.[48] The lord–vassal contract was based on a free relation of personal fealty which 'involves reciprocal obligations of loyalty, to be sure, on a legally unequal basis'.[49] The lord–vassal relationship was one aspect of the feudal relations of production. Another was the relationship between the vassal and his dependants, the serfs, and is denoted by the term 'seigneurie'.[50] The economic surplus was paid by the serfs to the knightly vassals in the form of a rent.

Based on this understanding, it can be said that feudalism was a mode of production in the Malay–Indonesian Archipelago. This is not to say that Malay feudalism was identical to European feudalism. Nevertheless, Malay feudalism had several of the traits of feudalism as it was found in Europe, the most important of which was the fragmented nature of sovereignty due to the independence of the datuk (district chief). What is not present in Malay feudalism is the lord–vassal relationship, the institution of knighthood. As long as the differences between European and Malay feudalism are noted it is perfectly reasonable to refer to the riverine exchange economies of the archipelago as being a variant of feudalism in the sense of a decentralized tributary mode of production.[51] Following Wolf, the tributary mode of production is one in which the 'primary producer, whether cultivator or herdsman, is allowed access to the means of production, while tribute is exacted from him by political or military means'.[52] Tributary modes of production range from decentralized to highly centralized systems.[53] Malay feudalism represents a decentralized version of the tributary mode of production in which power was held by local chiefs and rule at the top was relatively weak. On the other hand, the tributary modes of production found in Java, discussed below, represent centralized versions in which power was concentrated in the hands of a ruling elite located at the apex of the system.

Coming to the agrarian-based economies of the inland states in the archipelago, various attempts at conceptualizing the economic system have been made. The most notable are Tichelman's application of the theory of the Asiatic mode of production to Java and Bakker's application of patrimonial–prebendalism also to Java.[54]

In the Asiatic mode of production, power is centralized in the state. The entire economic surplus is appropriated by the state and the state is the legal owner of landed and manufacturing property.[55] Such a state is extremely strong when it controls a strategic element in the production process such as irrigation works or an army of superior military ability.[56] In addition to the centralization of power in the state, the Asiatic mode of production is defined in terms of the absence of private property in land,[57] and the combination of agriculture and manufacturing within the self-sustaining small community.[58] The basic ingredient of historical progression, class struggle, is missing and Asiatic societies are, as a result, stagnant.[59] Abrahamian, in his discussion on the Asiatic mode of production in Qajar Iran, finds two separate explanations for the power of the Asiatic state in Marx and Engels: '(1) the public works were the business of the central government; (2) the whole empire, not counting the few larger towns, was divided into villages, which possessed a completely separate organization and formed a little world in themselves'.[60] In the first explanation, the state is strong by virtue of its having a large bureaucracy to administer public works. In the second explanation, the state is strong by virtue of the existence of a weak and fragmented society. This is the distinction between what Abrahamian calls the theory of bureaucratic despotism and the theory of fragmented society.[61] Regarding the latter, while it is true that states in centralized tributary modes of production may derive power from the existence of a weak and fragmented society, this does not mean to say that these societies were stagnant. Class struggle is present in all class societies. What varies is the form of class struggle and the ways in which the state brings it under control. Centralized tributary modes of production may not have experienced a revolution in productive technology such as that under capitalism, but they did develop military technology, bureaucratic structures and state institutions. The Asiatic mode of production is part of the dynamic change that tributary modes undergo, oscillating between centralized and decentralized phases.

We are now in a position to consider the relevance of the theory of the Asiatic mode of production to the case of Java.

Clearly, two traits stand out as being irrelevant. These are the prominence of large-scale public works and the absence of classes and class struggle. The centralized state of Java derived its power neither from the administration of large-scale public works (theory of bureaucratic despotism) nor from the existence of a fragmented, classless society (theory of fragmented society). There were no large-scale public works for the state to administer and Java was not a classless society, this being a mythical view of 'oriental' societies.

Another trait of the Asiatic mode of production concerns the extraction of surplus directly from the dominated classes. In the Asiatic mode the state is both landlord and sovereign. Taxes and rent coincide in the sense that there was no tax that differed from ground-rent.[62] The tax/rent couple is a result of the coupling of political sovereignty and landownership in the state which acquires the surplus-product through taxation which is simultaneously a land-rent.

If we understand the Asiatic mode of production to be one in which the state acquires the economic surplus directly from the populace then it will be clear that the Javanese economic system cannot be characterized by this mode of production alone. As mentioned above, it was only from certain lands that revenue and labour services were remitted directly to the ruler, that is, the narawita and siti pamajegan dalem lands.[63] However, not all revenues, and labour services were directly available to the sultan. There were other forms of surplus acquisition pertaining to a different mode of production.

In the nagaragung and the mancanegara of the Mataram Empire administration and surplus acquisition were based on the granting of appanages (lungguh) and salary-fields (bengkok).[64] The lungguh, that is, an assigned region, the land which the assignee has a right to gain from in terms of taxes and labour services,[65] is similar to the benefice as defined by Weber. The benefice differs from the fief in that the granting of the former did not involve a contract of personal fealty carrying reciprocal obligations of loyalty. Rather the benefice was granted mainly out of fiscal considerations and existed in the general context of a despotic state where rule at the apex was strong. The economic system based on the granting of benefices was termed by Weber as prebendal feudalism.[66] In this system, the surplus was collected by assignees to land grants who did not legally own land but exerted control over it. It is mainly for this reason that I do not agree with Bakker's application of the patrimonial–prebendal model to Java. One of the traits of this model that he cites is the existence of prebendal officials 'who have no independent power base but must conform to the wishes of the patrimonial ruler'.[67] This, however, was not the case with the officials in Mataram whose autonomy from the centralized power derived from both their holdings of domains for their exclusive use and their personal armed forces.[68]

Apart from the existence of three modes of production there was also long distance trade in the archipelago. As Amin says, long distance trade is not a mode of production but is the means by which independent societies or social formations are linked together. Long distance trade allows for the transfer of surplus from one society to another. If the surpluses that the dominant classes can acquire in their own formation is limited, the monopoly position that they hold in long distance trade may represent a vital source of wealth for them.[69]

That there was a Malay and Javanese trading class that was well developed in the archipelago is an established fact. It is also a fact that this class as a dominant class began to disappear after the sixteenth century with the appearance of first the Portuguese and then the Dutch and British in the seventeenth century and later. This process has been elaborated elsewhere.[70] Here it is necessary only to state that since most of the great trading centres of the archipelago were to be found on the various Indonesian islands rather than on the Malay Peninsula, mainly because of the products found in these areas, the indigenous trading class continued to exist in what is today called Indonesia. In fact, during the early part of this century, indigenous traders rapidly expanded as a class in the Netherlands Indies. Many members of this indigenous merchant class came from aristocratic families who had turned to trade as a result of the increasing shortage of land.[71] This differs from British Malaya where population density was relatively low and where opportunities for profit in long distance trade were much less available.

In summary, then it can be said that the Malay–Indonesian Archipelago prior to the imposition of the colonial economy was dominated by the coexistence of three modes of production, the Asiatic, prebendal feudal and feudal, which were linked by long distance trade.

The arrival of the European mercantilist era, in the form of Portuguese expeditions in the late fifteenth century, followed later by the Dutch and British did not fundamentally alter the pre-capitalist modes of production. In 1511, the Portuguese conquered the Malacca sultanate on the west coast of the Malay Peninsula, which had hitherto monopolized trade passing through the Straits of Malacca and extracted tribute from other port-cities in the archipelago. This conquest, however, did not alter the existing relations of production. A new state just entered the competition for the hegemony of the trade of the archipelago in particular and the Indian Ocean in general. At the beginning of the seventeenth century, the Dutch East India Company, referred to as the VOC (Vereniging Oost-Indische Compagnie) succeeded in monopolizing some of the trade in the archipelago and occupying some port-cities, beginning with Batavia in 1619.[72] The Dutch, then, competed with the various local states. The British entered into this competition when they took formal possession of Penang Island off the northwest coast of the Malay Peninsula in 1786 and went on to control several VOC possessions in the archipelago.[73] After the Dutch took Malacca from the Portuguese in 1641, the two European powers in the Malay–Indonesian Archipelago were the British and the Dutch, but they co-existed with various indigenous regional powers, some of which remained independent until as recently as the latter part of the nineteenth century.

COLONIAL ECONOMY AND SOCIETY

The more immediate concern of this chapter is the period of the establishment of the colonial economic system, when the British and Dutch went beyond the mere monopoly of trade in the archipelago to the large-scale investment in the acquisition of agricultural and mining products and raw materials.

As the British advanced their interests in the Malay world with the founding of Penang and Singapore in 1786 and 1819 respectively, their commercial contacts with Sumatra began to expand. Thus, there was a need to avoid Anglo–Dutch conflict in the Straits of Malacca which led to the Treaty of London in 1824. Defining British and Dutch spheres of interest, the former consisted of the Malay Peninsula while the latter encompassed the island of Sumatra.[74] This treaty also provided the basis for the contemporary boundary between Malaysia and Indonesia as the British forward movement made its way into the Malay Peninsula and North Borneo and the Dutch increased their territorial holdings in the rest of the archipelago toward the end of the nineteenth century. In order to discuss the nature and impact of colonial rule on the economy and society of the archipelago it is necessary to consider the distinction between two forms of colonial rule, that is, direct and indirect rule. The following discussion on the two forms of rule, as it was imposed during the nineteenth century, will provide the political context in which to present an overview of the colonial economy.

The advent of European colonial exploitation brought with it two distinct forms of colonial rule. One was the policy of direct rule in which the European authority established in the colony operated within a European administrative framework that came into direct contact with every individual in the local population. The officials of this administrative system consisted mainly of locals but they were appointed by top European officials.[75]

In the policy of indirect rule the local states and their administrative frameworks were to be preserved.[76] It was an alternative form of colonial administration which recognized that the simplest and cheapest way a European power could gain economic control over a region was indirect rule through the local elite, from the ruler to the village head.[77] Indirect rule was especially suited to the procurement of local produce and the development of European enterprise in the colonies as the local elite could provide land and labour much more readily and cheaply than European officials could, by continuing to govern along local lines within the indigenous administrative framework.[78] Indirect rule also meant that the burden of maintaining colonial authority could be borne by the indigenous rulers and their officials who had, of course, more access to the loyalty of the population than the Europeans.[79] For both the Dutch and British the dominant policy was indirect rule.

In the Malay Peninsula direct rule was established in Penang, Province Wellesley, Malacca and Singapore which in 1826 were combined to form a single administrative unit called the Straits Settlements.[80] Indirect rule was established in the Federated Malay States (FMS) and the Unfederated Malay States of the Malay Peninsula. The four states of Pahang, Perak, Selangor and Negeri Sembilan constituted a region that was of great economic importance to the British due to their rich tin deposits. It was in these states that indirect rule was first established. In 1896 these states were brought together to form a single administrative unit, the Federated Malay States (FMS) with the capital at Kuala Lumpur.[81] The Unfederated Malay states, consisting of Johor, Kedah, Perlis, Kelantan and Trengganu did not form a single political entity. These states, with the exception of Johor, were brought under British indirect rule as a result of increasing Siamese interest, formally in 1909.[82] Around the same period, Johor lost its independence when in 1914 the General Adviser was legally made responsible to the Singapore Governor rather than the Sultan of Johor.[83]

In the Netherlands Indies, the nominally directly-ruled regions constituted about 93 per cent of the area of Java and large parts of the Outer Islands.[84] Nevertheless, in these areas what was really in place was a system of indirect rule, whereby, 'the regents, who are the highest officials in the native civil service, are as far as possible drawn from the old-established aristocratic families, in principle on the basis of customary rules of hereditary succession, and the subordinate officials are likewise those with a traditional claim to the allegiance of the people they govern'.[85] The rest of the Netherlands Indies consisted of the native or Indonesian states in which indigenous princes and rulers continued to rule with a measure of independence.[86]

The reasons for the establishment of direct rule in one area and indirect rule in another are as follows. In the area of direct rule in British Malaya, a policy of free trade was followed where there were no important raw materials. On the other hand, the regions of indirect rule were more significant from the point of view of the procurement of raw materials and the establishment of Western enterprises which required the enlistment of the support of the indigenous rulers and elite. This latter point holds true also for the indirectly ruled regions of the Netherlands Indies as opposed to those regions which were less important economically.

The British and the Dutch believed that it was necessary to retain the loyalty and trust of the Malay and Javanese elite in order that their hold on the region remained secure. The result of this belief was the policy of indirect rule which in practice constituted a hierarchy of authority based on an upper-level European administration and a lower-level indigenous one.

The Netherlands Indies, taking Java as an example, was divided into a number of residencies, each of which was headed by a Dutch resident.[87] Each residency was in turn divided into regencies.[88] Each regency was headed by a regent, the bupati of the prebendal feudal organization of pre-colonial Java. The regency itself was divided into districts and subdistricts and its administration was entrusted to district and assistant district chiefs from the indigenous population and Dutch controllers. Finally at the desa (village) level responsibility fell upon the headman. The officials of the indigenous administration were drawn from the elite priyayi class, the regents coming from among the top families of the priyayi.

In British Malaya, taking the Federated Malay States as the example, each was divided into districts. The sultan of each state was to receive a British Resident whose advice was to be sought in all matters other than those pertaining to Islam and Malay custom. The village headman (penghulu) of the Malay feudal system now came under a British officer in charge of the district and was responsible for the administration of the district or a subdivision (*mukim*) of it.[89] This brief introduction to the nature of indirect rule in British Malaya and the Netherlands

Indies provides the political backdrop against which the general features of the colonial economy can be discussed. This is dealt with in what follows.

Beginning with the Netherlands Indies, the sources of acquisition of the economic surplus were agriculture, mining and, to a lesser extent, manufacturing industry.

In agriculture, the economic policy that dominated the nineteenth century in the Netherlands Indies was the *cultuurstelsel* (cultivation system). Since 1820 the government of the Netherlands Indies had been running deficits which increased after 1825 as a result of the war with the sultan of Jogjakarta. By 1830 the Netherlands Indies debt was 30 000 000 florins with an annual interest of more than 2 000 000 florins.[90] The one who came to the rescue was van den Bosch, governor from 1830 and inventor of the system of forced cultivation, the cultuurstelsel. By this system, indigenous cultivators were required to set aside one fifth of their land for the production of cash crops (for example, coffee, sugar, tea, pepper, tobacco). This produce was bought by the colonial government at a low price or paid up to it as taxes in kind. It was then sold in the Netherlands for a high profit by the Netherlands Trading Company (Nederlandsche Handelmaatschappij).[91] From a fiscal viewpoint, the cultuurstelsel was successful.[92] As the production of commercial crops expanded the importance of the old spice trade receded. In fact, so successful was the cultuurstelsel that the colonial government was able to remit 15 million florins to the Dutch exchequer in 1851.[93]

The conflict between conservative and liberal forces in the Netherlands over the cultuurstelsel led to its eventual demise as liberal political views became more dominant after the 1850s.[94] As it led to impoverishment among the peasantry, the claims of the liberals were strengthened.[95] By the end of the nineteenth century the cultuurstelsel survived only in the cultivation of coffee.[96] In 1870 the Agrarian Law was passed. By this law leases of up to 70 years could be granted to subjects and inhabitants of the Netherlands as well as to members of companies registered in the Netherlands Indies. Thus, the legal basis for the extension of private enterprise into the plantation economy was laid and agriculture was left largely in private hands.[97]

During the period of the cultuurstelsel the provision of labour was based on various kinds of compulsory service. With the onset of the liberal system in 1870 slavery and debt-bondage were replaced with a labour-contract system whereby penal sanctions were imposed upon labour failing to observe contracts of service.[98] While in Java the regulation pertaining to this sanction was repealed in 1879, in East Sumatra and the rest of the Outer Islands coolie ordinances enforcing the penal sanction were passed in 1880 and after. It was only in 1942 that the system of penal sanctions was finally abolished.[99] While labour continued for the most part to be under the penal sanction in East Sumatra and the outer islands, in Java it was based more on the hiring of free labour.[100] Because of the relatively low population density of Sumatra in particular and the outer islands in general labour was scarce in these regions. This, coupled with the fact of subsistence agriculture as an alternative, led to the need for the importation of Chinese and Javanese workers into East Sumatra. In Java, however, plantation industries were based on the hiring of free labour.[101] The sugar factory owner, for example, rented land from the desa (village) community for 18 months after which the land reverted to indigenous use.[102]

While, for the most part, the production of commercial crops was undertaken by Western-owned and to a lesser degree Chinese-owned enterprises, there were also indigenous smallholdings involved in such production. For example, in 1929 as much as 41 per cent of the rubber output of the Netherlands Indies came from smallholdings.[103]

The next source of surplus acquisition was the mining industry. During the second half of the nineteenth century mining was opened up to private enterprise. Nevertheless, the colonial state continued to be a substantial investor in mining. Tin mining was almost exclusively in state hands, while the state also owned and operated coal mines and a gold and silver mine and was a partner in oil mining.[104]

Finally, in manufacturing, there was some degree of local production at the level of cottage industry as well as modern industry. However, it was only in the 1930s that significant industrial growth began, due to the collapse in the prices of primary products. The colonial government was active in the encouragement of both the indigenous craft industry and modern manufacturing. This involved, for example the provision of credit to small-scale concerns, and technical instruction to local craftsmen.[105] Import restrictions were introduced to protect local manufacturers. The 1930s saw the growth of the textile industry as well as miscellaneous industries (soap, shoes, tyres, torches, batteries, cigarettes, bicycles, phosphate). By the latter part of this decade most large industrial concerns in Indonesia were either branches of great Western manufacturing establishments or were controlled or even owned by locals.[106] Furthermore, most large and medium scale industry was in the hands of Western and to some extent Chinese capitalists.

Coming to the economy of British Malaya, in contrast to the Netherlands Indies where commercial crops (sugar and rubber) were the most important sources of revenue, it was tin that was, in the beginning, the basis of the colonial economy. During the early stages of its development most of the tin mining industry was in the hands of Chinese merchants who supplied the capital and brought in Chinese workers to work the mines. Western mining companies came into prominence only in the twentieth century.[107] After 1884, during the imposition of British indirect rule in the Malay Peninsula, a number of Western companies began to establish themselves in tin mining but it was only after 1912 with the introduction of dredging by the Europeans, that they took the lead in the industry. Dredge-mining was more capital-intensive and required more technical knowledge and large-scale management than other mining methods.[108] By 1937, the European share of tin mining had risen to more than two-thirds.[109]

In agriculture, both Chinese and Western attempts to engage in the cultivation of commercial crops such as spices, sugar and coffee were never successful in the long run.[110] It was rubber that bestowed importance to the field of agriculture in British Malaya. In the early years of the twentieth century it was with the take-off of the motor age that the rubber boom began. Large-scale rubber estates were in the hands of Europeans with smaller concerns being run by the Chinese. A significant proportion of rubber was grown on smallholdings, predominantly Malay.[111] Two other commercial crops that attained importance in the twentieth century were pineapple and oil palm.[112]

The labour in agriculture, particularly in the rubber estates, was predominantly Indian in the sense that they constituted the largest ethnic group, being 67.7 per cent of the total estate labour force in 1937 although this figure dropped to 47.8 per cent in 1962.[113]

In both the mining and agricultural areas the initiative came mainly from private enterprise and the colonial government was involved mainly in the building of infrastructure such as a railway, a road system, the implementation of irrigation schemes and the setting up of village agricultural schools.[114]

The development of manufacturing industry in British Malaya received its impetus mainly from the fall-off in imports during the First World War. For the most part Chinese rather than European capital took the lead in the 1920s. Among the prominent industries were pineapple-canning, rubber shoe, cement, and plywood roofing manufacture, most of which saw greater European interest after the Second World War.

In both the Netherlands Indies and British Malaya it was mining and agriculture that dominated the colonial economy. Through indirect rule the Dutch and the British were able to prescribe the kind of industry that was lucrative to them. For example, the cultuurstelsel was based on the persuasion of indigenous officials, headed by the bupati, to produce and deliver the prescribed commercial crops. The picture of the class structure of the two colonies that we have on the eve of independence, then, is as follows. The dominant class was composed of the executives and administrators of colonial government industrial undertakings and privately-owned enterprises. The members of this class were generally Westerners including British, Dutch, other European, American and Australian nationals. Among the local inhabitants, there were Chinese immigrants in the dominant class, but indigenous capital was insignificant. Below the dominant class is what we may call the professional–managerial class. It consisted of technical and managerial personnel in enterprises, public servants in colonial state and military administration, as well as independent professionals under contract in state and private companies. In Malaya English-educated Malays and Indians dominated state and military administration while mainly Europeans and Chinese made up the personnel in commercial enterprises. In Indonesia, Indonesians controlled the state and military administration at the level of the professional–managerial class while both Europeans and Indonesians were in mid-level positions in commercial enterprises. Also to be found in the Netherlands Indies and British Malaya were the old and new middle classes. The old middle class generally comprised small producers, artisans and merchants. They were almost exclusively Indonesians and Chinese in the Netherlands Indies while in Malaya they were mostly Chinese. The new middle class is to be distinguished from the old middle class in that members of the former were not owners of the means of production. Rather they were simply employees. They were generally employed in occupations usually thought of as office jobs. In both countries the new middle class consisted mainly of Indonesians and Malays. The working class consisted of proletarianized peasants who still engaged in subsistence agriculture, peasant smallholders and plantation and mining wage labourers, often immigrant Chinese and Indians.

In concluding this chapter, there remains the issue of how to conceptualize the economic systems of the Netherlands Indies and British Malaya. Were they capitalist economies, dual economies or do these economic systems deserve to have their own conceptual categories?

Modern economic science began as a theoretical justification of economic liberalism. Classical economists saw in laissez-faire economics the means to growth. Both classical economists and Marx saw the peripheral areas as extensions of the capitalist core, and it was believed that capitalism as a mode of production would spread to these areas from the West.

Classical Marxist theories of development of which Marx, Lenin, Hilferding and Bukharin were the propounders, believe in the progressive role of capitalism in developing the forces of production in backward areas. Development here is defined as capitalist development, that is, development based on the production of exchange value by free wage labour for sale on the market.

Marx's works were essentially on closed, capitalist societies. Hilferding, Bukharin and Lenin were the main figures behind the classical Marxist theories of imperialism. They wrote on the tendency to monopoly and the intensification of competition on a world scale between monopoly capitals of nation states. This was to accelerate capitalist development in backward areas. Lenin's contribution to the theory of imperialism was based not only on Hobson's work[115] but on those of Hilferding and Bukharin. To Bukharin must be given the credit of placing Hilferding's analysis of finance capital within the context of the world economy in which there was the tendency to monopoly, the development of finance capital and the integration of capital in a single world economy.[116] He applied Marx's observations on the tendency for the rate of profit to fall saying that this tendency led to the outflow of capital to backward areas, promoting capitalist development there. Lenin's main contribution to the conceptualization of national development was to insist that imperialism was a stage of capitalist development, rather than just a policy pursued by capitalist states. Capitalist development became capitalist imperialism at a high stage of its development.[117] Hilferding, Bukharin and Lenin defined development as the global spread of capitalist relations of production.

The theory of the dual economy was a critique of classical and Marxist economics for trying to apply Western economic concepts to the study of the underdeveloped world. The theory of the dual economy found its most coherent expression in the works of the Dutch economist, Boeke,[118] who defines dualism as the 'clashing of an imported social system with an indigenous social system of another style'.[119] The imported system is usually capitalism but could just as well be communism, socialism or a combination. An ardent critic of the theory of the dual economy was Andre Gunder Frank. His denial of the existence of dual economies was made in the context of criticism of those who posited that feudalism still existed in Latin America. Frank, who popularized the works of the Latin American dependency school during the 1960s, argued that the capitalist mode of production embraced the entire economies of countries in Latin America. He was, therefore, denying that capitalist and feudal modes of production coexist in the same economic system.[120] This view was criticized by Ernesto Laclau who called into question Frank's usage of the term capitalism. According to Laclau, Frank could subsume feudalism under the capitalist mode of production because he excluded the relations of production in his definitions of capitalism and feudalism.[121] As a result, the nature of exploitation of diverse groups such as the Peruvian peasantry, Chilean tenants, Ecuadorian sharecroppers, West Indian sugar plantation slaves and textile workers in Manchester all come under the notion of capitalism.[122] Laclau's point is that if the relations of production are taken into account, then it can be seen that both capitalist and feudal modes of production exist in Latin America.[123] During the last 20 years there have been numerous contributions to the conceptualization of modes of production that stress the coexistence of modes of production in an economic system.[124]

Laclau's point is certainly well taken. He agrees with Frank's criticism of the theory of dual economy, as well as with his insistence that capitalist development generates underdevelopment.[125] In fact this latter point was made long before Frank.

If capitalist development can occur simultaneously with pre-capitalist forms of surplus appropriation, do we define the whole system as capitalist or do we posit the coexistence of capitalist and pre-capitalist modes of production? A solution to this problem is provided by the world-system perspective. The world-system perspective argues that capitalism as it is found in the core (developed) regions differs from capitalism as it is found in peripheral (underdeveloped) regions in terms of their relations of production. Core production is characterized by wage labour and peripheral production by relatively coerced forms of labour. The core specializes in 'capital intensive production using highly paid skilled labor, and peripheral areas specialize in labor intensive production using low wage (or coerced) and relatively unskilled labor'.[126] The capitalist system as a world system is understood in terms of core and peripheral capitalism. The world-system perspective has advantages over that of Frank.

In contrast to Frank, the world-system perspective does not subsume all pre-capitalist modes of production under the heading of capitalism but instead refers to peripheral and core forms of capitalism, as well as the coexistence of modes of production. The new specification of the capitalist mode of production offered by the world-system perspective includes core/periphery exploitation along with class exploitation.[127] Peripheral capitalism is necessary for core capitalism in that the former made significant contributions to capitalist accumulation in the core in prior centuries while today it continues to have its effects on politics there.[128] The crucial difference between core and peripheral capitalism lies in the forms of labour. The core/periphery hierarchy corresponds loosely to a continuum from protected labour through wage labour to coerced labour.[129] Core labour then is commodified while peripheral labour is 'partly commodified while also containing a large dose of politically mediated coercion'.[130]

The definition of the world-system as a world capitalist economic system, understood in terms of core and peripheral forms of capitalism, does not mean that elements of tributary modes of production cannot exist in this world-system. In other words, Wallerstein's totality assumption which implies that each world-system has only one mode of production can be dropped. As Chas-Dunn suggests, bringing the core-periphery hierarchy and the interstate system into the definition of capitalism allows us to show the connectedness of core and peripheral forms of capitalism without holding on to the totality assumption.[131]

Rosa Luxembourg, who unlike the classical Marxist theorists of imperialism did not believe in the necessarily progressive role of capitalism, is important for showing how capitalist development can take place simultaneously with the process of primitive accumulation in backward areas.[132] She is a precursor of the ideas of the Marx-inspired unequal exchange theorists, Amin and Emmanuel. For Emmanuel unequal exchange occurs because of differing levels of remuneration to labour between the core and periphery. Commodities produced in the periphery fetch lower prices on the world market and the exchange of commodities between the core and the periphery is in effect a 'hidden' transfer from the periphery to the core.[133] So, in the case of Luxembourg and the unequal exchange theorists, development refers to the simultaneous underdevelopment of the periphery. The world-system perspective, along similar lines, recognizes that underdeveloped countries cannot follow the same path as that of the developed countries because of the historical evolution of a highly unequal capitalist system of rich-country to poor-country relationships. Unequal power relationships between core and peripheral countries do not allow underdeveloped countries to experience independent, self-sustaining development. A large part of underdevelopment is attributed to the policies of industrialized countries and their extensions in the form of elite groups in the periphery. Furthermore, world-system theory sees the world as constituting a single division of labour, this division being hierarchical.

From various perspectives, therefore, there is much agreement on the negative effect that capitalist development has in the underdeveloped world. On this score there is agreement with Frank.

If Laclau and others agree with Frank in this respect and mutually reject the theory of dual economy, positing instead the coexistence of modes of production, Alavi and de Silva go further so as to refer to the relationship between capitalist and pre-capitalist modes of production in terms of a new conceptual category, the colonial mode of production.

According to Alavi, if it were correct to posit the coexistence of a capitalist and feudal mode of production, 'they would be dialectically related, in mutual opposition and contradiction'.[134] However 'feudalism' in the colonies and capitalism in the home countries are not in contradiction with each other, for it is the latter which gives rise to and supports the former.[135] Alavi further argues that the transformation that India underwent does not warrant referring to a feudal and pre-capitalist sector coexisting with a capitalist sector, as only the superficial forms of feudalism were retained based on a deformed commodity production.[136] Instead, a new mode of production comes into being, the colonial mode of production.

De Silva, in rejecting the theory of dual economy, goes so far as to say that the colonial economy is a conceptual category of its own and that capitalism is not found there.[137] He argues that the criteria of capitalism used to describe the colonial plantation economy as capitalist are insufficient, that these criteria do not conform to the classic notion of capitalism, and that the plantation system was a pre-capitalist form of production.[138] He argues that in the light of the generic features of capitalism the form of production in plantation economies cannot be regarded as capitalist. Citing Marx, he discusses two main features of capitalism. One is the capital-labour relation based on wage labour and the other is the production and accumulation of surplus value as the aim and motive force of production.[139]

On the capital-labour relation as a feature of capitalism what is crucial is not the mere use of capital but rather the increasing use of fixed capital that allows for the increase in the productivity of labour. This is capital that enters into the actual production process itself and is to be distinguished from working capital.[140] Also important, de Silva argues, is the content of fixed capital itself. The kind of fixed capital which allowed for greater productivity came from investment in plant and machinery which had the effect of reducing labour in relation to output, increasing the specialization of labour and capital, giving rise to internal and external economies of scale, and changing the organic composition of capital.[141] As opposed to the dominance of fixed capital in the capitalist mode of production, what is far more pervasive in colonial economies is working capital. Plantation economies do not belong to the capitalist mode of production, therefore, because the major part of their investment assumes the form of working capital.[142]

On the surplus generating capacity of the plantation economy, de Silva argues that it produces a large mass of surplus only because it employs a 'large labour force at a small surplus value per head'.[143] For de Silva, therefore, the plantation economy is not a capitalist economy because of the low proportion of fixed to working capital and the low surplus value generated.

The issue of the characterization of the economic system during the colonial period that surrounds the imposition of colonial rule and economic organization, then, has many critics, each of which can be objected to on different grounds, both in general terms and with particular reference to the colonial economies of the Netherlands Indies and British Malaya.

If we take the dualism thesis to mean that a primitive village subsistence economy exists alongside a modern one, then this thesis is wrong. However, neither is referring to the whole economic system as capitalist helpful, as Laclau has pointed out. Laclau is right to posit a coexistence of the feudal and capitalist modes of production but is incorrect in saying that this entails the rejection of the theory of the dual economy. This theory as it was originally formulated by Boeke is compatible with the theory of coexistence, including the recognition of the negative effects on the pre-capitalist world, brought about by the interaction of these two modes of production. In Boeke's definition of the dual economy, there is the 'clashing of an imported with an indigenous social system of another style'.[144] He was very conscious of the connection between the imported and indigenous systems as well as the change brought about in the latter. For example, he refers to how the Javanese villages lost their decision-making power when the Dutch combined them into rural municipalities.[145] The effect of the introduction of a money economy on immiseration is also discussed.[146] The crucial point here is that what Boeke means by a dual economic system is very close in form and content to what Laclau has in mind by conceptualizing Latin American economic systems in terms of the coexistence of feudal and capitalist modes of production.

A couple of remarks can be made with regard to Alavi's critique of Laclau. Laclau was criticized for positing the coexistence of modes of production. According to Alavi, these modes of production were not in contradiction with each other. Rather, the pre-capitalist mode of production was in the service of imperialism. Therefore, to accept Laclau's view would mean refuting the Marxist conception of necessary contradiction between coexisting modes of production.[147] First of all, the acceptance or rejection of coexistence of modes of production, to my mind, in colonial societies cannot be made on theoretical grounds. We do not reject Laclau's view simply because it is not in line with the Marxist conception of necessary contradiction. We would only reject it if it did not conform to empirical situations, which brings us to the second point. In some cases, the thesis of coexistence or dual economy (in Boeke's sense) applies, in others Alavi's colonial mode of production applies. In Java we find instances of both. In earlier periods of colonial rule capitalist and prebendal relations of production were in motion alongside each other while in later periods the prebendal feudal mode of production clearly had disintegrated. There will be more on this a little later, but for now it should be stressed that adjudication between Laclau's and Alavi's viewpoints is not to be entertained dogmatically on theoretical grounds. The colonial mode of production or colonial capitalism as it has been referred to is certainly a valid conceptualization if indeed the pre-capitalist modes of production were disintegrating. Only on these grounds can colonial capitalism be said to determine the nature of the colonial economic system and only then does the colonial economy need to be described in terms of its own conceptual category.

De Silva also says that the colonial economy must be seen in terms of its own conceptual category. However, this economy is not capitalist to him. Again, a number of objections to this view can be made. First of all, everything else considered, the basic features of capitalism, that is, the production of exchange-values for a market, in which ownership of the means of production by one class enables them to buy wage labour which is severed from the ownership of the means of production, were present. De Silva is excessively stringent in drawing up the criteria of the capitalist mode of production. Given that the colonial plantation economy is characterized by a greater proportion of working capital and smaller surplus value per head, why does this make the economy less capitalistic? It is clear that such an economy would be less dynamic and more susceptible to the world market than economies in the industrialized world; but this does not mean it is not capitalist production that is in operation.

The various issues surrounding the characterization of the colonial economic system that have been raised above, can also be brought to bear upon the cases of British Malaya and the Netherlands Indies.

At the outset it should be stated that these economies could be seen to have the characteristics of the capitalist mode of production notwithstanding the fact of a greater proportion of working capital and smaller surplus value per head. This was especially true of Java where the high population density, relative to arable land, created the conditions for free wage labour. It was also true of British Malaya in the tin mining and rubber industries which relied on immigrants for a high proportion of their labour.

Regarding the issue of the coexistence of capitalist and pre-capitalist modes of production on the one hand and the existence of a unitary colonial mode of production on the other, the picture is more complicated.

It is correct to speak of the coexistence of capitalism and feudal or prebendal feudal modes of production in the colonies during earlier periods of colonial rule. In pre-colonial Java, holders of lungguh (benefices) that were appointed by the sultan were responsible for the acquisition of peasant agricultural surplus as well as for the exaction of labour services. Under the Dutch, especially in the period before the cultuurstelsel these officials continued to play similar roles as surplus appropriators with the main difference that a portion of the surplus had to be given up to the Dutch instead of to the sultan. Such prebendal feudal relations of production were visible even after the introduction of plantation economies. However, in the later years of the cultuurstelsel when it was more difficult for the peasantry to subsist from village agriculture, they were attracted to work in sugar mills.[148] Here, the role of the bupati as a receiver of peasant surpluses diminished as the peasantry began to make a switch in their means of livelihood. In British Malaya, in areas where British rule was less pervasive, that is in areas peripheral to the colonial plantation and mining sectors, the old feudal forms of surplus acquisition survived in spite of the fact that many among the feudal nobility received salaries from the British. In the Federated Malay States, however, the old feudal nobility was effectively converted into salaried officials and the peasants either became smallholders in commercial crops or remained aloof from the money economy. The dissolution of the feudal or prebendal feudal modes of production, then, left a capitalist mining and plantation economy in the colonies and this is what can be described as the colonial mode of production or colonial capitalism. What preceded colonial capitalism, however, was the coexistence of capitalism with feudalism or prebendal feudalism.

In fact, both the coexistence of capitalism with 'pre-capitalist' modes of production in British Malaya and the Netherlands Indies as well as the colonial mode of production there, represent phases of peripheral capitalism. Chase-Dunn refers to phases of the expansion of capitalism which reproduced 'pre-capitalist' forms of production and to other phases which replaced these 'pre-capitalist' forms with core-like production relations.[149] The coexistence of capitalism with feudalism or prebendal feudalism meant the maintenance of pre-capitalist forms of labour control for the production of commodities for export to the core. However, these pre-capitalist forms of production began to be supplanted by proletarianized labour, for the most part, in the mining and plantation economies, while coercive types of labour control did not disappear altogether.

CONCLUSION

The purpose of outlining the pre-capitalist and colonial social formations of the Malay–Indonesian Archipelago has been to provide an historical and sociological background to the emergence of the Malaysian and Indonesian post-colonial states, discussed in Chapters 4, 5 and 6. The three factors that I focus on, that is, the internal strength of the state, elite cohesion and armed resistance against the state, have their roots in pre-capitalist and colonial times. Furthermore, the kinds of peripheral capitalist societies that we find in British Malaya and the Netherlands Indies differ, especially in terms of how these factors emerged during the colonial period and after formal independence.

   The factors of the internal strength of the state and elite cohesion have their roots in the class structures established during the colonial period. The crucial difference between Malaysia and Indonesia during pre-colonial times was that there was a relatively strong indigenous merchant class in the latter while such a class was virtually non-existent in the former. Even prior to the colonial period, the great centres of trade in the archipelago were to be found in Sumatra, Java and on some of the other islands. But the case for indigenous traders in Sumatra and Java should not be overstated. The Malay–Indonesian world of maritime trade in pre-colonial days was characterized by the preponderance of West Asian, especially Arab and Indian traders. Indigenous traders were dominant in the interior of Java but maritime trade was dominated numerically and economically by foreign Asians. This was true of the whole archipelago.[150] On the Malay Peninsula, however, only Malacca was of any significance. In other words, for the most part, the Malay Peninsula had been a backwater of the archipelago, as far as the economic life of the region was concerned. As far as Javanese domination of the Malay Peninsula was concerned, the Javanese Majapahit State (1293–1521), located in East Java, claimed authority over various states throughout Sumatra, the Malay Peninsula and various other islands of the archipelago.[151] However, there is no evidence for this and it is more likely that rather than a centralized exercise of authority by Majapahit over other areas there were trading links with these areas. The state may have had a royal monopoly of the Majapahit end of this trade.[152]

The presence of an indigenous merchant class in the Netherlands Indies is important in that it helps to explain why post-colonial Indonesia and Malaysia differ over these factors of elite cohesion and the internal strength of the state. With regard to the former, the more complex class structure in post-colonial Indonesia, coupled with the fragmented power of the dominant classes, led to a more heterogeneous ruling elite as far as their class and ideological backgrounds were concerned. On the other hand, in Malaysia the state elite came from a similar class background and there was a great deal more consensus in Malaysia than in Indonesia on how the country should be run economically as well as politically.

Regarding the internal strength of the state, the presence of an indigenous merchant class from pre-colonial times had checked the growth of the Chinese merchant class and also gave rise to indigenous Indonesian capitalists who emerged after formal independence. This had the effect of fragmenting the overall power of the dominant classes. No one class or ethnic group was dominant enough to provide support for a democratic state. This is in contrast to Malaysia where there was only one dominant class at independence, that is, a Chinese capitalist class. The two factors of internal state strength and elite cohesion are discussed in Chapters 5 and 6 respectively.

Concerning the third factor of armed resistance against the state, the peripheralization of Indonesia and Malaysia took different forms. In Malaysia it was based on the importation of Chinese and Indian labour by the British, leaving a vast Malay peasant population out of the money economy. In Indonesia, on the other hand, a far greater degree of proletarianization of the indigenous population took place during Dutch rule. This is discussed in more detail in Chapter 4.

Thus, the three factors of the elite cohesion, the internal strength of the state and armed resistance against the state, have their origins in the pre-capitalist and colonial social formations of Indonesia and Malaysia which have been outlined in this chapter.

4 Peasant and Labour Opposition to the Colonial and Post-colonial State

PEASANTS AND MASS MOVEMENTS

The purpose of this chapter is to discuss the relative potential for revolutionary action against the colonial and post-colonial state to be found among the peasantry and labour during the period of the nationalist movements in Malaya and Indonesia.

While Marx generally placed the industrial proletariat at the centre stage of revolution, he by no means relegated the peasantry to a mere object of history. In his studies of the peasantry of republican France after 1848, Marx notes how peasants revoked their support for Bonaparte after a new wine tax was imposed upon them through the instrument of the petition.[1] Similarly, Engels documented peasant mass movements. In trying to account for the defeat of these movements, he agrees with Marx that peasant rebellions can succeed only in the context of a proletarian revolution.[2] Furthermore, both Marx and Engels envisioned the gradual sinking of the peasantry into the proletariat.[3] This view was echoed by Lenin, referring to the dissolution of the peasantry after the destruction of feudalism.[4]

It was Mao who recognized that the peasantry could constitute the major force behind a revolution. His observation of the peasant uprising in Hunan led him to assert that 'in a very short time several hundred million peasants in China's central, southern and northern provinces will rise like a tornado . . .'[5] At the same time Mao believed that the leadership of the peasantry should be in the hands of the proletariat.[6]

The potential for revolutionary action among the peasantry was not only cited by revolutionaries, however.[7] Barrington Moore, Jr. has been largely responsible for getting the social sciences to take note of the role of peasants in the history of state formation.[8] At a time when the active role of the peasantry in state formation is being discovered, the cases of Malaysia and Indonesia warrant a more traditional stance regarding the revolutionary potential of peasants. Peasants were by no means principle actors in the nationalist movements of Malaysia and

Indonesia, which is not to deny that to a greater or lesser degree they were participants.

THE TYPOLOGY OF PEASANTS AND THEIR POTENTIAL FOR REVOLUTION

In asking the question of which circumstances produce revolutionary peasants, Alavi distinguishes between three sectors of the rural economy. In the first sector land is owned by landlords who do not themselves cultivate the land.[9] The second sector is made up of independent smallholders who own the land they cultivate. They are what is referred to as middle peasants.[10] The third sector of the rural economy is made up of capitalist farmers who own land. They are distinct from landlords in that the former hire wage labour while the latter leases his land to landless sharecroppers.[11] The mass of the peasantry generally fall under these two categories, wage labour and sharecroppers.

There are extremely divergent views on the relative propensity of different sections of the peasantry for revolutionary action. Scott argues that isolated village-dwellers, have the greatest propensity for revolutionary action because of the cultural and organizational autonomy that they possess. There is to be found among these middle peasants 'the strongest resistance to capitalism and to an intrusive state'.[12] There is a contradiction in values between the dominant class culture of the ruling elite and the pre-capitalist culture of the smallholders. Wolf would concur with Scott regarding the type of peasant most prone to revolution, but has different reasons in mind. 'Ultimately, the decisive factor in making a peasant rebellion possible lies in the relation of the peasantry to the field of power which surrounds it'.[13] Thus, middle peasants who own their land and are outside the direct sphere of control of landlords are more likely to rebel than poor peasants, such as sharecroppers and wage labourers who are more dependent upon landlords.

In appraising these various views, Skocpol distinguishes between two patterns of revolution. In the first pattern, exemplified by the French, Russian and Mexican cases, the breakdown of the old regime state was followed by spontaneous widespread local peasant revolts that served to undermine the landed classes and other conservative forces. Consequent upon the consolidation of a new state organization, then, was not the mobilization of the peasantry, but rather their coercion.[14] The second pattern is exemplified by the Chinese, Vietnamese and Cuban cases, in which peasants were directly mobilized by revolutionary organizations whether before or after the fall of a regime. The result of this direct mobilization was peasant participation in new-regime state building. A significant difference between the two patterns is that the first is characterized by spontaneous and autonomous peasant behaviour and the second by direct mobilization and participation. The latter is more favourable to peasant interests due to the direct links established between peasants and revolutionary organizations.[15] The question of which peasants are more prone to revolution takes on a different meaning in the light of these two patterns. Skocpol rightly points out that, according to the second pattern, 'many different kinds of peasants – subsistence smallholders in marginal areas, landless laborers or tenants, even solidary villages of peasants alone, or else villages of landlords and peasants together can potentially be mobilized by revolutionary movements'.[16]

The case of British Malaya and the Netherlands Indies clearly comes under the second pattern in which there were attempts to directly mobilize peasants into revolutionary action. This is not to say that there had been no instances of spontaneous peasant insurrections, revolts and rebellions but their impact on the colonial and emerging post-colonial states was minimal, as I intend to show later.

We can proceed further to specify the kinds of peasants that participated in revolutionary activities in British Malaya and the Netherlands Indies. What Paige has to say is certainly more relevant than the views of Scott and Wolf in this regard. For we do not find in the two colonies the most active participants against the colonial state to be from among the middle peasants but rather landless labourers and sharecroppers. The orientation which supposes that the participation of various classes and groups in revolutionary movements can be explained in terms of economic interest and the social circumstances in which these groups find themselves is a useful one which can be better specified with recourse to Paige's work.[17]

He attempts to understand the nature of mass movements in terms of the combined effects of the political behaviour of both the upper and lower classes. A mass movement is a result of the 'interaction between the political behavior associated with the principal source of income of the upper and lower agricultural classes'.[18] The various combinations of income sources are in turn associated with particular forms of agricultural organization and lead to particular types of social movements. These various combinations of income sources can be presented in terms of the case of the nationalist movements in British Malaya and the Netherlands Indies. Of the four combinations that Paige discusses, three of them are found in British Malaya and the Netherlands Indies. I will discuss the former first.

Here, the combination of income sources are that of a dominant class dependent on income from capital and a working class dependent on income from wages. According to Paige, in such a situation a strong bourgeoisie is able and willing to make concessions to a well-organized, conscious working class, in order to direct revolutionary currents into reformist channels.[19] The result is a reformist labour movement. The mining and plantation sectors in British Malaya were based mainly on immigrant wage labour. Nevertheless, the initial result was not a reformist labour movement but a radical one that eventually retreated to the jungle and carried out guerilla warfare. In fact, Paige refers to the case of Malaya as an exception to the rule. He attributes this to the idea that rubber estate owners faced declining productivity and competition from smallholders and were, therefore, unable to make concessions to workers. The workers then resorted to revolutionary warfare.[20] Any militant elements in the Malayan labour movement were crushed by the British, and the Communist Party of Malaya (CPM) was declared illegal in 1948. Anti-colonial activity among labour did not cease altogether, needless to say, but took on the form of a reformist movement. While we would not describe this movement as revolutionary, it was the only organized working class movement that offered resistance to the colonial state. The destruction of labour militancy in British Malaya was to have profound consequences for the formation of the post-colonial state and serves to bring out a core difference between democracies in developed and developing economies. In the former, the working class pushed for the establishment of democratic institutions, whereas in the latter it is the destruction of mass movements that partly creates the conditions for democracy. To say more on this, however, would be to anticipate the next chapter.

Turning to the Netherlands Indies, two of the combinations of income sources discussed by Paige are relevant. The first is where the dominant class is dependent on commercial capital and the peasant classes on land. The latter are smallholders producing a supplementary cash crop.[21] In the Netherlands Indies, the direct producers of commodities marketed by the merchant class were also involved in share-cropping and estate wage labour. The pressures of this involvement drew them away from commodity production which created the basis of a reform commodity movement led by the indigenous commercial class. This movement later became radicalized and sought the destruction of the colonial state.

The second combination relevant to the Netherlands Indies is where the dominant class is dependent on the income from land and peasants are dependent on income from wages. Such peasants are involved in sharecropping and migratory estate systems of production.[22] The pressures on the peasantry due to such systems of production create the conditions for greater class solidarity and anti-colonial revolutionary movements.[23]

Indeed, it was precisely the merchant class, peasant sharecroppers, and peasant wage labour that were the most active anti-colonial forces in the Netherlands Indies. This raises an interesting question of whether the post-colonial authoritarian state in Indonesia emerged out of the need to crush a mass movement on the one hand or a revolting middle class on the other. In addition, it could be said that the authoritarian state functioned to mediate between the interests of the indigenous merchant class, the Chinese capitalist class, the military and foreign capital. This would seem to be the more plausible of the answers. As we shall see in the following chapters, the threat to the Indonesian post-colonial state, as perceived by the elite, was not only organized mass movements but middle class and elite groups as well. The creation of the repressive post-colonial military and bureaucratic apparatus was both to quell a mass movement as well as respond to pressure from the middle classes. While in British Malaya, mass movements were all but destroyed by the British and were not to be a significant force, in Indonesia they played a vital role in the form of armed resistance against the state. In the following section, I will discuss the various ways by which the peasantry experienced immiseration, the anti-colonial movements which emerged, and their appeasement by the colonial states.

ECONOMIC CONDITIONS AND PEASANTS AGAINST THE COLONIAL STATE

Because of the differing importance of the peasantry in the colonial economies of British Malaya and the Netherlands Indies, the economic systems varied.

In British Malaya, Lim Teck Ghee identifies three types of peasant economies in the Federated Malay States. These are the modified traditional subsistence, the mixed subsistence–commercial and the commercial peasant economy.[24] The modified traditional subsistence economy was predominant during the early period of colonial rule and did not differ significantly from the pre-colonial subsistence peasant economy with the exception of occasional cash-earning activities, especially in areas close to mining and other commercial ventures.[25] In other words, the main difference between this and the pre-colonial subsistence economy was a greater level of monetization and market relations while the basic structure of the subsistence economy remained the same. *Padi* (rice) production, which was the principle economic activity of the modified subsistence economy, hovered around subsistence levels.[26]

The mixed subsistence–commercial peasant economy was characterized by peasants who were much more integrated into the market economy. While still engaged in subsistence food production, resources were also allocated to cash crop production which yielded incomes much larger and more regular than those derived from the modified subsistence economy and less subsistence-oriented patterns of consumption.[27] The third type of peasant economy in British Malaya was the commercial one. In this economy, peasants were engaged full-time in commercial crop cultivation and were, therefore, more vulnerable to fluctuations in market prices.[28]

One of the most serious problems faced by peasants, especially those involved in commercial activities, was the need for credit and indebtedness. There were basically three forms of peasant indebtedness. One was where poor peasants would borrow money from rice millers with their incoming crop as security.[29] Secondly, peasants would obtain loans from *chetties* (professional moneylenders from Northern India) on the security of the land.[30] Thirdly, they would obtain goods from Chinese shopkeepers in exchange for agricultural produce.[31] The problem of debt affected all peasants and took a turn for the worse between 1913 and 1917 when the large-scale commercialization of peasant activities took place.[32] In 1920 and 1921 indebtedness had resulted in a 'flurry of foreclosures by their creditors'.[33] In addition to the problems of debt faced by the peasantry, the mining and rubber industries also had their share of economic problems as far as the workers were concerned. The majority of workers in the estate and mining sectors of the economy were of Indian and Chinese origin. They faced drastic reductions in wages during the depression.

Turning to the economic conditions faced by the peasantry in the Netherlands Indies, it too was victim to the establishment of a money economy. First of all, peasants were subject to recurring indebtedness in much the same way as they were in British Malaya. While the Dutch were able to prevent the loss of lands as a result of indebtedness they failed to protect the peasantry from incurring debt.[34] The impoverishment of the peasants arose for several reasons. The increase in Western demand for village agricultural produce certainly did benefit the economically strong among the peasants but the majority faced impoverishment because of price inflation.[35] Furthermore, there was the loss of skill and talent from the village to the Westernized towns and estates as youth, planters and craftsmen searched for greater opportunities.[36] Also, as peasants were more and more integrated into the money economy misery encroached when there was no money to pay for the imported necessities of life. As Boeke pointed out, such necessities which could only be procured by money imported into the village had increased dramatically in the twentieth century.[37] The way involvement in the money economy adversely affected village life is described by Boeke as follows:

> In this connection a vicious cycle presents itself. Rice mills, oil and cassava factories buy up an increasing proportion of the village products. So large a proportion in fact, that the producers are later obliged to buy back a certain amount of it. But for this purpose they cannot use the money obtained from the previous sale, as this left the village immediately to settle outstanding outside obligations. Hence new financial means must come from beyond the village limits.[38]

This results in more and more credit on progressively heavier terms which in turn results in a greater proportion of village products leaving the village. The end result is that the village is 'swallowed up in the dualistic traffic'.[39]

That various forms of economic hardship fell to the lot of the peasantry and immigrant workers whether in the plantation sector, in the village agricultural sector, or the mining sector does not need to be dwelled upon. What is more important is why the protest movement that these hardships yielded were not to play significant roles in the attainment of formal independence.

Peasant uprisings and worker protest were by no means unknown in the two colonies. There had been several instances of peasant rebellions in British Malaya and the Netherlands Indies as well as militant and reformist worker activities against the colonial state.

Peasant uprisings in British Malaya occurred throughout the Malay Peninsula. In 1891 an anti-British uprising broke out in the district of Semantan in the state of Pahang and spread to several areas within the state. The rebellion was not suppressed until 1895 and resulted in the abandonment of villages and the neglect of cultivation. A peasant rebellion in another state, Trengganu, led by one Haji Abdul Rahman

Limbong was not only anti-British and anti-tax-reforms but also against the chiefs. These chiefs were seen as exploiters of the *rakyat* (masses) through the exaction of taxes. This took place in 1928.[40] There was also the Tok Janggut rebellion of 1915 in the state of Kelantan.[41]

Similarly in the Netherlands Indies peasant protest was not uncommon. There were widespread peasant revolts in Java in the nineteenth century, caused by the excesses in exactions of the colonial economy. In the nineteenth and twentieth centuries of colonial Indonesia, the peasant movements were of various kinds including anti-extortion, messianic, revivalist, sectarian and pan-Islamic.[42]

Apart from rural peasant-based protest movements there were also urban and plantation estate-based labour movements, some more militant than others.

In British Malaya, the Societies Ordinance of 1909 established the basic right of association for all groups.[43] However, it was not until 1936 that labour unrest began to spread in the colony beginning with the strike of 13 000 coolies working in the Sanitation Department in Singapore.[44] Later in the same year Indian and Chinese workers of the Singapore Traction Lines were on strike for higher wages and shorter working days. A month later there was a serious strike of 4000 Chinese miners at the Malayan Collieries which brought mining operations to a standstill for several days.[45] Their demands, too, were for higher wages and a shorter workday as well as for better working conditions. In 1937 Chinese estate labourers went on strike to voice dissatisfaction at the restoration of depression wage cuts in spite of the prosperity enjoyed by the rubber industry after the depression.[46] After the Second World War the General Labour Unions (GLU) were established throughout Malaya and the Straits Settlements. This led to the formation of the Pan-Malayan General Labour Union in 1946[47] At this time, the Communist Party of Malaya was very active in organizing strikes.[48] In 1947 as many as 291 strikes were organized involving some 69 217 workers and resulting in 696 036 workdays lost. These strikes were closely connected to the activities of the CPM and the Pan-Malayan Federation of Trade Unions (PMFTU).[49] This was when the CPM was in its legal phase. During its illegal phase, after June 1948, the CPM organized the Malayan Races' Liberation Army (MRLA) as well as 'Blood and Steel Corps' which engaged in extortion, intimidation, raids and robberies.[50] After a wave of murders in which Chinese Kuomintang leaders as well European estate managers were murdered, a state of emergency was declared by the British on June 18th, 1948. The state of emergency lasted for 12 years. During this time the activities of labour organizations were severely limited by emergency laws. The outlawing of the CPM and the dissolution of the PMFTU led to a leadership vacuum in the labour movement.[51] In spite of resorting to guerilla and terrorist tactics during the emergency period, the CPM was still unable to make any inroads in leading a mass movement against the colonial state.

In the Netherlands Indies, the first labour union was formed in 1908 by railroad and tramway employees. This was followed in 1911 by the formation of a union by customs officials, and in 1912 by functionaries of the Departments of Education and the Treasury.[52] The same decade saw the burgeoning of labour unions which by the end of 1919 reached a total membership of 72 000.[53] Throughout the 1920s strikes called by labour unions were seen by the colonial government as communist instigated and attempts to restrict union activities finally led to the banishment or imprisonment of labour leaders.[54] This was after the failure of the 1926–7 Communist rebellions when some 13 000 people were arrested and deported to the Tanah Merah concentration camp in New Guinea.[55] Also active in supporting labour activities against the colonial state were the nationalist organizations, Budi Utomo and Sarekat Islam.[56]

In 1923 the Netherlands Indies Labour laws limited the right to strike. It was stipulated that any labour activity that violated the public order or contravened a labour contract was liable to penalization. This legislation was fairly successful in keeping down the number of strikes. Between 1936 and 1940 the largest number of workers involved in strikes in a year was 2115.[57] During the Japanese occupation of 1942–5, the labour movement continued to be relatively inactive and it was not until after formal independence that labour activities stepped up.

In view of the fact that the peasantries and labour movements had particular grievances against the British and Dutch and there were several instances of overt resistance to the state, their actual impact on anticolonial state activities and on the nature of the emerging post-colonial state was minimal. In elaborating this point, however, it will be necessary to establish the criteria according to which the significance for state formation of peasant and labour movements can be assessed.

PEASANTS, LABOUR AND FORMAL INDEPENDENCE

To establish these criteria we need to make the distinction, following Skocpol, between the causes and outcomes of revolutions.[58] To be more specific, a distinction can be made between two patterns of revolutions as discussed above. To recapitulate, the first pattern involved spontaneous peasant revolts that served to undermine the landed classes and other conservative forces. In the second pattern, peasants were directly mobilized by revolutionary forces. The outcome of revolutions of the former type saw the coercion and repression of peasant lower classes while that of revolutions of the latter type saw the mobilization of peasants to participate in new regime state building. Having made this distinction, the following questions can be asked. How were peasants involved in the causes of the revolution? That is, were they directly mobilized in the revolution and brought in to participate in the building of the new state? In the cases that Skocpol studied, peasant involvement in the revolution followed both patterns and was significant in that the peasantry was a force that the declining old regime and emerging new regime had to reckon with. How was the peasantry a force to be reckoned with in Skocpol's cases and can the peasant and labour movements in Indonesia and Malaysia during the struggle for independence be seen to have constituted such a force?[59]

Europe had seen revolutions with very wide peasant and labour participation. In France, the fall of the Bastille in the summer of 1789 must be understood against the background of labourers roaming the cities looking for arms and grain and demanding both bread and liberty.[60] During the collapse of the Romanov autocracy in Russia in March 1917, it was the crucial link between workers and the army that neutralized upper class resistance.[61] These revolts, rebellions and outbursts among the lower classes were directed against a specific class, the landlords. While there had always been in these countries local and sporadic revolts against the landed classes what was new in the French, Russian and Chinese revolutions was that peasants had 'achieved a successful, widespread, direct assault on the property or claims of landlords'.[62] This included even the seizure of seigniorial property. In France, feudal records and grain stores of local seigneurs were seized.[63] In Russia, the peasantry acquired possession of land formerly belonging to landlords. The average increase in land held by peasants was estimated at three to five acres per household.[64]

In those revolutions in which peasant participation was spontaneous and autonomous, it was the peasantry that was responsible for pushing the revolution beyond levels required by liberal and bourgeois interests. In France various feudal practices and institutions such as seigniorial dues, the venality of offices, tax immunities, hunting rights and court pensions were all surrendered. But, as Skocpol notes, 'the liberal nobles and Third Estate representatives assembled at Versailles would never have initiated this session of sweeping reforms had not a spreading agrarian revolt against the seigniorial system forced their reluctant hand'.[65] In other words, as participants in bringing about revolution the peasants had succeeded in pushing for such radical reforms. So forceful were they that they later became targets of coercion by revolutionary forces who demanded supplies of grain and military conscription.[66]

In revolutions in which peasant participation was a result of direct mobilization by revolutionary organizations, as in China, peasants provided support, military as well as non-military, because they were made to feel that the Chinese Communist Party was fighting for their interests. Peasant support was vital and it amounted to the Communist Party 'treating peasant lives, property, and customs with scrupulous respect'.[67] Not only were peasants important in the revolutionary initiative but they also featured prominently in the outcome, playing active roles in new regime building. Communist leaders were recruited from among the deprived classes after the revolution[68] and emphasis was placed on developing small rural and medium-scale industries for the benefit of peasant consumers.[69] The peasantry was not left unprotected by the state, or at the mercy of market forces.

In both patterns of revolutions (spontaneous peasant rebellions or directly mobilized peasants) there was widespread participation of the peasantry that proved to be vital in bringing down the old regime. So powerful were these forces that they either had to be repressed during the aftermath of the revolution or brought into the process of state formation. This contrasts with the case of Malaysia where the participation of the peasantry and labour was not focused against particular dominant classes or the colonial state during the periods of struggle for independence.

In Indonesia the significant force in the war of independence came from the various parties and organizations whose leadership came from professionals and bureaucrats, mainly Dutch-educated Indonesians placed in the colonial civil service, and which were able to mobilize mass followings. These movements against the colonial and later postcolonial state took the form of armed rebellion and regional separatism. While it is being argued here that authoritarianism in Indonesia was partly a response to threatening armed revolts and separatist movements, there had also been the mobilization of the masses to support authoritarianism. Consider the failure of the Madiun rebellion of 1948. The Central Labour Organization of All Indonesia (SOBSI) and members of various socialist parties had not supported the idea of a revolution against the government and, therefore, were not behind the unsuccessful Madiun coup[70] planned by the Communist Party of Indonesia (PKI), even though SOBSI and the socialist parties were communist-oriented themselves. They did not support the coup because many socialists were loyal to Sukarno, whereas the PKI was attacking leaders like Sukarno who had become symbols of Indonesian independence from the Dutch.[71]

Nevertheless, this did not lead to a ban on the PKI as Sukarno chose to include the communists in his system of Guided Democracy. The communists would be especially useful in counteracting the power of the orthodox Muslims and the military.[72] To strengthen their position as political partner, the PKI sought to mobilize the peasant population which, among other things, meant the undertaking of activities that directly related to the alleviation of everyday problems. For example, the PKI revived the traditional village custom of mutual aid in the repair and construction of roads, bridges, irrigation works and houses, fought for lower interest rates on loans, and pushed for more favourable terms for sharecroppers and for raising agricultural production.[73] As a result, the PKI was able to obtain 16 per cent of the votes in the general election of 1955, only seven years after the communist revolt of 1948, and was one of the four largest parties in the country.[74] Further inroads were made in the provincial elections of 1957 and ten years after the Madiun affair the PKI had more than a million peasant members.[75] In other words, when mobilization of the masses did take place, it was in support of Sukarno and not against the state, and in the context of an already phased out parliamentary democracy.

In Malaysia, there was no war of independence and the lower classes were neither participants nor sources of pressure in the negotiations between the British and the Malayan elite for self-rule. The only militant element in Malayan labour was associated with the CPM. The emerging Malaysian government, however, had refused to accept the legal existence of the CPM in an independent Malaysia. Meanwhile, during the period of the emergency imposed by the British from 1948 for a period of 12 years, the CPM had failed through guerila and terrorist activities to gain the support of the masses.[76] It was condemned to outlaw status in independent Malaysia as well and never made any inroads in the labour movement.

At this point some mention must be made of covert resistance to the state. To say that peasant and labour organizations did not play significant roles in the struggle for independence in Malaysia is to say that they offered little resistance to the state, whether overt or covert. I have already indicated that they provided little overt resistance against the colonial state, at least during the period of the struggle for independence, and did not have a significant impact on new regime building. My position is that the same can be said of covert resistance. There has been increasing attention to these forms of resistance which refer to 'flight, sectarian withdrawal, or other activities that minimize challenges to or clashes with those whom they view as their [peasants'] oppressors . . . '[77] Without denying that such forms of protest or resistance existed or were even prevalent it would be extremely difficult to claim that they had any appreciable effect on state formation. The speeches, works and activities of the various anti-colonial and nationalist movements do not reveal awareness of covert resistance as a problem. Therefore, the formation of the post-colonial state in Malaysia cannot be understood in terms of a response to such resistance.

ARMED REBELLIONS IN INDONESIA AND MALAYA

Thus far, the point has been to show that the newly-independent state of Malaya did not inherit oppositional mass movements that might have led to the reactive establishment of authoritarian regimes, while the rise of an authoritarian state in Indonesia is to be explained in terms of the presence of oppositional mass movements. This is, therefore, a crucial difference between the two states.

Indonesia was beset by a series of armed revolts both during and after the colonial period. The Indonesian post-colonial state inherited armed rebellions which originated from colonial times. In Malaya, the only armed rebellion of importance came from the CPM, while a number of secessionist attempts occurring between 1948 and 1957 in Johor, Kelantan and Penang did not reappear after independence.[78] Among other things, it was the presence of widespread armed revolts that gave the Indonesian military a prominent role in politics, as will be discussed in Chapter 6.

In Malaya, the credit for the success of the government counter-insurgency policy against the CPM must go to the British as the greater part of the emergency period lasting from 1948 to 1960 was during the period of colonial rule. In fact, in 1956, a year before independence, Tunku Abdul Rahman, the nation's first prime minister, declared that the government would only build up a small army so as not to sap the resources of the country.[79] This indicates that the emerging government of independent Malaya did not see the CPM as a great threat to the security of the country or to the state. There were no plans to build up the armed forces and the police on a scale necessary to fight communist insurgency. After the British left, there was no great expansion of the armed forces and police. It does seem to be the case that the government of post-colonial Malaya 'did not bestir itself unduly over the military threat posed by the CPM ... '[80] The left was heavily suppressed, but most of this suppression took place during the British period. By the time of formal independence, there was not much left of an anti-government movement to suppress.

In Indonesia the situation was very different. Indonesia was plagued by widespread armed revolts and separatist movements from colonial times[81] which have lasted till today. Most of these revolts took place after 1945 and the various separatist movements survive till today: the PKI-planned Madiun rebellion in 1948; the Darul Islam movement in West Java which proclaimed the Islamic State of Indonesia (Negara Islam Indonesia) in 1949 and survived as a regional rebellion from 1948 to 1962; the South Moluccan Republic (Republik Maluku Selatan) movement in 1950; the establishment of a counter-government in Sumatra; the PRRI (Pemerintah Revolusioner Republik Indonesia – Revolutionary Government of the Republic of Indonesia) in 1958; the Free Papua Organization movement in Irian Jaya since 1962; the PKI coup attempt in 1965 which led to the downfall of Sukarno; Fretilin (Frente Revolucionaria de Timor Leste Independente – Revolutionary Front of Independent East Timor); and the Free Aceh Movement (Gerakan Aceh Merdeka) since 1976.[82] Many of these rebellions involved military units which broke away from the army. For example, the 1965 coup attempt involved four units from different services and their intelligence forces.[83] The problem of armed revolts in Indonesia added to the various forces of opposition against the government after independence.

Two kinds of movements can be identified in Indonesia as far as these armed revolts are concerned.[84] Firstly, there were those insurgencies which originated in the independence movement such as the PKI-planned Madiun rebellion. These movements were usually based on Islamic or Marxist ideology and had their roots in the indigenous merchant class which spawned various organizations and political parties since the early part of the century. For example, one faction of the Sarekat Islam (Islamic Union) led to the formation of the PKI. Undoubtedly, the presence of a strong indigenous merchant class which was the breeding ground for Marxist and Islamic nationalist organizations is a factor that distinguishes Indonesia from Malaysia. The effect that this factor had on the rise of the Indonesian authoritarian state is discussed in Chapter 5.

The second kind of movement were those insurgencies which originated in the decolonization process. These were regional separatist movements that were Dutch-sponsored. Examples are the South Moluccan Republic Movement, the Free Papua Organization and the Free Aceh Movement. These insurgencies took place at an early stage of the post-independence period.[85]

Democracy was implanted in Indonesia and Malaysia from without. One of the conditions under which it can survive is if there is no mass resistance to the democratic programme and state. While the Malaysian post-colonial state was not up against mass movements, Indonesia faced a series of armed rebellions contributing to the downfall of Indonesian democracy. The stability of the democratic Indonesian state was threatened and led to the reactive establishment of an authoritarian regime. How this took place is discussed in Chapter 6. For now it is important to note that the Indonesian and Malaysian democratic post-colonial states differ in that the former was brought down, in part, by armed revolts and the latter was not.

THE CAUSES OF THE NON-REVOLUTIONARY NATURE OF THE PEASANTRY AND LABOUR

It is true that the dominant element in peasant and labour opposition to the state was non-communist in Indonesia, and that communism failed to make significant inroads in Malaysia. This is due, in no small measure, to a number of factors that explain the non-revolutionary nature of the peasantry and labour and the weakness of class-based mass movements in these countries.

The fact that there were various governmental efforts at curbing the freedom of lower class protest in Indonesia and Malaysia prior to independence, such as the declaration of a state of emergency, the jailing of nationalist leaders and the banning of trade union activities, by itself does not explain why labour and the peasantry did not play significant roles in the birth of the post-colonial state as class-based movements. Revolutionary organizations do not take heed of legal restrictions against them when seeking to overthrow a state. What explains the non-revolutionary nature of the peasantry and labour?

Perhaps the most important is the economic factor. There is a lot to suggest that several mitigating factors lessened the debilitating impact of colonial capitalism on the peasantry. It will be recalled that in British Malaya three types of peasant economies coexisted. These were the modified subsistence, the mixed subsistence commercial and the commercial peasant economy. While it is true that peasants were affected in various ways by the vagaries of the market, as discussed earlier in this chapter, it is also true that there was significant peasant mobility between each type of peasant economy.[86] Because of the relatively low population density of the Malay Peninsula there was ample opportunity for peasants to withdraw into subsistence cultivation should cash crop cultivation fail or should creditors foreclose on their land. The same is true of Sumatra where the Dutch had to bring in Javanese and Chinese workers to work on plantations. Apart from the possibility of withdrawal into subsistence, another device that was designed to 'protect' Malay peasants was the Malay Reservation Enactment. Any land that was declared a Malay Reservation by the British Resident could not be sold, leased or alienated in any form to a non-Malay.[87] In this way peasants were protected from foreclosures on their land. As a result, great losses were incurred by non-Malay creditors whose advances were not recoverable under the Enactment.[88]

In the Netherlands Indies, particularly in Java, different factors had served to lessen the negative impact of colonial capitalism on the peasantry. Kahin notes that in spite of the fact that individual landownership was supplanting communal landownership, revolutionary sentiments did not emerge from among the peasantry or rural proletariat because of a minimum social security provided by the village.[89] Activities such as house building and harvesting took place on a cooperative basis, although the land might be owned individually. The village supported orphans, the aged and sick as well as those unemployed.[90] In other words, the pre-colonial peasant economy had responded and adapted to colonial capitalism by involution. Instead of capitalism resulting in the dissolution of the pre-colonial economic pattern it resulted in the strengthening of the communal attitude. As Geertz put it,

> The Javanese cane worker remained a peasant at the same time that he became a coolie, persisted as a community-oriented household farmer at the same time that he became an industrial wage laborer. He had one foot in the rice terrace and the other in the mill.[91]

The cane worker and wage labourer were not completely at the mercy of planters and factory owners. They partook of the economic pie of village society which was progressively divided into minute pieces. Geertz referred to this phenomenon as shared poverty.[92] Similarly, Boeke observed that 'every little windfall must be distributed without delay. The village community tolerates no economic difference but acts as a leveller in this respect, regarding the individual as part of the community'.[93]

Geertz's theory of agricultural involution has come under heavy attack.[94] While his theory can be seen as a prop for Boeke's dualist thesis, the anti-involution argument takes a class perspective. Against the view that the production of cash crops under the Cultivation System in Java in the nineteenth century obstructed the development of indigenous capitalism and resulted in the process of involution and consolidation of the dual economy, Knight argues that commodity production was developed in the Javanese countryside prior to the establishment of the Cultivation System to such an extent that it is reasonable to speak of the potential for capitalist development.[95] He further argues that the kinds of changes taking place in Javanese rural society when the Cultivation System was in place were capitalist rather than involutional in nature.[96] This view finds support in Aas' work on Java which suggests that the destruction of household industry, the spread of money, and the obligation to pay the *landrente* in money had led to the creation of voluntary wage labour which was widespread in some regions of Java after 1890.[97] Nevertheless, even by the mid-1850s, many sugar factories in Java were employing large numbers of voluntary wage labourers, including skilled labourers such as carpenters, smiths, factory hands and overseers, as well as unskilled workers.[98] By 1872, all state sugar factories in Java discontinued the use of conscripted factory workers, this move coinciding with the dismantling of the Cultivation System and its replacement by a system of production based on free enterprise and free wage labour.[99]

If it is true that there was a potential for capitalist development in nineteenth century rural Java, indicated by the emergence of commodity production and wage labour, this would require a relook at the theory of involution which rests, it is charged, on a dualist interpretation of Javanese underdevelopment. Alternatively, one could view the beginnings of a capitalist development or primitive accumulation as taking place in the 1850s or 1890s, during which time involutionary tendencies were still visible, even if they were to disappear as Java moved into the twentieth century. As Aas points out *instleute* or *numpangs*, that is, second-class villagers, were observed in Java at the beginning of the nineteenth century. They were absorbed into the economic and social organization of the village through mutual labour-aid and communal labour (*gotong royong* and *sambatan*), and through the frequently held ritual meals of *slametan*, and so on.[100] Elson notes that there were examples of 'work-spreading' or the granting of shares in existing village lands, although not for the purpose of communally sharing poverty but to reduce the per capita labour obligations borne by landholders.[101] The extent to which this state of affairs continued during the heyday of the Cultivation System is, of course, a point of contention between the involutionists and their critics. Mention must also be made of the work of the Alexanders who claim that the 'shared poverty institutions' of land distribution, sharecropping and exchange labour did little to establish equal access of peasants to land and, therefore, close the gap between the landowners and the landless. The data that is presented for this, however, is for after the 1880s and does not rule out that involution occurred in the decades of the Cultivation System.[102] Finally, Kingston suggests that the phenomenon of rural stagnation in the Javanese countryside was more a result of ill-conceived transmigration policies rather than involutionary behaviour.[103]

Whether the involution model or its critics are right, the fact remains that revolutionary sentiments did not emerge from among the peasantry or rural proletariat either because of a minimum social security provided by the village, as claimed by the involutionist/shared poverty thesis, or freed up workers were absorbed into the developing capitalist relations of production.

Another factor that worked against the emergence of revolutionary agrarian movements in British Malaya and the Netherlands Indies pertains to the nature of the plantation. Kahin is quite right to say that revolutionary sentiments were more likely to develop among plantation workers than peasant smallholders and sharecroppers, because they were marginal to the village core and tended to receive less of the shared poverty.[104] However, Jain has characterized the plantation estate as a total institution.[105] The plantation was a closed world in which 'labourers not only produce rubber for export but also grow up, marry, save and consume, quarrel and cooperate and die'.[106] Housing, family employment and social activities are all part and parcel of the organizational logic of domination on an estate. A certain degree of security found in the self-contained world of the estate would tend to make estate labourers less enthusiastic about venturing beyond it to an unregulated, unpredictable world.

Probably even more important than this factor, however, is the lack of revolutionary leadership. As was mentioned earlier, the declaration of the state of emergency and the outlawing of the CPM created a leadership vacuum in the labour union movement. In Indonesia, the PKI failed to make any inroads as far as politicizing the peasantry was concerned. In addition to this, two prominent Indonesian nationalist leaders, Hatta and Sjahrir, preferred to work with a small but politically conscious group of nationalists in the Golongan Merdeka (Independence Group) because of their conviction that association with mass movements would be detrimental to the nationalist movement. The logic of this was that the Dutch jailed any leader who had mass appeal. This was unhealthy for a movement that depended on a few men at the top of the leadership which would, therefore, crumble once these men were removed.[107] This indicates just how important the masses were considered for the task of independence by nationalist leaders.

Finally, another factor that can be seen to have worked against the emergence of revolutionary sentiments among the lower classes is related to the issue of class consciousness. While the lower classes did understand that they were being exploited by feudal leaders and colonial capitalists and had risen against them from time to time, they did so sporadically and never as a class espousing a class-based ideology. The reason is to be found in the mechanism of indirect rule which sought to maintain pre-colonial institutions by means of the patron–client relationship between Malay and Indonesian elites and the masses. The patron–client relationship was expressed differently around the period of the struggle for independence in Malaysia and Indonesia. Nevertheless, what they have in common is the phenomenon of *aliran*.

For some time it was common among Orientalists to speak of 'oriental' societies as stratified along the lines of vertical associations such as race, ethnicity and tribal origin. However, there is another form of vertical association that is known as aliran or ideological orientation in the literature on Indonesian political economy. The term was coined by Geertz who observed that Javanese society was divided vertically along the lines of ideological orientations or aliran, with each having a structural referent in an organization. For instance, the Javanese *priyayi* ideology was associated with the Indonesian Nationalist Party, while the ideology of the *abangan* (commoners) was associated with the PKI.[108] Wertheim's discussion on the concept of aliran is useful because he brings to light several ways in which an aliran is related to its material referent.[109] He understands the material referent to the aliran in terms of the patron–client relationship.

Behind the concept of aliran is the idea that sharing a common ideology does not always imply similar class origins. For example, landowners and peasants could belong to the same aliran. The PKI for instance was not a class-based organization but an aliran-based one because its membership and following came from landowners, rich and poor

peasants.[110] The same can be said of the followers of the United Malays
National Organization (UMNO, the ruling party in Malaysia at the time
of writing) as well as various other political organizations in Indonesia and Malaysia.

The tendency of alirans to form vertical organizations can be understood in terms of the conceptual frame of the patron–client phenomenon.[111] This relationship exists when there is a particular type of personal
bond between individuals or families that transcends the dividing line
of upper and lower classes. The aliran leader takes on the function of
patron for his following. The result is political activism on the basis
of patronage rather than class solidarity. For example landowners who
were members of the Indonesian Nationalist Party (PNI) could influence poor sharecroppers to commit mass murders, the victims being
also peasants.[112] In Malaysia, local UMNO party leaders who were
landowners could mobilize support from among peasants who were
their tenants or wage labourers against other peasants whose patrons
were members of another aliran, say, the PAS (Pan Malaysian Islamic
Party). Association along vertical as opposed to class lines was also
obvious in view of the fact that Malays and Chinese were unrepre-
sented in the Malayan Trade Union Congress (MTUC). Many Chinese
trade unions had declined to be affiliated with the MTUC because it
was allegedly dominated by Indians.[113] The pervasiveness of the patron–
client phenomenon, in addition to the other mitigating factors discussed
above, makes it clear how difficult it could be to muster united revolutionary support among the lower classes against the colonial state
and elite.

The various factors discussed above explain why revolutionary mass
movements did not emerge from amongst the Malay and Indonesian
peasantry and working class, prior to and during, the attainment of
independence. At this point, a note on the differences between the cases
of Indochina on the one hand and Malaysia and Indonesia on the other
is interesting.

The peasants and workers of British Malaya and the Netherlands
Indies were militant but their militancy did not reach the scale of mass
mobilization against the state as it did in Indochina. Above I have
discussed several mitigating factors which lessened the negative impact of the colonial economy on labour. Some of these mitigating factors were not present in Indochina. The possibility of falling back on
to subsistence or benefiting from the 'social security' provided by the
village that we find in British Malaya and the Netherlands Indies, which
Scott refers to as the 'traditional shock-absorber', were absent in Cochin

China.[114] To a great extent this was due to differences in colonial policy. The Malay Reservation Enactment in Malaya and the agrarian laws in the Netherlands Indies[115] gave some protection to the peasantry. In Cochin China, on the other hand, lands that had once been available to the poor were legally claimed by local officials and notables under colonial rule.[116]

Turning to the estate and mining sectors, a major difference between the two regions, apart from the absence or presence of the mitigating factors discussed above, is the ethnic composition of workers. In British Malaya and the Netherlands Indies, a significant immigrant population of Chinese and Indians were working on plantations and in the mines. In Indochina, too, there were large numbers of coolies hired from Annam and Tonkin to work on the rubber plantations in Cochin China.[117] In fact Murray refers to the 'divide and rule' tactic of the French colonial government of separating workers into different residential camps according to ethnic background.[118] Nevertheless, the level of ethnic dissimilarity of labour in Indochina was certainly less than it was in British Malaya or the Netherlands Indies. Without denying there are cultural differences among workers from Cochin China, Annam and Tonkin, the differences are certainly less than those among Malay/Javanese workers on the one hand, and Chinese and Indian workers on the other. All workers in Indochina share very similar backgrounds in language, religion and cultural practices. In British Malaya and the Netherlands Indies, workers of different ethnic backgrounds come from different civilizations with extremely diverse languages, religions and customs. The point being made here is that in such situations of cultural diversity it is more difficult to achieve the level of unity required of mass movements. Such a movement was possible in Indochina where patriotism and communism were unified in the anti-colonial struggle[119] but extremely difficult in areas of great cultural diversity.

A final word on ethnic diversity is necessary. It should be noted that ethnic diversity in Malaysia was not solely a consequence of a British 'divide and rule' strategy, as the segregation of workers here predated the British arrival. There were migrations of Chinese workers to the area before the British period. However, it would be wrong to say that the British did not use methods to perpetuate already existing ethnic cleavages and to prevent solidarity across ethnic lines. The most important tactic was the establishment of Malay reservations which had the effect of keeping the Malays in the rural sector. But the effect of such tactics should not be exaggerated as ethnic cleavages existed prior to British intervention.

Peasants and workers in Indonesia and Malaysia were not inert or passive. Throughout the history of British Malaya and the Netherlands Indies peasants and workers had been involved in uprisings against both colonialists and indigenous leaders. But due to certain mitigating factors discussed in this chapter, they did not form class-based mass movements during the struggle for independence in the two colonies.

5 Nationalism and the Struggle for Democracy

In this chapter I will be discussing the principal causes behind the independence movements in British Malaya and the Netherlands Indies as well as the democratic outcomes of these movements. The post-colonial states of Indonesia and Malaysia emerged as democratic ones, even if their natures were quite different.

In the previous chapter, the role of the peasantry and of labour movements in the struggle for independence was noted. In this chapter, the parts played by the indigenous elite (who were converted to salaried officials under the colonial state), capital and the middle classes (old and new) in the emergence of the post-colonial state are discussed. Here, the issue of the internal strength of the state as a factor in post-colonial state formation is discussed. In the next chapter, the question of elite cohesion and the conditions under which democracy survived on the one hand, and gave way to authoritarianism on the other, are discussed. This and the next chapter, therefore, are concerned with two paths to post-colonial state formation and the basis of democratic stability.

Although both Indonesia and Malaysia emerged as parliamentary democracies upon independence in 1949 and 1957 respectively, they differed in terms of the internal strength of the state. The Malaysian state had from the very beginning been internally strong relative to the Indonesian state, if internal strength is understood in terms of strong class support for the state. This support was derived mainly from the Chinese fraction of capital and was manifested chiefly through the politics of coalition. The Indonesian state, on the other hand, was characterized by the lack of strong class support as Chinese capital could not play the political role that it did in Malaysia while, at the same time, both Chinese and indigenous capital had to contend with the military as a political force. This chapter elaborates on the question of the internal strength of the state. Before doing so, however, some remarks on the nationalism and the growth of the independence movements are in order.

CLASS, RACE, IDEOLOGICAL ORIENTATIONS AND THE NATIONALIST IMPULSE

The most obvious difference between Indonesia and Malaysia is that the former achieved formal independence through a revolution. It is necessary, therefore, to detail the meaning of revolution. My point will be to show that the different paths that the two countries took has less to do with the fact that there was a revolution in one than with particular class and ideological configurations that would nonetheless have made similar impressions in the absence of a revolution.

Rather than present a one-line or one-paragraph definition of a revolution, it would be more fruitful to list its ideal type traits:

(1) A change in the material relations of production.
(2) A change in the state structure.
(3) A change in the ruling class.
(4) A change in world-view.

The first point refers to various degrees of change within a particular economic system or to the establishment of a new economic system. Examples of the latter are the French and Russian revolutions. Such revolutions do not always mark the end of one mode of production and the beginning of another. Rather they are manifestations of the conflict between the forces of production and the old relations of production. Examples of revolutions that involve changes within an existing economic system are the Indonesian and Iranian Revolutions. The Iranian Revolution of 1979 involved drastic changes in the ownership and control of the means of production and in economic institutions even if the economy remained a capitalist one.

The second point refers to alterations in political institutions. It may involve the supplanting of one institution for another, radical changes in existing ones, or the invention of political institutions. For example, the Iranian Revolution of 1979 resulted in the abolition of the monarchy which was supplanted by a clerical regime.

A change in the ruling class occurs when revolution brings to dominance a new class which assumes state power as well. Such a change may occur independently or in the absence of a change in the state structure. For example, a capitalist class could supplant a middle class in dominating the state.

Finally, a change in world-view usually accompanies a revolution. In Iran today the ideology of the ruling elite is that of Shi'a Islam, specifically Ayatollah Khomeini's articulation of it. It supplanted a Western and capitalist-oriented monarchist state.

The Indonesian Revolution does exhibit these traits. The overthrow of the Dutch colonial state was accompanied by the expression of various nationalist ideologies from the left to the right, and the handing over of the economy to local personnel. It involved the supplanting of the colonial state by a democratic regime headed by a new ruling elite. What is also true, however, is that the Malaysian struggle for independence exhibited these traits but is never referred to as a revolution. This is probably due to the fact that independence was achieved without violence. This difference, however, may be trivial in that the magnitude of change in the four criteria listed above is similar in both cases. What sets the Malaysian and Indonesian cases apart, whether in the outcome of the struggle for independence or later developments, is not the fact that one country went through a revolution while the other did not. Whether or not Malaysia is said to have gone through a revolution and in spite of the fact that there was no violence between the principal actors, the changes brought about by the rise of the Malaysian post-colonial state were just as basic and significant as those brought about by the rise of the Indonesian state. This will be made clear as this chapter progresses.

There were attempts by the colonial powers to actively prevent the creation of nationalism through the importation of non-indigenous peoples and the suppression of nationalist organizations. In British Malaya, the Malay Reservations Act was designed to keep the Malays underdeveloped in the rural sector and isolated from the predominantly Chinese and Indian working class. The Dutch classified Arab (mostly Hadhrami) immigrants in the Netherlands Indies as *vreemde oosterlingen* (foreign orientals) in order to practise the policy of divide and rule amongst the predominantly Muslim population of the colony.[1]

The nationalist impulse in the Malay–Indonesian Archipelago first made itself known in Java. The first Indonesian nationalist organization was established in 1908. Budi Utomo (Pure Endeavour), however, was dedicated to the cultural advancement of the Javanese as opposed to the Indonesian people as a whole and did not call for the establishment of an independent nation-state.[2] Nevertheless Budi Utomo did have its conservative and liberal elements that corresponded to the class background of its leadership. The priyayi from which the Dutch recruited civil servants and administrators can be divided into the higher and the lesser priyayi. The higher from among the priyayi tended to form the conservative element of Budi Utomo and avoided confrontation with the Dutch colonial state which guaranteed their high status as administrators and civil servants. The liberal group in Budi Utomo were of lesser priyayi background. These were mainly the younger sons and relatives of the higher priyayi who did not succeed in gaining positions in the colonial administration and were, therefore, a disaffected group. Many of them were intellectuals trained in Dutch schools. This group eventually came to dominate Budi Utomo, but the most radical among them, headed by Dr Tjipto Mangoenkoesomo and Soewardi Soerianingrat, left the organization to form the Indische Partij (Indies Party),[3] a decidedly political party. The Indische Partij pushed for an independent Indonesia to be led by Indonesians and Indo-Europeans (those of mixed Dutch and European ancestry). The colonial government failed to grant the party legal recognition and in 1913 its leaders were exiled from Indonesia.[4]

In the Islamic sphere the most outstanding nationalist organization was the Sarekat Islam (Islamic Union), founded in 1912. By 1919 its membership had grown to two and a half million. On its political agenda was self-government for Indonesia which was to be attained by force if required.[5] The party had its origins in the Sarekat Dagang Islam (Islamic Commercial Union), founded in 1909 for the purpose of countering Chinese trading activities.[6] When Sarekat Islam was established in 1912, its goals did not include self-government. It was mainly concerned with the advancement of Indonesian commercial and spiritual interests. Its leader, Tjokroaminoto, himself expressed satisfaction with Dutch rule and proclaimed loyalty to the colonial government.[7] Sarekat Islam grew throughout Java, especially in rural areas. Governor General Idenburg in 1913 refused to grant legal status to the central body of Sarekat Islam. This move was ostensibly to protect Sarekat Islam from 'a series of legal complications which might have led to either its suppression or its rapid demise'.[8] It is more likely that because Idenburg saw the mass appeal for Sarekat Islam, the conferring of a legal and independent status for each branch of Sarekat Islam would weaken the hold of the central Sarekat Islam over the movement. Legal status was eventually conferred upon central Sarekat Islam in 1915.[9]

During the same period, the Indische Social-Democratische Vereniging (ISDV), that is, the Indies Social Democratic Organization was established in 1914. This was later to become the PKI (Indonesian Communist Party) and played a crucial role in the radicalization of Sarekat Islam. ISDV members had membership in Sarekat Islam branches as well, and by 1916 controlled the Semarang branch of Sarekat Islam. At the First National Sarekat Islam Congress held in 1916, many moderate views such as those held by Tjokroaminoto were expressed. But one Sarekat Islam member, Hasan Ali Soerati, a capitalist of Arab origin, raised the issue of combining Islam and socialism. Others who thought along similar lines pressed for the establishment of labour unions.[10] At the Second National Sarekat Islam Congress Tjokroaminoto spoke of the establishment of the Volksraad (People's Council) as a move in the direction of self-government.[11] Meanwhile, a radical of Sarekat Islam, Agus Salim, spoke of uneven capitalist development and the exploitation of Indonesia.[12] The socialist tendencies of Sarekat Islam leaders became more prominent in their basic platform published in *Neratja* (*The Balance*), a newspaper edited by Agus Salim. Included in the platform was the pledge to oppose sinful capitalism.[13] The implication was that foreign capitalism was exploitative while indigenous capitalism could be good.

Another radical of Sarekat Islam, Abdul Muis, asserted openly the quest for independence.[14] This was well taken by the ISDV which, however, stressed the need to strive not just against political oppression but economic exploitation.[15] The gap between Tjokroaminoto and the radical faction of Sarekat Islam widened at the Third National Congress when two leaders of the Semarang chapter of the organization, Semaun and Darsono, threatened to break off from Central Sarekat Islam. Tjokroaminoto succeeded in maintaining unity by bringing Semaun into the central steering committee and by making Darsono an official propagandist.[16] By the time of the Fourth National Congress of Sarekat Islam the idea of an association of labour unions to combat capitalism and foreign domination was proposed.[17] As Marxist elements within Sarekat Islam sought to minimize the role of Islam and stress class struggle against capitalism, another group led by Agus Salim espoused an Islamic socialism.[18] In December 1919 the Union of Labour Movements (Persatuan Pergerakan Kaum Buruh – PPKB) was formed, headed by Semaun and Agus Salim. Further disagreements over the use of the strike weapon occurred. In addition to this, several small local strikes and an abortive general strike failed to impress many and the prestige of Sarekat Islam plummeted. When the Sarekat Islam focused its activities on labour unions it came into direct competition with the ISDV (which became the PKI in 1920). This had a debilitating effect on Sarekat Islam because several of its members were also part of the ISDV. An attempt to bridge the differences between the Marxist and Islamic factions was made prior to the Fifth National Congress. At a pre-meeting agreement a new platform incorporating Islamic and communistic elements was formulated by Agus Salim and Semaun.[19] However, the communist faction finally withdrew from the Central Sarekat but still attempted to gain control of local chapters. From here on, the Sarekat Islam and PKI went their separate ways. The split was due to competition over control of the labour unions, the role of Islam in the struggle, and the issue of class struggle. After the split, the communists attempted to wrest control of the Sarekat Islam chapters by establishing sections of Red Sarekat Islam wherever a Sarekat Islam chapter existed. The Red Sarekat Islam was later called Sarekat Rakyat (People's Association).[20]

The ISDV was formed in 1914. At their first meeting on May 9th that year moderates and radicals split over the function of the organization. Most of the membership was Dutch and many were recent immigrants to Indonesia.[21] The moderates were not in favour of the ISDV participating in Indonesian politics and they saw socialist principles as relevant only in countries with a matured industrial proletariat. The radical wing came to dominate the ISDV, the task of which they saw to be the implantation of socialist ideas in Indonesia.[22] By 1916, Indonesian members of the ISDV had joined Sarekat Islam. Adolf Baars, editor of *Het Vrije Woord*, the organ of the ISDV, recognized that despite the anti-socialist position and bourgeois tendencies of Sarekat Islam, it signified progress in Indonesia because it brought people to self-assertion and independent thinking.[23] The Muslim–Communist encounter in terms of both cooperation and antagonism first made itself known in the history of the Sarekat Islam and ISDV/PKI, but was to continue through other organizations in the future.

Various strikes organized by Sarekat Islam and the ISDV failed to make any inroads in the struggle for independence. The PKI rebellion of 1926–7 was a disaster for various reasons discussed in the previous chapter. The attempt to start a revolution in the rural areas of West Java and West Sumatra only resulted in the banning of the party and the imprisonment of thousands of its members. The PKI was never again to be a force in politics until after independence. Meanwhile Sarekat Islam fizzled out into a relatively insignificant organization after a great number of its members opted for non-political Islamic activities by joining Muhammadiyah, a non-political organization that stressed education and social services.[24]

The most powerful nationalist organization to emerge after Sarekat Islam and the PKI was the Indonesian Nationalist Party (Partai Nasional Indonesia – PNI). Formed in June 1927, it was headed by a young engineer by the name of Sukarno. Although Sukarno was a protégé of Tjokroaminoto he did not believe in an Islamic basis for the party as not only Muslims but also Christians had independence as their goal.[25]

The PNI grew rapidly with many of its members coming from the Sarekat Rakyats and the formerly communist-dominated labour unions. It was also supported by leaders of the Sarekat Islam. With the latter's support a federation of major nationalist organizations was established.[26] In September of 1930 several PNI leaders including Sukarno were imprisoned for their anti-government and anti-capitalist activities and the PNI was outlawed.[27] The membership of the PNI then flowed to three new organizations. One was the Partai Rakyat Indonesia (Indonesian People's Party), established by Muhammad Tabrani. It advocated cooperation with the Dutch and the struggle for independence through parliamentary means. Most of the old PNI membership, however, joined the new Partai Indonesia (Partindo) led by one Sartono. The party advocated non-cooperation in the struggle for independence. A minority group from the old PNI who opposed Partindo for various reasons established the Golongan Merdeka (Independence Group). Headed by Sutan Sjahrir and Muhammad Hatta, both of whom played crucial roles in the revolution, Golongan Merdeka was the closest to the PNI in terms of its programme.[28] Both Hatta and Sjahrir were arrested and detained without trial from 1934 to 1942.

When Sukarno was released from prison he joined Partindo after an unsuccessful bid to unite Partindo and Golongan Merdeka. Under his leadership Partindo grew in membership. Alarmed at its rapid growth and its relationship with the masses, the colonial government arrested Sukarno and exiled him to Flores and then to Benculin where he remained till 1942. Thereupon Partindo was dissolved and a new party Gerindo (Gerakan Rakyat Indonesia – Indonesian People's Movement) emerged. Gerindo grew to become the powerful left wing of the nationalist movement under the leadership of Sartono, Amir Sjarifuddin, A. K. Gani, Sanusi Pane and Mohammad Yamin.[29] Gerindo took the position that while independence was a goal that could not be compromised, the immediate concern was a limited cooperation with the Dutch to combat the threat of Japanese fascism.

In 1939 the major Indonesian nationalist organizations were brought together to form the Federation of Indonesian Political Parties (Gabungan Politiek Indonesia – Gapi). Its common programme was as follows: (1) the right to self-determination, (2) nationality based on political, economic and social democracy, (3) a democratically-elected Indonesian parliament and (4) solidarity between Indonesian national organizations and the Netherlands for a strong anti-fascist front.[30] The Wiwoho Resolution passed in the Volksraad in February 1940 called for self-government, but within the Netherlands constitution. The Netherlands response to this was non-committal. Disillusioned with the Dutch attitude, the major nationalist organizations did not support them against the Japanese who occupied Indonesia in March of 1942.

Turning to the beginnings of the nationalist impulse in Malaya, this was preceded by the rise of a religious revivalist movement at the turn of the present century. In 1906 a Malay periodical by the name of *Al-Imam (The Leader)* began to be published in Singapore. Started by Syed Sheikh Ahmad Al-Hadi, it was the first Malay newspaper that discussed issues of social change and politics.[31] Inspired by the Muslim modernist movement during the latter part of the last century and led by Muhammad Abduh in Egypt who was Syed Sheikh Al-Hadi's teacher, the movement behind *Al-Imam* was first and foremost a religious one. Notwithstanding the general Islamic stance that there is no separation between religion and politics, *Al-Imam* was concerned more with the latter. Al-Hadi sought to uplift the lot of the Malays by exhorting them to return to the practice of Divine Law, and to use reason and rationality to develop themselves culturally, economically and politically. But Al-Hadi and *Al-Imam* had not called for an independent Malaya.[32]

Syed Sheikh Al-Hadi and his group came to be known collectively as Kaum Muda (Young Faction) as opposed to Kaum Tua (Old Faction). The latter consisted of the state religious hierarchy and the conservative Malay elite who derived their status from cooperation with the colonial state. The Kaum Tua sought to maintain their positions under colonial rule. If there was any quest for an independent entity it would be along the lines of pre-colonial Malay society. In other words, to them Islamic revival meant the revival of the pre-colonial aristocracy. On the other hand, the Kaum Muda advocated the rejuvenation of Malay Muslim society along the lines of Western notions of progress. To them this did not mean becoming Westernized or inculcating Western values or forms of behaviour. Rather, it meant the use of Western science and technology for the purpose of solving the various problems of Malay society.

The Kaum Muda began to become politicized during the mid-1920s.[33] Through the organ of two journals, *Seruan Azhar (Voice of Azhar)* and *Pilehan Timoer (Choice of the East)* published by Malay and Indonesian students at Al-Azhar University in Cairo, nationalist issues were raised. While religious topics pertaining to the purification of the faith were raised, the politicization of this group could be seen in their discussions of Pan-Malayanism, and anti-colonial nationalism. The Pan-Malayan movement referred to the idea of a union between Malaya and Indonesia. The first editorial of *Seruan Azhar* called on the peoples of Sumatra, Java, Borneo and Malaya to 'unite with one heart for progress and prosperity'.[34] Various articles stressing the facts of a common language and religion and comparisons between the two colonies in terms of economic development, education and political conditions appeared.[35] The call for independence within the context of the unification of Malaya and Indonesia was made explicitly and bluntly. The Kaum Muda movement, therefore, had turned its attention to agitation along the lines of nationalism.

The year 1926 saw the establishment of the first Malay political party, the Kesatuan Melayu Singapura (Singapore Malay Union). Its goal was to advance the social and economic interests of the Malays, to encourage the Malays to participate in politics and administration and to take an interest in higher education. An early achievement of the Kesatuan Melayu Singapura was the acquisition of a piece of land in Singapore for Malay settlement which was granted by the Government of the Straits Settlements in April of 1929.[36] At first this party did not push for independence. In fact it was supported by the colonial government because it pledged to obey the laws of the colony. This picture of cooperation with the British began to change, however, as immigrant demands for equal rights and privileges began to be heard more forcefully. After the split between the Kuomintang and the communists in China, the Chinese of the Straits Settlements began to ask for recognition as citizens, which meant equal treatment with the Malays.[37] In a land where the Malays were beginning to become numerically outnumbered such talk of equality led to the fear of racial extinction. Some Malays sought to lessen this challenge by aligning themselves with the Pan-Malayan movement which included Indonesia as part of the Malay world. This group never gained a following of import and was the forerunner of the left wing Malay party, the Kesatuan Melayu Muda (Malay Youth Union). This group was very much under the influence of the Sukarno-led Partai Nasional Indonesia. The Kesatuan Melayu Muda was especially attracted to the PNI because it was a period when the PNI was demanding independence for Indonesia and the former felt that Malaya was a part of Indonesia. The Kesatuan Melayu Muda was established in 1937 by Ibrahim bin Yaacob and Ishak bin Haji Mohammad, two journalists.[38] The party advocated independence for Malaya, unity with Indonesia and non-cooperation with the colonial government. Just as defiant, anti-colonial agitators were arrested and detained in Indonesia by Dutch authorities, so were leaders of the Kesatuan Melayu Muda.

In both Malaya and the Netherlands Indies, most of the leaders and active members of the political parties that arose in opposition to the colonial state came from the professional–managerial class comprising members of the nobility who had been converted to salaried officials and members of lower-class families who had gained ascendancy in the colonial administrative system through education either in Dutch/English or Indonesian/Malay schools. In both British Malaya and the Netherlands Indies, rightist and leftist tendencies were present in the independence movements. In the Netherlands Indies, the rightist groups consisted of members of the higher priyayi who stood to benefit from the continuation of the status quo. In Malaya, they consisted of the English-educated professionals and administrators who sought to protect the interests of the Malays, particularly the elite Malays, from the encroachment of immigrants and colonialists alike. The left-wing in the Netherlands Indies consisted of those individuals who stood to lose from the continuation of colonial rule and they came mainly from lesser priyayi and merchant families. In Malaya, they came mainly from peasant families and gained status through the procurement of educational credentials from Malay schools. The militant, anti-colonial left in Malaya and the Netherlands Indies were supported by the Japanese during the occupation. Nevertheless, it was only in Indonesia that the left emerged strong and able to challenge the Dutch when they regained possession of Indonesia. In Malaya they fizzled out into insignificance after the British returned. The reasons for this will be dealt with after the period of the Japanese occupation is discussed in the next section. In concluding this section, I would like to make some comments on the differences between Malay and Indonesian nationalism prior to the period of Japanese occupation.

The only comparison between Malay and Indonesian nationalism that I have seen was made by Soenarno.[39] He began by correctly noting that since the establishment of Sarekat Islam in 1912 the Indonesian movement 'proceeded step by frustrating step towards the achievement of political independence. Its growth was spectacular and its strife was dramatic'.[40] The growth of Malay nationalism, on the other hand, 'was so slow that it gave the impression that nationalism among the Malays was an evolutionary rather than a revolutionary attitude'.[41] Soenarno accounts for this in terms of the class bases of the nationalist movements in the two colonies. In Malaya the dominant force that led the colony to independence was an English-educated professional and administrative class whose members were connected with royalty and highly placed families in the Malayan social hierarchy, whereas in the

Netherlands Indies nationalist leaders emerged from not only the aristocracy, but also from the middle class of merchants, teachers and government servants and even the peasantry. The elite origin and status of the Malayan nationalists had caused a restraining effect on political development while in the Netherlands Indies they were not tied down by traditionalism.[42] I concur with this.

A reason that Soenarno cites as even more important was that Malay nationalism was still embedded in the feudal social structure in that the pre-colonial elite was left intact after the imposition of colonial rule.[43] This has already been discussed in connection with the colonial system of indirect rule in a previous chapter. In Indonesia too, the indirect system of rule was imposed, but the various sultans were either eliminated in wars or pensioned off. The reason for this is that the Malay peasant economy was less important to the British than the indigenous peasant economies were to the Dutch in Indonesia. Indirect rule was, therefore, more direct in Indonesia than in Malaya. Soenarno argues that the allegiance of the masses was transferred to the new Dutch-educated elite in Indonesia as the old elite receded into the background. This was contrary to the case of Malaya where the old elite remained intact and preserved the social structure. The result was that 'Malay nationalism during the pre-war days was more of an attempt of a feudal society to adapt itself to the new world order of democracy and socialism, rather than a national uprising of a people seeking political freedom from the domination of others'.[44] This view, however, is based on the faulty assumption that there was a national uprising in Indonesia. I have tried to show in the preceding chapter that mass participation in Indonesia was limited and sporadic. That the masses had given their overwhelming support to the emerging new Indonesian elite does not hold up to the facts. This being the case it cannot be said that the differences in vitality between the Indonesians and Malayan nationalist movements stem from the differences in mass support. A related reason cited by Soenarno to explain the differences in the two nationalisms is that in Malaya the nationalists upheld the feudal social structure. This was an impediment to the progress of nationalism because it 'became entangled with feudal consideration for vested interests of a particular class'.[45] This was in contrast to Indonesia where the more radical changes in the indigenous economy and society led to a mass-based nationalism. Again, I cannot agree with this explanation for two reasons. First of all, that Indonesian nationalism was mass-based has already been questioned. Secondly, it is not entirely true that before the Second World War Malay nationalism sought to preserve the feudal social structure. There was a move to maintain the institution of the sultanate with reduced powers and not within the old feudal economic system. In fact, nationalists whether on the left or right were pushing for a modern economy and society run along Western lines.

Finally, Soenarno attributes the difference between Malay and Indonesian nationalism to the relationship with the colonial state. He says that the political aims of Malay nationalists were unambitious when compared to those of Indonesian nationalists because the former cooperated with the colonial state while the latter opposed them for the most part. But cooperation of the Malay nationalists cannot be taken to mean lower political aspirations on their part. The British were more predisposed to the idea of an independent Malaya than the Dutch were to an independent Indonesia. There was little need for militancy in the Malay nationalist movement when the British increasingly made it clear that an independent Malaya was on their agenda. Britain was a signatory to the Atlantic charter declaring the right of nations to self-determination. In Indonesia, however, the Dutch had always vehemently opposed the idea of an independent Indonesia even after the signing of the Atlantic charter. This I believe is a crucial point that explains the differences between Malay and Indonesian nationalism.

Another factor that explains the greater vigour to be found in Indonesian nationalism, particularly in the years prior to the Second World War, was the fact that it was significantly more heterogenous in class composition, comprising elements from aristocratic, commercial and peasant backgrounds. This had caused a lot of internal disagreements as well as a broader base of support. In spite of this, the struggle for independence was not a mass movement in either Malaya or Indonesia.

JAPANESE OCCUPATION AND FURTHER DEVELOPMENTS IN NATIONALISM

The Japanese occupied Malaya in December 1941 and the Netherlands Indies in March 1942. Japanese policy was to encourage nationalist elements in Malaya and Indonesia to support Japan in her war effort against the British and Dutch. Japanese propaganda sought to promote the Greater East Asia Coprosperity Sphere and the Japanese presented themselves as the 'light of Asia' ready to liberate Asia from Western aggression. The case of Japanese involvement in the development of Malay and Indonesian nationalism illustrates very clearly the significance of the international geopolitical context in the internal development of nation-states. The favourable Japanese policy towards the nationalist movements in Malaya and Indonesia must be understood within the international context of the conflict between the imperialisms of Japan and the West.

The Japanese encouragement of and impetus to the nationalist movements of Indonesia and Malaya took the forms of (1) bringing in more indigenous personnel to replace Europeans in the civil service, (2) the support of militant anti-colonial groups in the nationalist movement and (3) promising self-government for the two colonies. While Japanese policies in the two colonies closely resembled each other they did not lead to the same results. The nationalist forces that the Japanese aided in Indonesia went on to gain independence after the Dutch regained control of Indonesia after the war. In Malaya, the Japanese-sponsored forces declined to insignificance after the war. There are several reasons behind this which will be discussed once the effects of the Japanese occupation on the nationalist movements in Malaya and Indonesia is detailed.

By bringing in more indigenous personnel to fill in posts in high levels of the civil service that Europeans vacated after the Japanese occupied the two colonies, the Japanese laid the ground work for the indigenous takeover of the state after the war. It created a situation whereby the civil services of the colonies were filled by nationalist-minded personnel giving nationalist forces some bargaining power with the British and the Dutch when they regained their former colonies. As Kahin says, 'almost all such Indonesian personnel found themselves advanced at least one and frequently two or three ranks in the hierarchy in which they had been employed'.[46] Even those members of the upper priyayi who had secured positions in the Dutch colonial civil service and therefore had reason to support the Dutch, found themselves occupying even higher positions under the Japanese which they never dreamed of occupying under the Dutch.[47] Similarly in Malaya the Japanese brought in Malays to replace British civil servants at high levels.[48]

The Japanese also realized that in order to enlist the support of Malayans and Indonesians, they would have to work through nationalist leaders and organizations. Thus, their support of nationalism was a matter of expediency. The nationalist leaders that they supported were decidedly anti-British and anti-Dutch. Shortly after the Japanese occupied the region they released Sukarno and Ibrahim Yaacob, the latter being the leader of the radical KMM (Kesatuan Melayu Muda – Malay Youth Union) in Malaya, who had been detained and arrested by the Dutch and the British respectively. When Sukarno was released he made contact with two other nationalist leaders, Hatta and Sjahrir. They made the decision to carry out the nationalist struggle at two levels – legally and underground. At the legal level, Sukarno and Hatta would work with the Japanese while Sjahrir was to organize the underground resistance.[49] When Ibrahim was released he revived the KMM in Malaya and forged ties with the CPM and the MPAJA (Malayan People's Anti-Japanese Army). This resulted in the Japanese banning the KMM in June 1942, but this ban was only formal. The Japanese needed their cooperation in the war effort. Thus, the KMM was operating at two levels – above ground in 'cooperation' with the Japanese and underground in cooperation with the CPM[50] and the MPAJA. As Soenarno notes, this tactic of 'cooperation' was a copy of what Sukarno was doing in Indonesia.[51] An important manifestation of this cooperation was the establishment of Pembela Tanah Air (Peta – Avengers of the Country) in both Malaya and Indonesia. Peta members were trained along the lines of the Japanese army, but the officers as well as the rank and file consisted of Malays and Indonesians. Peta was disbanded in Malaya in the wake of the Japanese defeat.

While the Japanese supported the nationalist movements of Malaya and Indonesia to enlist local support in their war effort the question of granting independence to Malaya and Indonesia did not arise till after Japan suffered major setbacks at the Battle of Midway in June 1942 and at Guadalcanal and Buna in Papua in January 1943.[52] The promise of independence, then, was another effort in enlisting the support of Malayans and Indonesians against the Allies. In March 1943 in Indonesia the Pusat Tenaga Rakyat (People's Power Center) was established. It was an umbrella organization for all nationalist organizations in Java and Madura. This was followed in September with the establishment of a Central Advisory Board, with Sukarno as president.[53] To the Japanese, the Pusat Tenaga Rakyat was a means of enlisting Indonesian support in the war, but for the nationalist leaders it was a means to further the nationalist cause. As Japanese defeat became more and more imminent, they accelerated their plans to establish an independent Indonesia. In March 1945 the Investigating Committee for the Preparation of Independence (Badan Penyelidik Usaha Persiapan Kemerdekaan) was established. Its members included Sukarno, Hatta and other important nationalist leaders, as well as seven Japanese.[54] On August 17th, 1945 amidst rumours of Japanese surrender to the Allies, Sukarno read the declaration of independence. What followed closely was the appointment of the first cabinet of the Republic of Indonesia with Sukarno as president and Hatta as vice-president.

As Indonesian plans for independence in 1945 were underway, the Japanese in Malaya who were sympathetic to the idea of a united Malaya and Indonesia (Indonesia Raya) decided to support Ibrahim Yaacob and the KMM. They confessed to the KMM that their policy towards the Malay nationalist movement had been wrong all the while and that they would now support nationalist goals of independence.[55] However, the Japanese withdrew their support for Indonesia Raya at the last moment to avoid creating any obstacles for peace with the Allies.[56] Meanwhile, Ibrahim had established the KRIS (Kerajaan Rakyat Indonesia Semenanjung – Government of Peninsula Indonesians). However, the Indonesians had made the declaration of independence without the knowledge of Ibrahim and the KRIS and before any concerted attempt at independence could be made the Japanese had surrendered. When the Allied troops landed in September 1945, the British Military Administration was established and it arrested and jailed all the leaders of the KMM, KRIS and Peta.[57] In other words, the Japanese had delayed their commitment to the independence of Malaya until it was too late. But perhaps even more importantly, the Indonesian nationalist leaders could act decisively and in unity to declare an independent state because of the unequivocal Dutch position against an independent Indonesia. In Malaya, however, the anti-colonial forces were not of one mind. The group around Ibrahim Yaacob and the KMM were nurtured by the Japanese but failed to declare an independent state because they were not supported by the English-educated Malay elite and the MPAJA, neither of which resisted the return of the British because the latter had promised to work towards the granting of Malayan independence.

FORMS OF NATIONALISM IN BRITISH MALAYA AND THE NETHERLANDS INDIES

At this point, it would be useful to outline the two forms of nationalism that were to be found in the Malay–Indonesian world prior to formal independence. Apart from the nationalist movements that had evolved a sense of nationhood, understood in the modern sense, and wished to see Malaya and Indonesia as independent nation-states, there was also Pan-Malayan nationalism which called for the unification of British Malaya and the Netherlands Indies into one independent state. There were also various regional movements to be found in the Netherlands Indies.

The regional movements, which postulate the existence of a people based on regional and cultural affiliations, were prominent in the Netherlands Indies although the Malays in Malaya were also very much under the influence of regional loyalties. In the Netherlands Indies, the 1910s and 1920s saw the rise of numerous organizations among the educated elite which were based on regional/ethnic identities. Examples are the Sarekat Ambon (Ambonese Union), Jong Java (Young Java), Pasundan, a Sundanese version of Budi Utomo, Sarekat Sumatra (Sumatran Union), Jong Minahasa (Young Minahasa), Timorsch Verbond (Timorese Alliance) Kaum Betawi (The People of Batavia), and Pakempalan Politik Katolik Jawi (Political Association of Javanese Catholics).[58] In British Malaya, where the vast majority of the indigenous population consisted of Malays, there were no regional movements. Nevertheless, the Malays had not yet evolved a sense of common nationhood and, instead, owed their loyalties to the sultans of the various negeris (states).[59] Furthermore, in both British Malaya and the Netherlands Indies, loyalties were also based on the patron–client relationship discussed in Chapter 4.

The rise of nationalism in the Middle East, especially in Egypt, in connection with the development of the Islamic modernist movement there was an important factor in the appearance of Pan-Malayan nationalism.[60] The Pan-Malayan idea, also known as 'Indonesia Raya' or the 'Greater Indonesia' nationalist idea, was initiated by Indonesian and Malay students at al-Azhar University[61] in the 1920s who argued that the people of the Netherlands Indies and British Malaya should occupy one state as they shared a common language and religion.[62] Proponents of the Greater Indonesia idea, such as Ibrahim Yaacob, joined Sukarno's Indonesian National Party (PNI). On the Indonesian side, Sukarno had called for the inclusion of Malaya in the territory of an independent Indonesia.[63] Further impetus to the development of the Greater Indonesia idea came from the Japanese side. During the Japanese occupation, Malaya and Indonesia were united through the setting up of a joint administrative unit of Sumatra and Malaya which was under the jurisdiction of the 25th Japanese army.[64]

Nevertheless, the idea of a Greater Indonesian state which included Malaya was not realized due to Japanese opposition in the end. The territorial claims of the Indonesian nationalists could not be recognized by the Japanese. Japanese acceptance of an Indonesian state which encompassed the former territories of two Allied powers may have constituted an obstacle to peace with the Allies.[65] And so, the Indonesian state declared by Sukarno and Hatta consisted of just the former Dutch colonial empire and excluded Malaya.

Apart from Pan-Malayan or Greater Indonesian nationalism, there were also Malayan and Indonesian nationalisms which sought to establish Malaya and Indonesia as independent nation-states. The factors which led to the emergence of Indonesian and Malayan nationalisms were different in the two countries. In both British Malaya and the Netherlands Indies, ethnic and regional organizations stood in the way of the evolution of a sense of common nationhood. These obstacles were overcome through different means in the two colonies.

In Indonesia, it was initially the Islamic modernist movement which had influenced the rise of Indonesian nationalism and a strong anti-colonial movement. Whereas ethnic and regionally-based organizations such as Budi Utomo called for an improvement in the conditions of particular groups, and did not have nationalist political endeavours, modernist Islamic movements such as the Sarekat Islam and Masyumi called for the establishment of an independent Indonesian state. In addition to those Muslim organizations, there was the PKI which rose as a result of competition with the Sarekat Islam for a rural constituency. It was the nationalist tendencies of the Islamic and communist movements that eventually gave birth to the Indonesian independence movement that formed around Sukarno. Sukarno had met many of the early political leaders associated with Muslim and leftist organizations such as Tjokroaminoto, Haji Agus Salim, Sneevliet, Semaun and Musso, but eventually became interested in the synthesis of Hindu, Buddhist, Islamic and Western ideas as the ideology of Indonesian nationalism. In 1933, Sukarno offered four principles as the basis of the independent Indonesian state. These were internationalism, nationalism, democracy and social justice.[66] This was restated in 1945 as the Pancasila (Five Principles). These were nationalism, internationalism or humanitarianism, deliberation or democracy, social prosperity and belief in God.[67] These five principles could be reduced to three, according to Sukarno, in which case they became the Tri Sila (Three Principles). These were socio-nationalism (consisting of nationalism and internationalism), socio-democracy (consisting of democracy and social justice) and belief in God.[68] These three principles could be, in sum, reduced to one.

> If I compress what was five to get three, and what was three to get one, then I have a genuine Indonesian term, the term 'gotong-royong' (mutual cooperation). The state of Indonesia, which we are to establish, should be a state of mutual cooperation.[69]

With this formulation of the Pancasila, Sukarno attempted to create an 'umbrella philosophy' that was based on elements of humanism, Islam, Marxism and Javanese culture, the dominant culture of Indonesia. Nevertheless, the foundation, as far as the creation of a sense of common nationhood is concerned, was laid by the Islamic modernist movement as well as by the left.

The creation of a sense of common nationhood in Malaya did not have its roots in the Islamic movement there. In British Malaya, Islamic nationalism was expressed in terms of the Greater Indonesia idea. While Malayan Malays, Chinese and Indians were exposed to the ideas of nationalism not only through the Islamic modernist movement, but also through developments in China and India, nationalist aspirations were communally isolated prior to the Second World War. After the war, when a sense of common nationhood began to emerge, leftist and anti-colonial nationalist forces failed to receive much support from the dominant classes and the masses, as preparations for independence through negotiations with the British were underway.

What led to serious efforts at nation building through cooperation of the various races of Malaya was the Federation of Malaya scheme. In the face of communist insurgency, Malayan nationalist leaders tried to convince the Malayan Chinese community that the Communist Party of Malaya consisted mainly of China-born Chinese who were not looking out for the welfare of locally-born Chinese.[70] Efforts were also made to get the non-Malays to think in terms of a Malayan identity. This was encouraged by citizenship concessions and national constitutional progress.[71] As Malayan citizenship became available to the non-Malays, they became aware of their Malayan identity, rights and responsibilities.[72] As far as national constitutional progress was concerned, when the colonial secretary in 1952 stated that Malayan independence would not be granted until the different ethnic communities achieved unity,[73] a strong incentive for cooperation between Malay and non-Malay leaders was created, and this helped to make the myth of the Malayan nation a reality. Contrary to commonly accepted belief, the concept of Malaysia appeared before 1961 and did not emerge merely as a result of the attempt to solve the 'Singapore problem'.[74] As early as December 26th 1955 Tunku Abdul Rahman invited Sarawak, Brunei, North Borneo and Singapore to join the Federation of Malaya in achieving independence as one nation.[75] The press reported this as referring to a 'Greater Malaya'[76] and the 'Republic of Malaysia'.[77]

INTERNAL STATE STRENGTH AND THE BIRTH OF TWO DEMOCRACIES

The Japanese-supported anti-colonial forces in Malaya and Indonesia did not face similar circumstances after the return of the Allies to the region. The Indonesian nationalists were able to step into the shoes of the Dutch before they returned to Indonesia. There was a political vacuum for the nationalists to fill in the event of the Japanese surrender to the Allies. In Malaya, however, the anti-colonial forces sponsored by the Japanese did not have the opportunity to establish a government. The most important reason for this difference lies in the colonial response to the nationalist movements. The Dutch were not willing to grant independence to Indonesia. As Governor-General B. C. de Jonge said, 'we have ruled here for 300 years with the whip and the club and we shall still be doing it in another 300'.[78] On the other hand in Malaya, Britain had agreed to begin a process of negotiation that would lead to self-government. The Indonesian militant nationalist movement was united in the face of Dutch opposition to their struggle, while the Malayan movement was divided between those who advocated negotiation with the British and those who wished to declare independence when Japanese surrender was imminent. As we saw above, this latter group surrounding the KMM, KRIS and the Peta was neutralized and did not receive support from other factions in the nationalist movement when the BMA (British Military Administration) was established after the war. For example, the MPAJA decided not to resist the returning British because the British had indicated that they would negotiate for an independent Malaya. Similarly, Datuk Onn bin Jaafar, the founder of UMNO (United Malays National Organization – the dominant component of the present ruling National Front), said that before speaking of political independence 'we must improve our economic standards first. We must make use of Malay lands, build up agriculture and establish cooperatives. We must endeavour to achieve economic independence first.'[79]

Despite the fact that the British were willing to grant formal independence to Malaya unlike the Dutch in Indonesia, both colonies had to struggle for an independent and democratic state. In Malaya the struggle was waged through negotiation while in Indonesia it was waged through both negotiation and war. The period of negotiation and fighting that commenced after the conclusion of the Second World War had resulted in crises, because the emerging ruling elites of these two states had battles to fight on two fronts. On the one hand, there was the struggle against the colonial powers and, on the other, against the internal fragmentation of the nationalist movements. These crises were ultimately resolved in terms of the emergence of two parliamentary democracies. In this section, I discuss these crises and how they led to parliamentary democracy with two very different futures.

The general principle guiding the following discussion is very elementary. Given that the emerging elites in a colony had been nurtured in the democratic tradition of government and had come to believe in democracy as an ideal to be cherished and achieved,[80] these elites would strive for an independent democratic post-colonial state because this is the model best known to them. This is especially the case if these elites were Western-educated and derived benefit from their positions in the colonial administration or aspired for positions in it. In fact, Anderson goes so far as to say that 'parliamentary democracy survived in Indonesia until about 1957 simply because *no other form of regime was possible*' (italics in the original).[81]

Apart from the fact that the democratic model was the one best known to the emerging elites, it was also true that some democratic institutions were already in place in the colonies long before independence. The appearance of various councils such as Regency Councils, State Councils, the Volksraad and the Federal Legislative Council, while generally advisory bodies that conferred little power upon the indigenous elite, nevertheless gave them an understanding of the workings of democratic institutions.

Another point, made by Feith, is that national self-respect caused indigenous elites to strive for democracy as this was one way that they could show the colonizers that they were capable of self-government along democratic lines.[82]

Finally, the importance of the inculcation of democratic values in men like Datuk Onn in Malaysia and Hatta, Natsir, Sjahrir and Sjafruddin Prawiranegara in Indonesia cannot be underestimated in explaining the paths to democracy taken.

Given that democracy was valued, placed on the nationalist agenda and fought for, what were the material conditions that conditioned its emergence as an institutional reality? The guiding principle in mind here is that the forces that seek a democratic state will attain their goals if (1) there is no armed resistance to their programme. In the case of Indonesia and Malaysia, it has already been established that mass resistance was not an important factor in the struggle for independence in both countries, but that armed resistance was widespread in Indonesia; (2) the state is internally strong; and (3) there is a high degree of elite cohesion founded in part on similar class and ideological backgrounds.

In this chapter, the focus is on the internal strength of the state, defined in terms of strong class support. As far as this is concerned, it operated in Malaya and Indonesia in different ways.

The internal strength of the state can be defined in terms of the resources that it can mobilize in situations when its power is challenged,[83] as well as in terms of the support it receives from the dominant classes, whether industrial or merchant capital, or the landed classes. A democratic regime that is internally strong can withstand opposition without having to respond by suspending the democratic process altogether. Moore referred to the strong bourgeois impulse as a requirement for democracy. What is important is the general principle behind this, that is, strong class backing for the democratic state.

In Malaya, the economically dominant class, predominantly Chinese capital, was allied with the emerging Malay ruling elite which was supported by the British in the establishment of a constitutional democracy. In Indonesia, the economically dominant Chinese had not been able to wield political power in order to exert themselves as a ruling class until after independence, in the late 1950s and early 1960s. This is because Indonesia, unlike Malaysia, had a strong indigenous merchant class which allied with the emerging ruling political elite against the Dutch. Taking the Malay–Indonesian Archipelago as an entity, historically Java was a centre of indigenous trade in spices and textiles, with other regions, Malaya included, being backwater areas. Thus, in Malaya, the Chinese did not encounter resistance in establishing themselves as the eventual Malaysian domestic capitalist class while in Indonesia indigenous merchant capital had been organized against Chinese capital since the establishment of the Sarekat Islam.

In both cases the foreign factor was important in the process of decolonization. British capital, which was dominant in the colonial economy of Malaya, continued to expand in the industrial sector after independence in terms of market share and employment and remained high in the primary sector during the 1960s.[84]

The Indonesians obtained foreign support from the United Nations and the United States, with Marshall Aid functioning as a catalyst in the decolonization of Indonesia.[85]

The first crisis that the Malay nationalist movement experienced came from the idea of the Malayan Union. Before the conclusion of the Second World War, the British had devised a scheme that would unite the Federated Malay States, the Unfederated Malay States, Penang and Malacca as a single crown colony with the aim of eventually granting independence to this entity. This was referred to as the Malayan Union.

What alarmed Malay nationalist leaders about the scheme were the provisions it made for the political and cultural equality of non-Malays with Malays. In a country where the Malays were barely a majority in their own land and were economically backward, this spelled disaster. Malays from various backgrounds came together on May 11th, 1946 under the *Mentri Besar* (Chief Minister) of Johor, Datuk Onn bin Ja'far, to establish the United Malays National Organization (UMNO). In the light of these developments, Britain could not proceed with the Malayan Union scheme. Not only did it face the possibility of open rebellion from amongst the Malays but even the Chinese and the Indians gave little support to the scheme because it could not guarantee rights along communal lines. A democratic union without such guarantees was not acceptable. The Malayan Union scheme was scrapped. What emerged in its place was the Federation of Malaya proposal the details of which were worked out together by the Malay elite, the rulers (the various sultans), and the British. In the proposed federation, the states involved would be the same as in the Malayan Union scheme. The new conditions, however, were that (1) Malay cultural domination would be established, and (2) Malays would wield political power.[86] Accordinging to its report five principles were followed by the working committee: (1) the need for a strong central government, (2) the need to maintain the individuality of each Malay state, (3) the need for new arrangements leading to self-government, (4) common citizenship for those who regarded Malaya as their home and were loyal to her and (5) recognition of the special position of Malays and their rights which must be safeguarded.[87] The need for the recognition of the special position of the Malays was stressed because 'the Malays live in a country in which they, owing to the influx of *foreign immigrants* [italics in the original], are numerically inferior. It is important to emphasize that the Malays have no alternative homeland, while the remainder of the population, with few exceptions, retain in varying degrees a connection with their country of origin, and, *in very many cases* [italics in the original] regard that country and not Malaya as the primary object of their loyalty and affection.'[88] This argument had strong emotional appeal even though the Malays were only slightly inferior in number, constituted the largest ethnic group, and benefited from the delineation of constituencies favouring UMNO.

In 1949, the Malayan Chinese Association (MCA) was established. It was an association, the class nature of which was capitalist. The UMNO–MCA alliance during the 1952–3 municipal election as a preparation for independence began the ruling elite–capital alliance that has characterized Malaysian political economy to this day. The Alliance, as it was known, won 94 out of a total of 119 seats over a two-year period.[89]

The British were not pleased with this trend in Malayan politics, however. An alliance between communal parties tended to strengthen communal politics. An UMNO–MCA convention was organized and made demands to the effect that elections to the Federal Legislative Council he held in 1954.[90] A debate at the Convention illustrates very clearly two opposing views amongst the Malays. A delegate of the Peninsula Malays Union criticized the UMNO for making a meaningless alliance with a race of those whose sincerity to this country had not been challenged. Furthermore, he accused the Chinese of participating in this alliance for the sole purpose of protecting their wealth.[91] In the language of sociology, the delegate was accusing the UMNO of being the committee that manages the affairs of the Chinese bourgeoisie, represented by the MCA.

This is not to suggest that the famous expression that the 'executive of the modern state is but a committee for managing the common affairs of the whole bourgeoisie'[92] applies to the Malayan case. The Malay-dominated newly-independent state agreed to sustain the conditions for the operation of a laissez-faire economy and not to encroach upon Chinese economic superiority. The situation differed from Marx's characterization of the capitalist state in that in Malaya the ruling elite did not emerge from among the economically dominant class. The Malayan Chinese dominant class which had the means of production at its disposal did not rule politically, nor did it aspire to do so. As far as the running of the state is concerned it was and is a junior partner. According to Wood, the capitalist state 'divested the appropriating class of direct political power and duties not immediately concerned with production and appropriation, leaving them with private exploitative powers purified, as it were, of public, social functions'.[93] Gulalp observes that this can be understood in terms of the 'separation of capital accumulation into its "public" and "private" moments'.[94] In the Malayan state the private moment of capital accumulation was almost entirely in Chinese hands while the Malay-dominated state attempted, especially after 1969, to engage in state capital formation. But during the struggle for independence and immediately following it capital accumulation was strictly an affair of private capital, the conditions of which were maintained and reproduced by the Malay-dominated state. Here, the question of why the Malay political elite and Chinese capital did not move against each other arises. There are a number of reasons for this.

First of all, cooperation between the Malays and the Chinese was a condition of being granted independence imposed by the British. In 1952, the colonial secretary stated that 'Malaya was unfit to receive any major political concessions, and that independence would not be forthcoming until unity between the different communities had been achieved'.[95]

Apart from this condition, as Ratnam observes, cooperation was necessary due to the relative numerical strength of the Malays and the Chinese.[96] In 1957, the year of formal independence, the population of the Federation of Malaya was 6 278 763, of which about 50 per cent were Malays and about 37 per cent were Chinese.[97] Had the Malay political elite moved against Chinese capital, they would be up against 37 per cent of the Malayan population. This is because communal politics is such that a move against Chinese capital would have been construed as a move against the Chinese community.

Furthermore, there were benefits to be gained from cooperation. It was advantageous for the Malay elite to have Chinese capital on their side. In the Kuala Lumpur municipal elections of 1952, UMNO candidates were placed in predominantly Malay constituencies while MCA candidates were put up in Chinese-dominated constituencies. This arrangement proved to be successful when up against non-communal opposition parties, since voting was almost always communal.[98] This state of affairs continues till today.

Ratnam suggests yet another reason to explain cooperation between the Malays and the Chinese. Since the Chinese were not concentrated in any particular part of Malaya they were more apt to compromise. Citing the examples of Sri Lanka and Canada he says that minorities that are territorially concentrated do not cooperate as easily as those which are territorially dispersed. This may be because territorial concentration increases the feeling of distinctiveness.[99] With cooperation and compromise possible, the Malay elite felt that excluding the Chinese from the franchise was not a desired path to take.

In the year prior to formal independence the success of the Chinese capital–Malay elite alliance was first gauged from the results of municipal elections held in several urban areas in 1952–3. In the first national election for legislative council seats held in 1955 the Alliance won 51 out of the 52 seats and thus became the government that led the country to independence.[100] The alliance formula worked as follows, as far as elections were concerned: the MCA provided funds while the UMNO allocated some seats for the MCA to contest. This is the essence of the MCA–UMNO alliance to this day and is the basis of Malaysian democracy in the sense that the Malay ruling elite have the support of the economically dominant Chinese capital in the running of a democratic state. This is true, notwithstanding other forms of support that capital extends to the Malay-dominated state via the stock exchange, taxation and so on.[101] On August 31st, 1957, the Federation of Malaya was proclaimed an independent state and a member of the British Commonwealth.

In Indonesia, independence was not obtained so easily. The newly-proclaimed republic in 1945 had a temporary constitution, a central National Committee of 135 members, a cabinet, and a functioning military. Administration was established throughout most of Indonesia.[102] After the Allies landed, Sukarno, Hatta and Sjahrir tried to negotiate with the Dutch, but were not able to prevent large numbers of Dutch soldiers from entering the country. In 1946 the Dutch succeeded in establishing control over several cities in Java and Sumatra and over much of the other islands. Most of Java and Sumatra was under the government of the Republic. Political parties were established and a parliamentary cabinet was set up under Sjahrir.[103] The new government was almost immediately beset by internal problems. In July 1946 there was a failed attempt to stage a coup d'état by the communist, Tan Malaka.[104] In November 1946, the Sjahrir government and the Dutch signed the Linggadjati Agreement according to which the Dutch recognized Indonesian authority in Java and Sumatra and the ultimate granting of independence to the country within the context of a Netherlands–Indonesian Union.

Meanwhile with 150 000 Dutch troops in Indonesia, the fighting continued. Accusing the Republic of not living up to the Linggadjati Agreement the Dutch succeeded, through military action, in capturing strategic territory including estate, mining and food-production areas in Sumatra and Java. In 1948 the Renville agreement was signed but it only 'reflected the weaker military position of the Republic'.[105] By then the Dutch controlled more than half of Java, most of Sumatra, Kalimantan and East Indonesia which they set up as formally autonomous states that would later become part of the Republic under the terms of the Linggadjati Agreement.

When the prime ministership of the Republic was taken over by the leader of the Socialist Party, Amir Sjarifuddin, the PKI grew in power. Amir's cabinet fell in 1948 and was replaced by one led by Hatta and was composed mainly of nationalist PNI and Muslim Masjumi members. What crystallized was a conflict between this cabinet and the pro-communist coalition, Front Demokrasi Rakyat (FDR or People's

Democratic Front), led by Amir Sjarifuddin. The main point of contention was the manner of dealing with the Dutch.[106] At the same time in 1948, Musso, a communist leader from the 1920s returned from exile in Russia and organized the FDR into an expanded PKI which launched a failed rebellion against the government. This was known as the Madiun coup. The rebellion was suppressed and Musso was killed in the battle. Amir and other leftist leaders were executed.

Within months of the Madiun affair, the Dutch launched another attack against the Republic and captured its capital, Jogjakarta. Sukarno and Hatta were among those top leaders exiled on the island of Bangka. The Dutch had gained control over the main urban areas of Java and Sumatra and hoped to establish a federal Indonesia on their terms.[107] However, world opinion was not on their side. More importantly, the United States took a pro-Indonesian stance and on January 28th, 1949, the United Nations Security Council passed a US-sponsored resolution which ordered the Dutch to (1) return Indonesian Republic leaders to Jogjakarta, and (2) assist them in the arranging of elections for the transfer of sovereignty to the United States of Indonesia by July 1950.[108] The combination of armed Indonesian resistance, changing attitudes of Dutch business groups and increasing US-pressure on the Dutch (including the threat of suspending Marshall Plan Aid) led to a change of policy on the part of the Dutch.[109]

A ceasefire between the Republic and the Netherlands was called on August 1st, 1949. With the military phase of the revolution over, negotiations at the Round Table Conference at the Hague between the Republic, the BFO (Bijenkomst voor Federaal Overleg – Federal Consultative Assembly) and the Netherlands commenced.[110] Plans for the unconditional and irrevocable transfer of complete sovereignty to the Indonesians were made.[111] Among the various concessions that the Indonesians made at the Round Table Conference, the most heavy were in the economic field. First of all the Republic of the United States of Indonesia (RUSI) was to assume the debt of the former Netherlands Indies which amounted to 4300 million guilders. To the Indonesians this was payment for four years of Dutch military campaigns against them.[112] Furthermore, the Indonesians would be required to provide guarantees to Dutch capital in Indonesia that all the rights, concessions and licences granted to them by the Netherlands Indies governments could not be expropriated except in accordance with the law.[113] Sovereignty was formally transferred on December 27th, 1949.

We have seen that the final struggle for independence involved internal struggles between Republican leaders and a struggle against the

Dutch. The emerging Indonesian state was based on a coalition of merchants and intellectuals 'competing in the social and economic fields with the upper class or with those groups which had already consolidated themselves in various functions'.[114] The newly-emerged Indonesian state can be described as relatively autonomous. In fact, the state like that under Bonaparte, represented indigenous Indonesian capital as well as the peasantry. Sukarno called his ideology 'Marhaenism', after a peasant named Marhaen who had told him about his extremely sober, but not truly proletarian, life as owner of a small plot of land, with a hut and a few tools of his own. This ideology is very remote indeed from a Marxist type of analysis stressing class conflict. In Sukarno's view, the great majority of the Indonesian people was composed of 'Marhaens', either rural or urban small owners, experiencing a community of interests in which class conflict was absent.[115]

At the same time, the democratic state during Sukarno's time tried to foster the growth of indigenous capital. By representing diverse classes, the state had some autonomy. In the context of the lack of peasant mobilization against the state, at least one condition for a democratic state was fulfilled for a brief duration.

In both Malaya and Indonesia in the period following independence, the context of a functioning democracy was that of emerging indigenous elites who were educated in the Western tradition,[116] who were already participating in democratic institutions even prior to independence, and who did not have to contend with overwhelming mass mobilization. Nevertheless, parliamentary democracy could not survive in Indonesia due to the prevalence of armed and separatist movements, the absence of an internally strong state and the lack of elite cohesion, problems not seriously encountered in Malaysia. In the following section the question of internal state strength will continue to be addressed while a treatment of elite cohesion will be found in Chapter 6.

ETHNICITY AND THE INTERNAL STRENGTH OF THE STATE

As far as Indonesia and Malaysia are concerned, the question of internal state strength, and the support that the state receives from the dominant classes in particular, cannot be viewed in isolation from the ethnic factor for the simple reason of the predominance of domestic Chinese capital. Therefore, our understanding of the internal strength of the state will have to take into account both the class and ethnic aspects of dominant class support for the state. For example, Chinese capital finds itself in a particular set of relations with the state due to its being both Chinese as well as owners/controllers of the means of production. As has been said earlier, the Malaysian state was internally strong in comparison to the Indonesian state and this is accounted for by the fact that dominant class support was forthcoming in the former while it was absent in the latter.

Dominant class support for the state in Malaysia is obvious from the following facts. As far as the class aspect of this support is concerned, this can be seen from patronage relations between the state and private sector and from the phenomenon of bureaucrat capitalists.

The form of capitalism that exists in Malaysia, and in Southeast Asia as a whole, is rightly described as ersatz capitalism,[117] that is, an economic system dependent on state patronage, the investment of transnational corporations and foreign technology. State officials and ruling party leaders, whether in their public or personal capacities, are in a position to extend various forms of favours to private capitalists. These encompass the provision of incentives, licensing, protectionism, concessions and joint-ventures. Very often, this involves a special relation between a politically powerful patron and a client who needs protection or favours due to the inadequacies of formal economic institutions. During colonial times, the Chinese were the clients of colonial patrons and after independence the state extended patronage to indigenous capital as well. There is a close working relationship between the state and private capital. For example, while it is not easy to trace the link between the corporate sector and a party, it is well known that UMNO has a significant corporate presence in publications, communications, banking, insurance, property development, construction, hotels, manufacturing and food retailing. The difficulty in seeing the link is due to the 'informal way in which party assets are held, that is, through trustees or nominees appointed by party leaders, often as a means of political patronage'.[118] There are also unverified reports that some Chinese capitalists who had emerged in the 1980s have close associations with the Malay political elite.[119]

In the early years after independence and prior to the launching of the New Economic Policy (NEP), the Chinese fraction of capital was dominant as Malay capital was significantly undeveloped.[120] But the NEP brought a new set of rules, regulations and constraints upon Chinese capital, which allowed for the emergence of politically-connected Malay private capital by way of 'Ali-Baba' arrangements, appointment to company directorships and the procurement of government contracts, not to mention the increasing role of foreign capital since the 1970s.[121]

In addition, Malay bureaucrat capitalists, that is, those who hold or once held bureaucratic posts and use such posts for initial capital accumulation[122] have made their indelible mark on the economic landscape. Nevertheless, in spite of the change in the ethnic composition of capital, and whatever the direction and magnitude of such change in state–capital business relationships since independence, the point is that the state has continuously had a solid financial basis and access to funds which has provided for some degree of democratic stability. This includes the provision of funds to UMNO politicians from Chinese capitalists, which is as true of the 1950s as it is of today.[123]

There is also an ethnic aspect to the role played by capital in maintaining the internal strength of the state. This was especially important in the early years of post-colonial state formation as far as Chinese capital was concerned. The MCA, as the political representatives of Chinese capital, helped to obtain a majority for the Alliance at federal elections.[124] This alliance, in the form of the Barisan Nasional (BN) today, is still important in spite of the relative loss of clout of Chinese capital. Although there had been a decline in support from the Chinese community of the MCA since 1959 and the implementation of the NEP resulted in the MCA losing ground to Chinese-based opposition parties during the last three decades,[125] as well as in the constriction of Chinese capital,[126] the ability of the MCA to bring in votes due to their link with capital is still significant because of the role that it plays in 'reinforcing Chinese ethnic identity and giving it concrete expression' in economic activity.[127] In spite of a history of Malay–Chinese antagonism, including the riots of May 1969, Malay sentiments towards the Chinese were not such that Chinese capital could not aspire to ruling class status.

The situation in Indonesia has been quite a stark contrast to that of Malaysia. On several counts, the Indonesian state can be said to have been internally weak. The weakness of the state in terms of the presence of secessionist movements and regional revolts has already been noted.

The Indonesian revolution was a contributing factor,[128] having taken its toll on the economy, and the new post-colonial state found itself saddled with inherited debts and few sources of revenue as the major conglomerates and oil-producing companies were in the hands of the Dutch, Americans and British. It is in this context that the indigenous and Chinese fractions of capital must be seen.

With respect to the question of dominant class support for the state, the crucial factor distinguishing Indonesia from Malaysia was the historical presence of an indigenous merchant class which aspired to become a bourgeoisie in post-colonial times. In Malaysia, the absence of widespread armed revolts and secessionist movements neither created the conditions for the reactive establishment of an authoritarian state nor provided a rationale for the military to play a dominant role in politics. Furthermore, the Malaysian state had the support of both local and international capital, even though the ethnic proportions of local capital changed after the implementation of the NEP.

In Indonesia, on the other hand, attempts to establish parliamentary democracy took place in the absence of any of the conditions of democratic stability, so much so as to raise the question of why parliamentary democracy lasted as long as it did.[129] The presence of an indigenous bourgeoisie, however weak, meant that it was politically unfeasible for the state to accommodate Chinese capital and while neither fraction of capital was capable of playing the role of dominant class supporter of the state, the army found itself to be indispensable as a political actor due to the prevalence of armed rebellions and secession attempts and the failure of capital to contribute to political stability. By the time both Chinese and domestic capital were able to forge stable ties of patronage with the state, this had become authoritarian and it would be appropriate to speak of dominant class support of an authoritarian state.

As has been said earlier, internal state strength implies that the state has the resources of the dominant class available to it, whether this is in the form of tax revenues, election funds or parliamentary support. These resources were not forthcoming to the state as indigenous capital was not a dominant class,[130] Chinese capital had no political clout, and there was intense rivalry between the two during the period of liberal democracy. While indigenous capital was too weak to constitute a basis of state strength, its very presence made it politically unfeasible for the young Indonesian state to consider an alliance or a more accommodative stance vis-à-vis Chinese capital.

Historically, the Javanese priyayi did not make the shift from rights of appropriation over land, labour and crop to private property and a landowning bourgeoisie did not develop.[131] While both Chinese and Javanese santri merchants[132] were active in trade up to the seventeenth century, the Javanese suffered from the establishment of the United East India Company (VOC) and the subsequent control of international trade by the Dutch. Javanese dominance in rural trade also diminished when the Dutch removed travel and residence restrictions on the Chinese between 1910 and 1926, resulting in conflict between indigenous and Chinese capital.[133] Sumatra faired better than Java as far as the rise of indigenous traders is concerned. Minangkabau traders developed a prospering trade in gambier, coffee and textiles in the late eighteenth and early nineteenth century. Sumatrans were involved in smallholder export production of rice and rubber in the early part of this century and a handful were able to expand beyond small-scale trade and move into import and export at the national and international levels, and even manufacturing in the 1950s, while at the same time spreading to Java.[134] Nevertheless, the lack of a basis for large-scale capital accumulation such as tax farming, pawn shops and wholesaling,[135] and easy money through the Ali-Baba economy, prevented indigenous capital from developing sophisticated business organizations with extensive ethnic networks that could lead to large-scale capital accumulation.

The presence of an indigenous capitalist class in Indonesia, however weak it was, had been partly responsible for anti-Chinese outbreaks in Indonesia in the sense that competition between indigenous and Chinese capital had created unfavourable attitudes towards the Chinese. These outbreaks include the 1959 ban on Chinese retail trade, the May 1963 riots of West Java, and the 1965–7 crisis,[136] and it is reasonable to advance the thesis that the root of such tensions are to be found in the economic competition between adjoining social groups.[137] This did not preclude cooperation between the *asli* (native) and Chinese fractions of capital, but the latter depended on the former for powerful political support due to their links with the ruling family and other patrons. In addition, the Chinese factor in getting the vote was never crucial due to simple demographics.

Chinese capital could not aspire to ruling class status as they were not acceptable by the masses as having a legitimate public political role, thereby limiting the possibilities for collusion with the newly emerging post-colonial state due to the general state of hostility towards the Chinese.[138] This is especially so in view of the 'sins' that Indonesian Chinese are said to have committed, according to the majority of asli Indonesians, including:[139]

(1) domicile exclusively in Chinese areas;
(2) preference for recruiting Chinese workers;
(3) wage discrimination in favour of Chinese workers;
(4) discrimination between Chinese and asli Indonesians in business relations;
(5) lack of social solidarity with asli Indonesians;
(6) weak sense of national identity;
(7) lack of assimilation to Indonesian culture;

(8) view of Indonesian citizenship purely in legal terms;
(9) superiority complex vis-à-vis asli Indonesians.

To be sure, such attitudes towards the Chinese were in part a result of Dutch use of the Chinese as middlemen in the exploitation of Indonesia's natural resources. The Chinese had become prominent in Indonesian trade during colonial times partly because colonial policy had placed restrictions on their entry into other occupations and the purchase of land.[140] This had the effect of establishing Chinese economic dominance in certain fields as well as isolating them socially from asli Indonesians.[141] The sentiments of the Indonesians with respect to the Chinese was reflected in government policies during the liberal democracy period which sought to Indonesianize the economy through a series of discriminatory measures designed to transfer wealth and control over the means of production from alien and Chinese hands into native Indonesian ones.[142]

Furthermore, capital's position vis-à-vis the state in Indonesia was further weakened by the position taken by the army contra the bourgeoisie. The military was an enthusiastic supporter of Guided Democracy and, therefore, the decline of parliamentary democracy. To the extent that parties like Masjumi represented the interests of Muslim merchants, this was a blow to indigenous capital. The close identification of Masjumi with the PRRI rebellion which the army suppressed only strengthened the view that the separation of the army from politics is 'a holy dream' which may be realized by the next generation, which had not participated in the revolution to free Indonesia from Dutch colonialism.[143] The state and army's strong apprehension of the incompetence of indigenous capital was quite clear in the takeover of Dutch firms by the army in 1957–8, which under other circumstances could have come under the control of indigenous capital.[144]

There was also the problem of a crumbling administrative discipline of the civil service after 1950 which was largely a result of the 'penetration of the state by society'.[145] There was a tenfold increase in the number of civil servants from 250 000 in 1940 to 2 500 000 in 1968[146] with certain offices and functions taken over by illiterates and incompetents.[147]

One of the consequences of such a large civil service in the 1950s was the generalization of corruption, both for personal as well as party gain and, as a result, diminishing state efficacy. The group of capitalists that have evolved this way are known in Indonesia as client businessmen.[148]

State involvement in economic development in terms of the role of political parties and client businessmen is potentially damaging to the economy because very often those who obtain rights, licences, franchises and the like are neither qualified nor competent in business. Patronage and rent-seeking represent major means by which such businessmen join the ranks of the economic elite. The disadvantage of this is that major corporations that were established through patronage or through political party connections are not up to standard as far as efficiency, technical know-how and entrepreneurship are concerned. In this sense, the role of the state in development is negative. Some of these effects that can be listed as follows are the reduction in government revenue, the reduction in efficiency and the concentration of capital.

A common means by which government experiences a loss of revenue through corruption is over-pricing. Another way in which government revenue is lost through corruption is mismanagement. Examples include the awarding of contracts without tenders, unvouchered payments, surcharges and abortive expenditures, illegal collection of fees and so on.

It is sometimes claimed that corruption may increase administrative efficiency because employees who receive this speed money would become more productive and may even work overtime, with no increase in salary. This is only partially true. Only those customers who are able or willing to bribe or to be extorted will benefit from the increased productivity of the official behind the counter.

Furthermore, it is usually the case that speed money does not buy efficiency but simply a service which would otherwise not have been produced. It also serves to lower morale and frustrate those officials who are honest and dedicated in their work, which in turn decreases the efficiency of the organization.

Corruption, particularly nepotism, plays a vital role in the increasing concentration of capital, that is, the degree to which a relatively small number of firms account for a significant proportion of production, employment or some other measure of size in an industry. One of the ways by which concentration increases is through nepotism. Economic elites are involved in the process of capital accumulation by virtue of their position in or connections with government.

While money politics and other forms of political business are to be found in Malaysia as well, there they became dominant factors in the context of a booming economy and reflect the economic strength of the state, while in Indonesia, kleptocracy in the 1950s was the outcome of a weak and economically burdened state that had the effect of diminishing state efficacy.[149]

The failures of the weak state in Indonesia to create political stability and economic prosperity, created the appropriate rationalization for the military to play a dominant role in politics. This is discussed in the next chapter in connection with the question of elite cohesion as a factor explaining the persistence of democracy in Malaysia and its demise in Indonesia.

6 From Democracy to Authoritarianism: Tendencies and Transformations

THE PARTING OF WAYS

In the last chapter, it was established that the emergence of democracy in the Malaysian and Indonesian states out of the experience of colonialism had different bases. In Malaysia the strength of the state was based on a coalition of ethnic parties, especially that of the MCA (Malaysian Chinese Association) and the UMNO (United Malays National Organization). This was an alliance between capital and the old elite which had been transformed for the most part into a class of salaried officials under the colonial administration and so were severed from the ownership of the means of production. The compliance of the British in this alliance must, of course, be remembered. The political elite, mainly Malay in composition, and Chinese capitalists agreed on a formula that granted privileges to the Malays, relative freedom to pursue their economic activities as they always had for the Chinese, and parliamentary democracy. The latter was achieved because the Malayan elite were educated and nurtured in this tradition and they faced no opposition in establishing it. In a sense, the Malay-dominated state was the representative of the capitalist class although it did see itself as the upholder of the rights of Malay society as a whole.

The case of the Indonesian state was very different. The basis of democracy there had some similarities with the Malaysian case in the sense that nationalist leaders were educated in the colonial tradition and imbibed democratic values as a result. A major difference was the role of mass movements during and after the process of decolonization. Furthermore, the class basis of the Indonesian state was quite unlike that of Malaysia. The Indonesian state was composed of members of the old elite as well as of the merchant class and belonged to different political parties with divergent views as to what the direction of the political economy should be. The state was not dominated by any particular group or class and was not the representative of any class. Therefore, from their inception there was more potential for consensus within the regime in Malaysia than in Indonesia. It was in this political context that economic factors, including those pertaining to participation in the capitalist world economy, took their toll on democracy in these two new states. The story of democracy in Malaysia and Indonesia is the story of the failure of private and then state-sponsored capital to solve economic and political problems that had beset these countries even before independence, and it is in this context that the question of elite cohesion and democratic stability will be discussed.

Malaysia and Indonesia were to pass through a number of crises that eventually led to the temporary suspension of parliamentary democracy in the former and its demise in the latter. What I attempt to show in this chapter is how and why Malaysia and Indonesia took divergent paths in state forms after both obtained formal independence as democratic states. This amounts to showing that the third condition of democratic stability, that is elite cohesion, that obtained in Malaysia around the time of independence continued to exert itself till the present while this condition in Indonesia during independence no longer did. The ethnic alliance at the level of the dominant classes persisted in Malaysia and was not seriously challenged from below. In Indonesia, the coalition of parties that reflected the alliance between elite nationalists, communists and merchant-based Muslim parties crumbled under the pressure of economic problems and left a vacuum for the army to step into and exert its influence. The periods that we are concerned with here are the following: in Malaysia parliamentary democracy was suspended in 1969 and was not reinstated until 1971. In Indonesia parliamentary democracy was replaced by what was euphemistically known as Guided Democracy in 1958, but which was really authoritarian in nature. With the overthrow of Sukarno in 1965 began the next period of authoritarian rule that continues to the present. In what follows, the failures of private and state capital in the context of international political economy to solve economic and political problems and, therefore, generate authoritarian tendencies and transformations will be discussed.

THE FAILURE OF PRIVATE CAPITAL

Following formal independence, the Malaysian and Indonesian governments sought to expand the role of private capital. In Indonesia this meant the creation of an indigenous capitalist class (that is, at the expense of Chinese domestic and foreign capital). In Malaysia, the expansion of private capital referred to domestic capital (both Chinese and indigenous) and foreign capital. In both countries, the state failed to create a sufficiently powerful indigenous capitalist class that could provide a strong basis of support for the state. Indigenous capital never developed sufficiently to the extent that it could control the state. This failure is discussed below.

Turning to Indonesia first, the role of the state in capital accumulation was primarily regulatory and infrastructural, although the state did enter into the process of production directly by the establishment of state enterprises. The most important aspect of the regulatory role of the state was in the area of financing. During the period of parliamentary democracy, the state transformed the Java Bank into the Bank of Indonesia. It also established the Bank Industri Negara (National Industrial Bank) and the Bank Negara Indonesia (National Bank of Indonesia). The former provided funds for industrial projects while the latter financed importers through the provision of foreign exchange. In addition to this, the state entered into the process of production through the procurement of a number of public utilities such as pawnshops, post, telegraph and telephone services, electricity, ports, coal mines and railways.[1]

The most important aspect of the state's bid to expand the role of indigenous capital in Indonesia was in the area of imports. The Benteng programme, first implemented during the Natsir cabinet (September 1950 – March 1951), gave preferential treatment to indigenous importers by reserving certain categories of goods for them to import and by the provision of funds from the Bank Negara Indonesia. The conditions for participation in this programme were that the importer had to be an Indonesian (that is, indigenous and not Chinese) and had to have a working capital of at least Rp 100 000, 70 per cent of which had to come from indigenous citizens.[2] Most of the beneficiaries of the Benteng programme were individuals with ties to powerful figures in the state bureaucracy or political parties who had authority over the distribution of licences and credit. To make matters worse, most licences issued under the Benteng programme were not utilized by indigenous importers to improve their standards as capitalists but were instead sold to Chinese importers at 200 per cent to 250 per cent of their nominal value.[3] In spite of government efforts to curb the abuses of the Benteng programme very few indigenous import companies were successful in their ventures, especially in the event of the decline of foreign exchange after the Korean war boom. The PSI, Masyumi and moderate members of the PNI all pressed for the end of the Benteng programme, arguing that a market-oriented economy was superior to state subsidy of indigenous capital as the former would yield greater efficiency in production and exchange.[4] Nevertheless, the Benteng programme continued and in 1956 under the Harahap cabinet (August 1955 – March 1956) was extended to include non-indigenous Indonesians as well. In 1957, under the Djuanda cabinet, the programme was ended. Whatever indigenous capitalists that existed, then, were dependent on credit, licences and contracts awarded to them by the state.

State involvement in capital accumulation went beyond its regulatory and infrastructural roles. Three levels of state involvement in the sphere of capital accumulation can be identified. The first has already been briefly described. It is the level of public policy where the state through the instrumentality of fiscal, monetary and legal policies influences the possibilities and outcomes of capital accumulation. The second level is where the state establishes state enterprises. In this respect the state was to take on a much more pronounced role from the period of Guided Democracy onwards, but state ownership of capital began during the period of parliamentary democracy. The third level at which state involvement in capital accumulation can be understood is that of corruption. At this level, state bureaucrats and politicians use their authority over the allocation of credit, licences, contracts and monopolies to establish personal sources of capital accumulation.[5] Bureaucratic capitalism, that is, 'capital owned by the officials of state and party bureaucracies, became a major feature of private capital ownership in Indonesia'.[6]

The result of the failure of state policies to generate an indigenous class of capitalists in the import and manufacturing sector of the Indonesian economy, left the bulk of indigenous producers, for want of political connections, unable to compete with Chinese production. For example, in the *kretek* (clove cigarette) industry those indigenous producers who had secured import licences through the state benefited through import trade profits or through the selling of import licences. The rest of the indigenous kretek producers suffered a decline. In 1950, up to 65 per cent of the production of *rokok putih* ('Western' cigarettes) was foreign or Chinese-owned and the greater part of kretek production was in Chinese hands.[7] The cigarette industry is just one example and similar circumstances obtained in the textile industry, traditionally the domain of indigenous capital. Schmitt sums the situation up:

The overvalued exchange rate benefited importers–bureaucrats who controlled the exchange allocations and their friends – but did not reduce costs for trading interest outside the import sector, to whom imports were resold at high and rising prices. Price controls added further irritation. Trading groups outside Java therefore won political allies among their less powerful counterparts within Java. In combination, the trading interests provided the core of indigenous support needed to put force behind the demand for retrenchment at the top.[8]

In 1956 a political body, Kensi (All-Indonesian National Economic Congress) was established to push for reforms in favour of indigenous capital. Kensi failed to obtain support from any major political party. The PSI and Masyumi parties had come to the realization that indigenous capital could flourish in the context of Chinese and foreign capital. The PNI refused to enact legislation that had a racial basis. Finally, the PKI did not make the distinction between indigenous and Chinese capital. What was of greater significance to them was the distinction between national and imperialist capital.[9]

The protest that the state encountered from indigenous capital was only part of a larger opposition launched against it from many fronts of which there were three major ones.

One was regional instability. Apart from armed rebellions and separatist movements cited in Chapter 4, from 1953–7 there was active banditry in regions like West Java and South Sulawesi that would last for several months. While the army at times succeeded in driving bandits from a particular region, the bandits would just re-establish themselves elsewhere. Even if bandit members had surrendered themselves, they did so on terms that were risky for the government. For example, it was often the case that surrendering band leaders were allowed to keep their organizations intact, resulting in their returning to banditry.[10]

Another major opposition force to the government came from the PKI. The PKI organized peasant and labour against the new Republic but was effectively put down by the government in 1950–1.[11] Because of the little support that the PKI received from peasant and labour, its leaders decided that what the party needed was an alliance with major political parties even if this meant the de-emphasis on class issues.[12] The alliance that was forged between the PKI and PNI and other parties was presented by the PKI as an alliance across class lines, that united the working class, peasantry, petty bourgeoisie and national bourgeoisie against imperialism, compradors and feudalism. In reality, however, it was just a political alliance between radical nationalist elites and communists.[13] Among the chief proponents of the dismantling of parliamentary democracy were those who sought to restrict the influence of the PKI.[14]

Finally, the third major opposition to the government during the period of parliamentary democracy came from the army. The army was in part prompted by the organizational superiority of the PKI into taking a more active role in politics and economics. Because the government was unable to solve pressing economic problems and because of rebellions in various regions of Indonesia, the army took it upon itself to urge Sukarno to dissolve parliament 'which would have placed them in a very strong position from which to make further political moves'.[15] The army accused the government of being weak, incompetent, corrupt and inattentive to military interests.[16] From 1956 to 1958, the Indonesian government was faced with rebellions. Several leading figures from the Masyumi and one from the Socialist Party (PSI) set up the Revolutionary Government of the Republic of Indonesia (PRRI) based in West Sumatra. The rebellions were successfully quelled by the army which more or less confirmed their future role in politics.

> By proving its indispensability in the crisis caused by the rebellion, the army leadership had underpinned its claim to a more permanent role in the government ... convinced that its participation in the government was necessary, and less inhibited by the old internal fissures, the army took advantage of the disrepute of the parliamentary system to press for a new government structure in which the army's place would be central.[17]

The opposition that the government faced from the army, the PKI and the regional revolts must be seen from the point of view of a fragmented government. The failure of the state to consolidate its power through the creation of an indigenous capitalist class, left it with two options, as summarized by Robison:

> (a) To retreat from nationalism and indigenism and look once again to foreign and Chinese capital as the main generating force of capitalist development. (b) To extend the process of economic nationalisation and socialisation by expropriating the remaining Dutch enterprises and using the state as the engine of national capital accumulation and industrialisation.[18]

The first option was supported by the PSI, Masyumi and moderate elements of the PNI. Sukarno and the PKI supported the second option. But it was Sukarno that the army supported and 1957–8 saw the dismantling of parliamentary democracy and the nationalization of Dutch enterprises. Thus began the period of Guided Democracy which was essentially presidential rule, lasting formally till 1965. Under the constitution of Guided Democracy the president was to have executive power and was not responsible to parliament. When the various political parties began to attack the government in 1959, Sukarno reacted by dissolving parliament in March 1960. In June of the same year he established a new legislature consisting of 283 members of political parties such as the PNI, NU (Nahdatul Ulama, a Muslim party) and the PKI as well as members of the armed forces. The Masyumi and PSI were excluded as they had been against the idea of Guided Democracy.[19] Guided Democracy was characterized by government encroachment into the everyday lives of intellectuals, students, workers and peasants alike. Political bodies such as the Masyumi, PSI, the Democratic League and several smaller political organizations were merged into organizations run by the government.[20] Also, there was no longer a separation of powers. In February 1960, the Chairman of the Supreme Court was made a cabinet member and six months later Sukarno denounced the principle of the separation of powers. Nevertheless, power at the top continued to be shared through the instrumentality of the coalition as under parliamentary democracy. In the period of Guided Democracy, this coalition was formulated as NASAKOM (Nasionalisme, Agama, Komunisme – Nationalism, Religion, Communism) which symbolized the alliance between Sukarno and the PNI, NU and the PKI.

The conflicts that plagued the Indonesian state and led to the demise of parliamentary democracy cannot be understood solely in class terms. While class interests certainly were issues of contention, the battles that were waged were mainly at the level of elite politics, between different alirans or ideological orientations represented by the PSI, PNI, PKI and the Masyumi parties. The respective ideological orientations of the parties did not consistently correspond to particular class positions, nor did their memberships derive from particular classes.

Coming to the failure of private capital in Malaysia, unlike Indonesia, the Malaysian state sought to expand the role of both domestic and foreign capital and did not discriminate between indigenous and Chinese capital. As in Indonesia, the state's role in Malaysia at first was primarily regulatory and infrastructural. During this period, which lasted till 1969 when a state of emergency was declared due to racial riots, the establishment of state enterprises and economic nationalism were not high on the agenda. The important aspects of the state's role in promoting private capital accumulation were mainly three.

One was the provision of funds. The Malayan Industrial Development Finance Limited (MIDFL) was incorporated in 1960 and reorganized in 1963.[21] Its share capital was held by the then Malayan government, established Malayan banks, several insurance companies, the Commonwealth Development Corporation (formerly the Colonial Development Corporation), the Commonwealth Development Finance Company and the International Finance Corporation (IFC) of the World Bank.[22] In this way local finance became available as loans to transnational corporations (TNCs). In addition to this, the MIDFL provided loans to companies without imposing the condition of management control. The MIDFL provided the bulk of its funds to large foreign concerns rather than small local ones, although the latter was its professed aim.[23]

Another area of the state's role was in the establishment of a stock market in Malaysia. The stocks of two subsidiaries of foreign companies were floated on the local stock exchange. In addition to the various benefits to be derived from financing via the stock market, the market served to establish 'a commonality of class interests important for foreign capital operations in alien situations'.[24]

Thirdly, the Malaysian state was very active in the regulation of labour that took the form of legislation restricting the right to strike. Legislation introduced in 1965 required compulsory arbitration for various 'essential services' which was broadly defined. Furthermore, government employees were prohibited from participating in labour disputes.[25]

Although the primary thrust of the policy of the state was to mobilize foreign as well as domestic private capital as a whole, it was not entirely unconcerned about the creation of an indigenous (Malay) capitalist class. Initial attempts, however, were feeble and unimpressive. The Rural and Industrial Development Authority (RIDA), established in 1953 by the colonial government, was responsible for Malay development in industry and commerce,[26] while the Ministry for Rural Development was responsible for the rural areas.[27] In spite of the establishment of these bodies Malay ownership of capital did not increase significantly following independence except in the transport industry, where the government made concerted efforts through preferential policies to increase Malay ownership.

In 1965,[28] Malay expectations were raised in the light of a number of events. The Majlis Amanah Rakyat (People's Trust Council – MARA) was created to replace RIDA. RIDA was merged with the Malay Secretariat in the Ministry of National and Rural Development.[29] 1965 also saw the convening of the first national Bumiputera[30] Economic Congress where dissatisfaction among Malay businessmen with government policy was voiced. They complained that the failure of the policy of increasing the participation of Bumiputeras in the economy was indicated by the lack of Bumiputera ownership of companies.[31] In spite of these criticisms of government policies Malay ownership in the industrial sector did not increase and was largely restricted to those with political connections.

While there was disaffection among Malay businessmen and political leaders at government policy on the one hand, there was growing inequality among the Malay masses on the other. From 1957 to 1970, the Gini ratio increased from 0.34 to 0.46. During the same period the income share of the top five per cent of Malay households increased from 18.1 per cent to 23.8 per cent while that of the bottom 40 per cent decreased from 19.6 per cent to 13 per cent.[32]

The result of dissatisfaction among Malay businessmen and political leaders on the one hand and the Malay masses on the other resulted in the May 13th race riot in 1969 following the general elections on the 10th, when the very basis of the Malay–Chinese Alliance was jeopardized. In fact, the government began to face serious problems much earlier. After independence in 1957, the Alliance government was faced with political and security problems. The Alliance government consisting of the United Malays National Organization (UMNO), the Malayan Chinese Association (MCA) and the Malayan Indian Congress (MIC) came to power in 1955 and facilitated a smooth transition to independence in 1957. In the 1959 federal elections however, it lost ground although it still remained in power. It had lost ground in the Malay rural areas and this gave rise to the realization that more would have to be done for the welfare of the Malay peasant. In 1957, while the Malays constituted 49.8 per cent of the population and the Chinese constituted 37.2 per cent, most of the Malays lived in rural regions of the northern and eastern areas of the country while the Chinese were concentrated in the more developed urban areas.[33]

A review of the events since the 1959 federal elections to the 1969 May upheaval is essential, for these events had a significant bearing on Malaysian economic development in the following decade of 1970–80.

In the 1957–9 period the Alliance government lost ground in local government and state assembly elections. The Prime Minister who was also leader of the Alliance and leader of UMNO, Tunku Abdul Rahman, temporarily resigned as Prime Minister at the beginning of 1959, before the federal elections of the same year to muster support in the Malay rural areas that might be vulnerable to the attack of opposition parties such as the Pan-Malayan Islamic Party (PMIP).[34] At the same time he was under pressure to make concessions to the MCA regarding the allocation of voting constituencies. Giving in to the MCA meant possibly losing ground to the PMIP. This is because the MCA was a predominantly Chinese political party and the PMIP would be an alternative to those Malays who might feel betrayed by the Malay party, UMNO, if the Prime Minister gave in to MCA demands. As it turned out UMNO did not do well in the elections losing control of the northeastern states of Kelantan and Trengganu. In spite of the Malay party of the Alliance losing ground to the PMIP, the Alliance was still in power after 1959. After the elections, concessions were made to the MCA, thus easing the conflict with the Chinese. This conflict existed in the first place because of the subordination of the MCA to the UMNO in the leadership of the Alliance.

But the dust did not settle. Further threat came from Singapore. The People's Action Party (PAP) led by Lee Kuan Yew, was based in Singapore which was predominantly Chinese. As a result, the PAP constituted a threat to the MCA as far as Malaysian Chinese representation in the Alliance was concerned.

The events preceding the 1964 federal elections were important. The Alliance made a comeback, gaining what it had lost in 1959. The PMIP, the PAP and other Chinese opposition parties were defeated. Then Lee Kuan Yew from Singapore organized a new coalition of opposition parties that carried the slogan of 'a Malaysian Malaysia'. This meant that no one community or race would have supremacy. The Malays were beginning to feel that their rights were being encroached upon. To restore stability Tunku Abdul Rahman decided that Singapore should leave the Federation of Malaysia and reluctantly in 1965 she did. The point to be gathered from all this is that anti-Chinese sentiments among the Malays were gathering momentum.

By the end of the 1960s the Malay leadership began to realize that the constitutional bargain agreed to prior to independence that had provided for special Malay privileges to raise their standard of living and participation in the economy had not resulted in the desired goals.

The lowest mean monthly household income of M$178.7 belonged to the Malays compared to a mean monthly household income of M$387.4 among the Chinese. Also 85.5 per cent of households that had an income of less than M$100 a month were Malay, while only 9.6 per cent were Chinese and 4.9 per cent were Indian.

The Malays showed their discontent at their economic inferiority by reducing their support for the UMNO, the dominant party of the Alliance. In predominantly Malay constituencies the UMNO share of votes fell from 66 per cent to 56 per cent. The opposition PMIP increased its share of votes among the Malays.[35] The MCA faired much worse than the UMNO winning only 13 of its 33 contested seats. It was then that the erosion in power of the Alliance and, therefore, UMNO was apparent.

The May 1969 communal riots took place immediately after the federal elections. The violence has been attributed to several reasons. Perhaps, the most important is that the Malays were dissatisfied with the pace at which the Alliance government was implementing programmes to improve their [the Malays'] lot.[36] A state of emergency was declared and the constitution was suspended, the country to be ruled by a National Operations Council (NOC).[37]

Although the May 13th affair had its roots in Malay–Chinese antagonisms that reflected both ethnic as well as class antagonisms, it cannot be said that it was the reason for the suspension of parliamentary democracy for almost two years. It is true that a state of emergency was declared immediately following the riots in order to effectively deal with racial tensions. But tensions had died down soon after and consensus on the future course of the country had been reached among most groups involved well before the state of emergency was lifted. The real cause for the suspension of parliamentary democracy for a prolonged period was intra-UMNO conflict. When the Alliance party lost its two-thirds majority in parliament there was much pressure on Prime Minister Tunku Abdul Rahman to resign. This pressure mounted after the May 13th riots, three days after the elections were held. The intra-UMNO conflict was between the opponents and supporters of Tunku Abdul Rahman. His opponents regarded him as having not paid sufficient attention to Malay problems and being too close to the MCA.[38] The government claimed that democracy had been suspended for 21 months because of racial tension and the need to arrive at a consensus to amend the constitution. But the government had the racial situation of the country under control within a few months of the riots. A plausible alternative explanation for the suspension of parliamentary democracy for 21 months, the banning of public meetings for political parties, the banning of general meetings of political parties and the banning of the publication of party journals, was dissension within the UMNO.[39] In spite of the fact that it was clear to all that the Constitutional Amendment Bill passed on March 3rd, 1971, could have been passed much earlier and was supported after May 13th, 1969 by all opposition parties, parliament was reconvened only in January 1971 after Tunku Abdul Rahman had resigned and the question of his successor was settled.[40] The relationship between the internal history of UMNO and the future of democracy in Malaysia will concern us again when the state is discussed in the context of the mobilization of state capital.

THE TRIALS OF STATE CAPITALISM

The failure of private capital to serve the interests of various political parties, classes and groups in Indonesia and Malaysia led to greater state involvement in the process of production.

Beginning with Indonesia, during the few years after 1957 the various institutions of parliamentary democracy were dismantled and an authoritarian regime was consolidated. This was known as the period of Guided Democracy although there was little about it that was democratic. Authority was no longer vested in an elected parliament but in the president. The chief bodies through which the president ruled were appointed. These were the cabinet, the Supreme Advisory Council and the Supreme War Authority. Not only was the power of political parties weakened by these appointed bodies, but also by the rise of functional groups in parliament. Functional groups were organizations that served various 'interest' groups comprised of youth, workers, peasants and religious organizations. In the 1960 parliament, out of a total of 283 members, 154 were appointed to represent functional groups while 129 were appointed to represent political parties. The army was included as a functional group.[41] The role of the army was crucial in March of 1957 when martial law was established in the face of regional revolts and the appropriation of Dutch companies. The military succeeded in gaining authority over former Dutch estates and trading companies as well as state oil companies.[42] The military ownership of state enterprises was the best way for the military to exercise direct control over the process and means of production.

In the economy of Sukarno's Guided Democracy the state continued its role as regulator but its role in the process of production was greatly expanded through the increase in state ownership of capital which came about mainly through the acquisition of Dutch enterprises in 1957–8. Towards the end of 1957 unions began to take over Dutch companies but later came under military supervision. The takeover of Dutch enterprises radically altered the structure of the ownership of capital in Indonesia. Ninety per cent of plantation output, 60 per cent of foreign trade, about 246 factories and mining concerns, as well as banks, shipping and some service industries were transformed into state enterprises. As Thomas and Panglaykim observe:

In the months between 'take-over' and nationalisation, private businessmen made a bid to persuade the Government to transfer certain of the ex-Dutch companies to the private sector. This was a rather forlorn hope because leaders of several political groupings had launched a strong attack on the performances of private enterprise at a National Economic Conference in November-December, 1957.[43]

Indeed, the handing over of ex-Dutch property to private capitalists was out of the question. Indigenous capital had proven its inability to develop as was evident from the failure of the Benteng programme. And it was political suicide to hand them over to Indonesian Chinese capitalists.

At the same time the state moved more decisively into production, steering away from its past emphasis on imports. In 1963, monopolies on the import of essential goods were removed from the state trading corporations which forced them to be more autonomous.[44] State banks were directed to channel 50 per cent of credit to the production sectors, effectively reducing credit to importers.[45] In 1964, the Berdikari programme was established. Along the lines of the strategy of import-substitution industrialization, this programme was focused on steel production, ship building and fertilizer production.[46] To further discourage importing, private businessmen were prohibited from importing except through government auspices. Instead they were to engage in production for export.[47]

As a result, the role of the domestic bourgeoisie in the economy diminished. Indigenous as well as Indonesian Chinese businessmen were subject to various controls, political and economic. Most of these controls were based on the ability of the state to allocate imports. Government coordinating bodies such as the Federation of Homogeneous Enterprises and the Organization of Homogeneous Enterprises were set up ostensibly to regulate and rationalize production. In reality they were the means through which government officials and political figures 'could make exactions from business in return for allocations of raw materials and other imports necessary to the production process'.[48] But it was not the whole of the domestic bourgeoisie that was negatively affected by state intervention in production. There was a section of Chinese capital which had access to the resources of the state and which had established partnerships with state civilian and military officials.[49]

The government's bid to stimulate a national industrial capitalism largely met with failure, mainly because of the lack of capital and poor infrastructure. Declining earnings from exports combined with an increasing debt and imports threatened to cause a serious balance of payments crisis.[50] To this must be added management problems. As Castles said, 'managers of state corporations were able to treat the property entrusted to them as in some respect private property and extract private profits from the abuse of their authority'.[51]

As Robison notes, by 1965 the workings of state capital in Indonesia had to be rethought. There were two possibilities. One was that the PKI would assume political power and provide the organizational and ideological leadership for state-owned production. The other possibility was a move back to the private sector where the overall responsibility for capital formation and production would lie.[52]

It was against this background that the coalition led by Sukarno collapsed. After private capital had been politically neutralized with the onset of Guided Democracy 'politics became principally a matter of conflict between different segments and "empires" of the civilian and military bureaucracies and their offshoots'.[53] This conflict was played out between the military and the PKI. For several reasons the PKI was at a disadvantage. First of all, the opposition they encountered came not only from the military but also from civilian bureaucrats. Secondly, its members, numbering up to three million, were not prepared psychologically, materially or organizationally for open confrontation with the military.[54] Furthermore, they were dependent upon the leadership of Sukarno for the position they enjoyed in the NASAKOM alliance. In August 1965, PKI chairman Aidit returned from China with a team of Chinese doctors who determined that Sukarno's health was fast deteriorating. If Sukarno was removed as the effective leader of Indonesia, the military would launch an attack against the PKI. To prevent this from happening the PKI, according to the official Indonesian version, conceived the September 30 Movement.[55] This was not a movement to establish a communist government as the communists were relatively too weak to do this. Rather their goal was to assassinate seven generals of the anti-communist army central command, of which there was a total of 12 members. When the assassinations were carried out, the plan was to urge Sukarno to appoint a new army leadership that was not anti-communist and that was pro-Sukarno. The communists had succeeded in assassinating six generals and Sukarno agreed to the setting up of a Revolutionary Council as a temporary centre of national authority as the PKI wished. Furthermore, Sukarno also put a stop to all operations in favour of or against the September 30 Movement.[56]

The Movement did not succeed mainly because the army disobeyed Sukarno's orders and continued operations against the Movement. By October 2nd, the army under Major-General Suharto had neutralized the Movement's forces in Jakarta.[57] Aiding the army were members and supporters of Muslim parties (Masyumi and NU), Christians and the PNI. During the next two and a half years or so Suharto had consolidated his position in the army and had weeded out Sukarno loyalists from important positions in the army. On March 28th, 1968, General Suharto was appointed as Indonesia's second president.[58] Sukarno remained under house arrest until his death in June 1970.

Thus the 1965 attempted coup by the PKI was met by successful resistance from the army, which installed a new regime under Suharto that survives till this day, that of the New Order (Orde Baru). The overthrow of Sukarno was orchestrated by those who sought to maintain authoritarian rule and who wished to preserve the capitalist order, which was under threat from the PKI and Sukarno. The reasons for authoritarian rule under Suharto are the same ones for authoritarian rule during the period of Guided Democracy. No class, or political party was powerful enough to determine the nature of the economy and the political system. In the midst of the failure of civilian governments to solve economic and political problems, at first through parliamentary democracy, then through Guided Democracy, the army stepped in, supported by Chinese capital, to determine the course of politics. If Sukarno had tried to mobilize indigenous (*pribumi*) capital, in the New Order period the new power holders would bring in their own 'money men'.[59]

Turning to the case of Malaysia, among other things, the result of the May 1969 riots, was the New Economic Policy (NEP) that was to constitute the Second Malaysia Plan, 1971–5 and the Third Malaysia Plan, 1976–80. The NEP had three main objectives. One was 'to reduce and eventually eradicate poverty by raising income levels and increasing employment opportunities for all Malaysians, irrespective of race'.[60] The second was aimed at 'accelerating the process of restructuring Malaysian society to correct economic imbalances, so as to reduce and eventually eliminate the identification of race with economic function'.[61] The third was to make it possible within a period of 20 years for Malays to 'own and manage at least 30 per cent of the total commercial and industrial activities of the economy in all categories and scales of operation'.[62] The NEP had the general aim of eradicating poverty and the particular aim of raising the standard of living of the Malays without provoking communal violence.

One of the main objectives of the NEP was to reduce and eventually eradicate poverty by raising income and employment. Since 1957 Malaysia has recorded high rates of growth. From 1961–76 the average growth rate of real GNP was seven per cent per year and rose to 8.5 per cent during the period of the Third Malaysia Plan. In spite of this impressive performance, Malaysian society has remained highly inegalitarian with income inequality increasing. This fact has been cited frequently in the literature, with recourse to Gini Ratios and income shares. Even after the implementation of the NEP the Gini Ratio had increased from 0.46 in 1970 to 0.57 in 1976/77. The income share of the top 20 per cent of households increased from 48.6 per cent of total income in 1957/58 to 61.9 per cent in 1976, whereas the income share of the bottom 40 per cent declined from 15.9 per cent in 1957/58 to 10.3 per cent in 1976.

At the same time, it has been recognized that, with respect to the restructuring of Malaysian society, this has been achieved at the level of the working class. More Malays have come into the industrial workforce and there is a greater ethnic balance here. At the level of the dominant and professional–managerial classes, however, the identification of race with economic function has not been eliminated.

As mentioned earlier, one of the main goals of the NEP was to create a Malay commercial and industrial entrepreneurial class. This does not refer to Malay shopkeepers and petty traders but to a Malay capitalist class. The merits of such a policy have been criticized from its inception. The Second Malaysia Plan states that the government will set up enterprises and train Malays to take them over. The criticism is that 'why should this private group lick the cream of the profit? Such a successful business run by government can ensure Malay participation and employment, but not ownership by a handful.'[63] This criticism of the NEP was made more than 20 years ago and the question that it raises is very pertinent to the evaluation of the NEP. Is the Malaysian government guilty of upholding the particularistic interests of a handful of Malay capitalists? Before giving a direct answer to this question a brief mention should be made of the relationship between capitalism and the state in Malaysia. After independence the economic system of Malaysia was managed along the lines of liberal capitalism. The role of government lay in the areas of the provision of infrastructure and the education and training of the labour force. In this context, the Malay dominant class made no headway as far as the accumulation of capital was concerned, particularly because of the relatively more established state of big Chinese capital. The Malaysian state can be understood in terms of the idea that the capitalist state is the committee that manages the affairs of the bourgeoisie, subject to the qualifications discussed in Chapter 5. In the case of Malaysia it was the Malay-dominated state that was the committee of the Chinese-dominated bourgeoisie prior to the implementation of the NEP. In fact this situation in newly-independent Malaya was quite different from the post-colonial circumstances of most other third world states which, unlike Malaya, did not have a strong local bourgeoisie. In these other countries, the state retained some degree of autonomy from the dominant classes, (that is, the landed aristocracy, the national bourgeoisie and foreign capital) and mediated between these classes. In Malaysia, however, the state did not face three classes with sometimes contradictory interests. Instead, it faced a Chinese bourgeoisie and it embarked upon policies that in general favoured the interests of large-scale capital.

After the riots of May 1969, the NEP was launched with a major aim being the creation of a Malay commercial and industrial entrepreneurial class. This was to be achieved through the establishment of state corporations, the transfer of equity shares to individual Malays, the provision of in-service training, and various other means. The embarkation of the state on this policy, however, did not alter its fundamental orientation, which is towards upholding the interests of capital. The difference now is that capital takes on a more multi-racial character. What this indicates is that the Malaysian state has continued to serve the interests of capital, the NEP merely changing the racial composition of capital. While it is true that Chinese capital had been put at a disadvantage under the NEP,[64] any conflicts that may have arisen between the Malay and Chinese fractions of the dominant class by no means indicate that they are not cognizant of their common class interests, and their common antagonistic position towards the dominated classes. What is fundamental is that the Chinese business elite rely on a close relationship with the Malay political elite and choose their Malay patrons and allies with great care.[65]

In fact, the main lines of challenge that the state has faced since the inception of the NEP have not come from Chinese capital, nor have challenges and opposition been all that threatening to the status quo.

An excellent example of the latter comes from the Islamic revival movement. This has been interpreted as an 'ideological response of the Malay middle and working classes against the Malay bourgeoisie'.[66] Nagata in referring to the difference between PAS (PMIP), ABIM and Arqam discusses the class background of its leaders and members

but concludes that Islamic ideology in Malaysia is relatively autonomous as a social force and does not reflect economic or social realities.[67] Her reason for saying so is that the ulama have their own
class interests in mind and that their contribution to the material and
social life of the peasantry would be minimal.[68] Shamsul Amri
Baharuddin, in criticizing Nagata for overemphasizing ethnicity, says
that Islam has become an ideological tool in Malaysia wielded by both
the elite and other classes.[69] Here Islam is seen as an ideology that is
employed by particular classes to further their interests. Certainly this
is a valid approach. It should be pointed out, however, that statements
to the effect that Islam is an ideological tool wielded by the elite to
minimize or suppress class conflict or that Islam functions as a protest
ideology for the masses should not be taken to mean that Islam mani-
fests itself in politics in Malaysia in ways similar to the Middle East.
After the Iranian revolution, some were fearful to speak of the potential for revolutionary action among Malaysian Islamic fundamentalists.
However, the parallels with Iran are totally unfounded. The class bases
of the Islamic movement in these two countries are entirely different.
In Iran, the old middle classes, the bazari and the ulama were fast
becoming a déclassé stratum and in this case Islam was certainly an
ideological tool employed by the middle class against the Pahlavi Shah.
In Malaysia, however, Islam as it is understood and practised amongst
Malays of the middle, and the professional and managerial classes, is
not to be understood in terms of a protest ideology against the state.
To a great degree it can be argued that the particular manner in which
these classes have articulated their Islamic ideology actually supports
the status quo. It is apparent that the Malay professional–managerial
and middle classes have, under the NEP, increased in size relative to
the Malay community as a whole. The point is that these classes as
carriers of *dakwah* (missionary) Islamic ideology and as beneficiaries
of the NEP have it in their interest to support the status quo. While
this can be inferred from their class position, we can go further to
examine their ideologies. The resonance of dakwah ideology and middle or professional–managerial class status is unmistakable. I say this
both of ABIM (Malaysian Muslim Youth Movement) and Darul Arqam.
In the case of Arqam this resonance is perceived from its preoccupa-
tion with religious rituals, the meticulous following of the life-style of
the Prophet, the adoption of Arabic customs and dress, and sometimes,
the retreat from secular affairs of the world. Only a middle class stratum can afford to practise Islam in this manner. This form of Islam
should not be understood in terms of a retreat from a world of harsh

socio-economic realities. Rather, it is a leisurely retreat from a comfortable world whose invitation to return is always open.

As far as ABIM is concerned, its apparent oppositional role towards the Malaysian state must be seen in the light of its overall agenda. Taking its views on Islamic economics, for instance, it is quite clear that the kind of economic system that it supports is not fundamentally different from a liberal capitalist economy. For Islamic economics is nothing more than neo-classical economics dressed up in Islamic terminologies. The evolution of a highly unequal world capitalist system has not been theoretically encountered by Islamic economics. Nor has Islamic economics seen fit to imbibe elements of existing theories of development which do offer constructive criticisms of the exploitative nature of capitalism. Certainly Malaysia is large enough for ABIM and the UMNO. While it is true that Islam is an ideological tool employed in the field of class contradictions within Malay society, the dominant Islamic trend in Malaysia is not a middle class reaction against the state but rather a conservative, if latent, approval of it.

ELITE COHESION AND DEMOCRATIC STABILITY

The question of why and how Malaysia's style of democracy emerged and stabilized and why Indonesia experienced a breakdown in parliamentary democracy can be addressed by recourse to an elite perspective on democratic stability. Such a perspective is not at odds with class analysis but highlights the role of elites as actors in their own right. Works on the question of elites and democracy can be divided into pluralist, power elite and Marxist perspectives.[70] Pluralist theories[71] focus on elite fragmentation in the context of a balanced power structure while both power elite[72] and Marxist theories[73] note the tightly integrated nature of elites.

Others have shifted the focus from fragmented balance and cohesive hegemony to consensual unity,[74] which is the approach taken in this chapter as well. The argument here is that the important elite groups participate in decision making and are able to reach agreements on the informal rules of the game and the worth of existing democratic political institutions.[75] Some of the characteristics of elite consensus that provide for democratic stability are the following: (1) disputes are settled through elite settlements or pacts,[76] (2) national elites are tightly integrated due to common interests and (3) the presence of a plurality of interests makes consensus among elites vital.

The ability of political elites to defend their democratic rights and positions of power and, therefore, the institutions of democracy depend upon their ability to come to settlements with each other over issues that would otherwise result in regime breakdown and the rise of undemocratic elements such as the military. Non-violent cooperation and compromise so essential to democratic stability exists to the extent that elites believe that such interaction is to their mutual benefit. In the case of many developing societies, the cohesion between private and state capital is due to the perception of mutual interest.

As we have seen above, the inability of the Indonesian state to achieve some measure of consensual unity was a major factor in the breakdown of parliamentary democracy in 1957–8 and the onset of the New Order period in 1966. Feith explains the instability of constitutional democracy in Indonesia in terms of the lack of cohesion between the solidarity makers and the administrative elite. The former refer to those possessing skills in manipulating symbols and organizing the masses while the latter to those with administrative, legal, technical and foreign language skills.[77] This rift coincided with the division between 'those who would risk financial stability to rid the economy of Dutch control' and 'those who preferred foreign dominance to monetary chaos'.[78]

Kahin states lack of consensus on important issues as a factor in the decline of parliamentary democracy. Issues that the elite became split over include secular versus Islamic state, regional autonomy versus centralism, and the role of the army in government. But the elite were even divided over such basic issues as the desirability of the parliamentary system.[79] There was also a disagreement over the possibility of creating a second chamber in parliament which would allow for representation on a territorial rather than population basis and correct the over-representation of Java in the first chamber.[80] To these we can add other examples such as the debate between Sukarno and the Masyumi leader, Isa Anshary, on the Islamic basis of the Indonesian state, and the sacking of senior bureaucrats sympathetic to the Masyumi and PSI by the PNI-dominated cabinet of Ali Sastroamidjojo (August 1953 – July 1955).[81] Goh points out that the blame for the failure of parliamentary democracy is to be put on the major parties, that is, the PNI, Masyumi, NU and PKI. For example, Masyumi's electoral strength lay outside Java in Sumatra and Sulawesi while that of PNI, NU and PKI was in Java. It was vital that Masyumi was in the cabinet in order to represent the outer islands. The withdrawal of five Masyumi ministers from the cabinet in January 1957, therefore, was a serious blow to the legitimacy of the government.[82]

Feith noted the view that the party system in Indonesia failed because it was not a two-party system but was instead based on the Dutch *verzuiling* (pillarization) model from which the notion of aliran was adapted.[83] This view necessarily begs the question as to why the Indonesian pillarization was a problem in Indonesia and not in the Netherlands as far as democratic stability is concerned. The stabilizing effect of the alirans on party life is undoubtedly tied to the problems of armed resistance and regional revolts, an internally weak state and a politicized military to begin with.

Many other works have cited the lack of elite cohesion and consensus in Indonesia.[84] A more theoretically informed analysis of the problem is provided by Brown, who looks at the tension between elite cohesion and elite factionalism in the context of neo-patrimonialism. In the neo-patrimonial state the leader provides an umbrella of patronage under which cohesive elites may be successful in mobilizing communalism for the sake of national integration. Alternatively, elite factionalism may result in the use of ethnicity to fuel elite factional rivalries, whether this is by disaffected elites seeking to pressure the neo-patrimonial leader or the leader seeking to discredit rival elites.[85] Since the neo-patrimonial leader cannot depend on traditional loyalty, resources must be continuously redistributed in order to contain elite disunity.[86] During Indonesia's period of liberal democracy, competing elites shared power and resources while acting as patrons to communal clienteles in the four major parties, the PNI, PKI, Masyumi and NU. The elite factionalism that unfolded in the struggle for power between these elite–patrons was seen in the cleavages between both the administrative elite and the solidarity makers as well as the *santri* and *abangan* elite.[87]

The inability of the political elite to resolve their disputes and deal with the pressing economic issues of their time, amidst problems of armed and regional revolts and an internally weak state, was deemed sufficient justification for the army to involve itself in political decision making. The ability of the army to weaken the military resistance of the separatist movements had sufficiently impressed Sukarno so that he was willing to give it formal representation in the emerging Guided Democracy regime.[88] In the words of Roeslan Abdulgani, Sukarno viewed the army as the 'most difficult to handle, the most difficult to domesticate but one willing to follow him in his capacity as Supreme Commander and as Proclaimer of Independence and as Father of the Nation . . .'[89] This was especially so in mid-1958 when the military had successfully defeated a rebellion in West Sumatra and North Sulawesi, thereby giving Sukarno and his army coalition much legitimacy.[90] There were several signs of military dissatisfaction with parliamentary democracy. In 1956, the commander of the West Java military region ordered the arrest of Foreign Minister Roeslan Abdulgani on a charge of corruption. In November, the Deputy Chief of Staff, Colonel Zulkifli Lubis attempted to overthrow the PNI-dominated government in a coup d'état in Jakarta. In December of the same year, the regimental commander of Padang had power transferred from the civil administration of the province of Central Sumatra to a military council.[91] The weakness of the political elite and the dissatisfaction of the military with parliamentary democracy, led to power being put in the hands of Sukarno, which he had to share with the military in order to oppose parties like Masyumi and the PSI which were vehemently against Guided Democracy.[92] The military, under the command of Nasution, gave their full support to Sukarno's dismantling of the cabinet and the establishment of presidential authority. The power of influence of the army stemmed from the fact that it was the only institution that was able to exercise influence throughout the archipelago.[93]

The periods of struggle for independence from the Netherlands (1945–9) and liberal democracy (1957–65) were crucial as far as the politicization of the military was concerned. The Indonesian armed forces were created out of armed groups which organized themselves even before the Allied forces landed in Java, and not on the initiative of the government.[94] As a result and because the armed forces played a vital role in the struggle for independence, many officers understood their responsibilities to be as much political as they were military and that their views merited special consideration by the government.[95] Although the military accepted its apolitical role with the onset of parliamentary democracy, the failure of civilians to solve economic problems and contain armed revolts throughout the country led the military leadership to pressure Sukarno into declaring martial law, thus ending the period of liberal democracy.[96] The army exercised martial law between 1957 and 1963, supported Guided Democracy up until 1965, and were instrumental in the subsequent downfall of Sukarno after the attempted communist coup of September 1965.[97]

The Indonesian problem of elite cohesion was in stark contrast to the situation which obtained in Malaysia both before and after the riots of May 1969 and the temporary suspension of parliamentary democracy. From 1957 to 1969, the UMNO, MCA and MIC had consensus on vital questions concerning the special position of the Malays, the status of Malay as the official language and citizenship for non-Malays.[98]

The alliance between the Malay and Chinese elite broke down temporarily when the Central Working Committee of the MCA said that the party would not join the new Alliance cabinet as Chinese voters 'rejected the MCA to represent them in the Government, if the result of the general elections reflect their wishes'.[99] Nevertheless, when the new cabinet was formed on May 20th, the MCA continued to be part of it, providing three 'Ministers with Special Functions'.[100] Although there was still talk of withdrawing from the cabinet when the situation returned to normal, the Chinese Chambers of Commerce were able to persuade the MCA to reconsider the question of participation in the cabinet.[101] The potential for a protracted elite factionalism between the MCA and UMNO was to be seen in the views of some UMNO politicians who were against continued alliance with the MCA. But what finally took place was a power struggle within UMNO itself. When Tun Tan Siew Sin announced that the MCA would not participate in the cabinet, he was openly supported by UMNO 'ultra' politicians such as Dr Mahathir Mohamad, Syed Ja'afar Albar and Syed Nasir Ismail who wished the UMNO to go it alone in the cabinet.[102] The elite factionalism was within the Malay leadership and not between Malays and Chinese. Tunku Abdul Rahman told the Malay weekly, *Utusan Zaman,* that Malay extremists within the UMNO wanted to topple him.[103] The MCA was eventually quite amenable to participating in the cabinet, but the reason for the suspension of democracy for up to 21 months was due to a power struggle between Tunku Abdul Rahman and those within the UMNO who had opposed him.[104] Nevertheless, the problem of leadership within the UMNO was resolved when Tun Razak replaced the Tunku as Prime Minister in September 1970. What is interesting to note is that whatever elite factionalism that surfaced during this period was intra-Malay rather than inter-ethnic. The 'ultra' Malay UMNO elite did not move to expel the MCA from the cabinet but simply supported the MCA's earlier decision not to be in the cabinet. The real conflict was within UMNO, with the MCA issue being used to discredit rival elites.

It should also be noted that the relative elite cohesion that obtained in Malaysia during the formative period of the post-colonial state was in the context of an internally strong state and a non-politicized military, unlike the case of Indonesia. Why did the military not seize power in May 1969 even though the conditions may have been right?

Concerning the lack of politicization of the military, there were a number of reasons for this. One, of course, is that the armed forces did not play a vital role in the struggle for independence and that the officers, therefore, understood their responsibilities to be exclusively military ones, not demanding that their views merited special consideration by the government. When parliamentary democracy was suspended, the military was included in the National Operations Council (NOC) from the very beginning, represented by General Tengku Osman Jiwa, Chief of Staff of the Armed Forces.[105] As a result there was no reason for military officers to feel that they were not taken seriously by the civilian elite.

It must also be remembered that the Malaysian military, unlike its Indonesian counterpart, lacked the opportunity to be become politicized as they were relatively newcomers on the scene of Malaysian history. During British rule in Malaya, locally- and Indian-recruited Sikh and Punjabi police were used to control riots and uprisings, even though a Malay Regiment Experimental Company was established in 1933. In Sabah and Sarawak, constabulary forces were employed and military units were established only in the 1960s.[106] In 1955, just two years before independence, the Federation of Malaya's armed forces consisted of only six battalions with no navy and air force.[107] After independence, there was still dependence on the British military which meant that the institutional development of the Malaysian armed forces would be lagging.[108]

In asking the question why the army did not seize power in May 1969 when they could easily have done so, some suggest that the then Chief of Staff, General Tengku Osman Jiwa, was a nephew of the Prime Minister, Tunku Abdul Rahman and was not about to stage a coup d'état against his uncle.[109] At the time of writing, when there was much talk about the possible ousting of President Saddam Hussein of Iraq by his son and sons-in-law, such a view may not be tenable but, nevertheless, warrants attention.

The fundamental difference between Indonesia and Malaysia is that in the former no one class or party was capable of wielding power and preserving a system that benefited capital. The condition was right for the military to step in to maintain the proper conditions for capital accumulation which in Indonesia, because of the opposition from various quarters, necessitated authoritarian rule. In Malaysia, on the other hand, the state was, as it were, politically homogenous if ethnically divided. But the ethnic divisions were and are politically united in the interests of state and private capital, and there was no serious threat to the status quo after 1969 that would have caused the demise of parliamentary democracy.

7 Historical Analysis and the Future of Democracy

HISTORICAL COMPARATIVE STUDIES VERSUS QUANTITATIVE CROSS-NATIONAL RESEARCH

Part of the significance of this study lies in the fact that there has not been any comparative work done on the state in Malaysia and Indonesia. Furthermore, the few works on the state in the two countries[1] tend to focus on issues not directly related to the question of the origins of the post-colonial state. Democracy in post-colonial states cannot always be explained in terms of its emergence because it is a given, having been introduced from without. What needs explanation is how and why democracy persisted in some post-colonial states and gave way to authoritarianism in others, or alternatively, why democracies lasted as long as they did. This study has been an effort in this direction.

The theoretical framework adopted in this work is based on an historical study of the emergence of the dominant elites and class forces that shaped the types of regimes found in the two countries. Both Indonesia and Malaysia emerged as democratic post-colonial states, this being due both to the establishment of democratic institutions during the colonial period and to the fact that nationalist leaders were educated and nurtured in the European tradition. In other words, the model states that were available to them were European parliamentary democracies. However, the forces that created viable and lasting democracies in Europe and the rest of the developed world were not always present in the colonies and the emerging post-colonial states. If new post-colonial democracies did emerge, they often failed to achieve stability and eventually gave way to more authoritarian forms of government. Malaysia and Indonesia are examples of post-colonial states which established democratic systems of government upon independence. However, in Indonesia the democratic process was suspended altogether and after about a decade of independence, an authoritarian state emerged there. Meanwhile, Malaysia still retains a functioning democratic system. The contrast between Indonesia and Malaysia, then, offers an opportunity to study the conditions under which democracy can be sustained in post-colonial states, which has been the focus of this study.

At this point, it may be interesting to comment on the apparent discrepancy between results obtained in historical comparative studies on the one hand and quantitative cross-national research on the other, on the question of democracy and socioeconomic development.

The experimental–statistical methodology of cross-national research restricts itself to the consideration of measurable variations of factors, which are translated into numerical codes. The objective is to cover a large enough number of countries so that law-like regularities can be discovered and general theories formulated. Historical comparative studies, on the other hand, do not study discrete variables but whole systems. There is attention to a host of factors while a small and manageable number of countries are studied. Such studies look beyond the linkages of variables at the genesis and structure of social and political systems.

The historical comparative method is valuable where quantitative cross-national research presents problems. One such problem is question-begging. The fact that there is a high correlation between various indicators of development and levels of democracy begs the question of the nature of the link between economic performance and regime type, the answer to which historical comparative research is well suited to provide. Secondly, historical comparative research may reveal cases which do not conform to general trends as suggested by cross-national studies. For example, a model theorizing the negative effect of economic dependency on democracy does not hold for the case of Indonesia and Malaysia. Thus, the historical comparative study of cases may serve either to provide deeper analyses of processes suggested by cross-national work or lend an understanding of deviant cases.

A disadvantage of historical comparative studies concerns the difficulty in establishing a hierarchy of causation. For example, the present study asserts that the three conditions under which democracy can survive in post-colonial states, based on the experience of Malaysia and Indonesia, are (1) the absence of armed resistance against the state, (2) an internally strong state, and (3) a high degree of elite consensus. It is difficult, however, to establish a hierarchy of importance among the three factors. The identification of these factors are a result of both common sense and theoretical arguments. Furthermore, what is suggested by common sense and theory is strengthened by the observation that the hypothesized conditions of democratic stability are present in Malaysia and absent in Indonesia. Nevertheless, the contrast-oriented historical comparative method enables one to tell a story of democracy quite different from that told in quantitative cross-national studies.[2]

THEORETICAL IMPLICATIONS

In this study on Indonesian and Malaysian post-colonial state formation, the comparative dimensions are armed resistance against the state, elite consensus and internal state strength.

Concerning the question of peasant and worker resistance against the colonial and emerging post-colonial states, the claim is not that they were inert or passive. While peasant rebellions and worker strikes were common in pre- and post-colonial Malaysia and Indonesia, what we do not find are widespread revolts amidst the breakdown of the colonial state. Nor do we find the mass mobilization of peasants and workers in post-colonial state building. Therefore, the question of the rise of authoritarianism in Indonesia as a response to mass opposition against the state does not arise. Nevertheless, Indonesia does differ from Malaysia in the sense that a series of armed rebellions had given a central role to the military in politics. No doubt this contributed to the prominence of the military in government.

Another important factor pertaining to resistance against the state, that helps to explain the persistence of the democratic state in Malaysia and its demise in Indonesia, is the left. The PKI continued to play a crucial role in Indonesian politics long after independence, while in Malaysia the CPM was effectively repressed during the colonial period and did not pose a threat to the democratic post-colonial state. In Indonesia, the PKI was involved in the independence movement and was an active participant in post-colonial nation building. The role that the party played in supporting the state, resisting the army, and making a coup attempt in 1965 contributed to the demise of democracy in Indonesia as it led to the rise of the army in politics to protect the interest of state capital. In other words, more effective colonial repression of the left is an important difference affecting the chances of maintaining democracy.

But the left was not the only force that opposed the state. The Indonesian post-colonial state lacked a homogeneous ruling elite and a high degree of elite consensus. There was no convergence of material and ideological interests among the ruling elite. As a result the state was plagued by internal conflicts and opposition between various groups of which the PKI leadership was only one. This problem of intra-state conflict was absent in Malaysia, the ruling elite being homogeneous. The relative autonomy of the state must be understood in terms of the homogeneity of the ruling elite. The existence of competing propertied classes and class fractions themselves do not bestow relative autonomy to the state. Effective state autonomy only comes into being when the state itself is internally united.

Equally important is the internal strength of the state which is indicated by the support it receives from the dominant classes. The Malaysian state by virtue of the strong support it had from the capitalist class could withstand opposition, which was minimal to begin with, without having to respond by suspending the democratic process altogether. On the other hand, in Indonesia, no one class or group was sufficiently strong to dominate or support the democratic state of the first decade after independence. The struggle between different ideological and political forces eventually led to the reactive establishment of an authoritarian regime.

Thus, the lack of armed resistance against the state, an internally strong state, and a comparatively high degree of elite consensus explains democratic stability in Malaysia, while their absence led to authoritarian outcomes in Indonesia.

With regard to the implications of those finding for other theories of the state and for the cross-national studies done on the state in peripheral societies, there are some interesting points to be made concerning how these studies relate to mine.

The post-colonial state theory of Alavi and others working on South Asia and East Africa, is unable to distinguish between the rise of democratic and authoritarian post-colonial states. The present study, however, has been an attempt to chart the paths of two forms of post-colonial regimes.

The imposition of colonialism upon the pre-capitalist societies of Malaysia and Indonesia left several classes with competing interests in these countries upon formal independence. The capitalist class consisted of not only the metropolitan and indigenous bourgeoisies, but also of an immigrant, ethnic minority bourgeoisie. In addition to this, there were the merchant classes which were divided between indigenous and immigrant fractions. The ethnic factor is crucial in distinguishing these cases from those of Pakistan and Bangladesh, and is a point that a post-colonial state theory for Southeast Asia must take into account.

Chase-Dunn notes important differences between semi-peripheral Latin American countries studied by O'Donnell and the peripheral Caribbean and African states studied by Thomas.[3] While both are discussing the emergence of authoritarian regimes, the causes that each suggests to explain this emergence are different and opposite. For O'Donnell, the aggression of the middle class and urban workers towards the state resulted in the reactive establishment of the bureaucratic–authoritarian regime.[4] For Thomas it is precisely the insignificance or absence of the middle and urban working classes which results in authoritarian regimes. All that is available is political exploitation through the control of the state apparatus, and competition over the state results in the establishment of an authoritarian regime.[5] These two theories are not necessarily contradictory. If, as Thomas says, the absence of a middle and urban working class leads to an authoritarian state, so can the presence of such classes. For the presence of a middle and urban working class will only lead to the establishment of a democratic regime if industrialization has favourable consequences for these classes. In other words, the rise of a middle and urban working class in the Caribbean does not mean that democratic states will emerge there. This will happen only with industrialization that favours these classes and, therefore, channels their support to the democratic state.

O'Donnell and Thomas offer two different sets of causes for the rise of authoritarian states. This study indicates a third.

In the present study, it is conflict among the political elite which leads to the reactive establishment of an authoritarian state. But this can only be understood within the context of the internal strength of the state and armed resistance against it. This conflict is due to the different material and ideological interests of the constituencies that the elite represent, ranging from Islamic fundamentalists to radical leftists. Furthermore, this conflict takes place when the state is plagued by armed rebellion and separatist movements. Therefore, the theory differs from Thomas' in which intra-elite conflict over control of the state is due to the absence of middle and urban working classes. In this study it is precisely the presence of such classes, divided into several ideological orientations that leads to conflict among the political elite and the demise of the democratic state. This is also different from O'Donnell's theory which stresses middle and urban working class aggression towards the state.

All three theories suggest two principles that operate in the demise of democracy or the establishment of authoritarian regimes. One principle is that pressure on the state whether from the middle or working classes, or from armed rebellions and mass movements, leads to the rise of authoritarianism. The other is that conflict among the political elite leads to the establishment of an authoritarian state, whether this conflict is due to underlying contradictions at the level of the middle and working classes or not.

Turning to cross-national studies on regime types, according to the world-system perspective, economic dependency has a negative effect on the level of democracy, as discussed in Chapter 2. Looking at the various indicators of economic dependency, we saw that Malaysia does seem to be a more dependent economy than Indonesia (see Chapter 2). Nevertheless, Malaysia is a democratic state while Indonesia is an authoritarian one. It may be that economic dependency did not have a negative effect on democracy in Malaysia due to the effects of state strength. As discussed in Chapter 6, greater state strength, measured by government revenues as a proportion of GNP in Malaysia, as compared to Indonesia, contributed to the resilience of democracy in Malaysia. Whether internal state strength contributed to maintaining a democratic regime, in spite of greater relative economic dependency, is a question for future cross-national research. It might be that economic dependency is inversely related to democratic performance in cases of internally weak states. This suggests yet another question for cross-national research.

THE FUTURE OF DEMOCRACY IN INDONESIA AND MALAYSIA

While this study has been concerned with the conditions of post-colonial democratic stability, it does suggest a number of points to be taken into consideration when speaking of democratization. The term openness, or *keterbukaan* as it is known in Malay and Indonesian, may remind many of us of *glasnost* and the accompanying revolutionary changes in Eastern Europe and the former Soviet Union. But whereas, in Eastern Europe and Russia serious attempts are underway to bring about fundamental changes in the political economy of these nations, this is not the case in Indonesia and Malaysia. The literature of the 1980s and 1990s conveys the impression that there is increasing pressure in Indonesia for democratization while authoritarianism is on the ascent in Malaysia, as if there were a convergence between the two.

Robison refers to the Indonesian middle class demands for more predictable and institutionalized government as an important stage in Indonesia's bourgeois revolution.[6] More optimistic is Max Lane, noting that there had been a weakening of Suharto's hold over the political agenda since the People's Consultative Assembly (MPR) of 1988. For the first time, there had initially been two candidates for the vice-presidency. This raised questions hitherto not dealt with, such as whether there was to be voting and the adherence to unanimity, a foundation of Pancasila democracy.[7] There were also organized grassroots-based campaigns protesting about land disputes and wage and human rights

issues, as well as media editorials and public comment.[8] It was believed that some of the ruling elite had begun to loosen restrictions on
criticism and dissent, an indication of which was the formation of groups
such as Petisi 50 in 1980, consisting of retired generals, civilian ex-
politicians, intellectuals and students. This group had criticized Suharto's
interpretation of Pancasila and the notion of *dwifungsi* (dual function)
of the Armed Forces.[9] The Democratic Forum (Forum Demokrasi), an
association of activists and scholars dedicated to the promotion of
democratization, was formed in 1991. In addition to this, there were a
number of other groups formed such as the Liga Pumulihan Demokrasi
(League for the Restoration of Democracy) and Forum Pemurnian
Kedaulatan Rakyat (Forum for the Purification of Peoples' Sovereignty).[10]

On the role of the military, it had been noted that its successful role
in maintaining economic and political stability created a dilemma among
those who recognized both the need for such stability as well as for
more democratic forms of government.[11] Nevertheless, a prominent figure,
former Armed Forces Chief Lt.-General T. B. Simatupang left a mes-
sage on his deathbed in January 1991 to the effect that the Armed
Forces' (ABRI's) doctrine of dwifungsi must not be allowed to take
the country towards militarism, authoritarianism and totalitarianism.[12]
More recently, the ABRI chief of socio-political affairs, Major General Mohd. Ma'ruf had said that ABRI would be taking a back seat in
politics in order to allow civilian forces to play a more active role in
politics.[13] Therefore, the view of the constitutional and legal role of
the military in non-military affairs in the context of dual function[14]
appears to be less entrenched than previously.

Nevertheless, the view that in Indonesia openness seems to be in
jeopardy and under threat of closure by the state is also prevalent.

A recent indicator of this was the spectacular ban on three leading
weeklies, *Tempo, Editor* and *Detik,* announced in June 1994. Seven
weeks after this, 'dissident' journalists signed the Sirnagalih Declaration which led to the establishment of the Independence Alliance of
Journalists (AJI), a rival of the government-backed journalists' association (PWI). The result was the expulsion of 13 AJI members from
PWI and the arrest of those AJI journalists responsible for the illegal
distribution of *Independen,* a magazine critical of the government.

The current global trend of democratization and the historic role
played by the middle classes in pushing for democratic reforms have
caused some to imagine that the Indonesian middle class can show the
way to democratization. Ardent critics of the New Order and those
most enthusiastic about democratic reform, however, tend to be scholars

and professionals rather than businessmen who have more to gain from an authoritarian and stable regime rather than a democratic but volatile one.

During the last few years, the Indonesian media carried many stories and discussions on democratization and liberalization in the country. These ranged from statements made by the political elite to the effect that Indonesia is well imbued with the spirit of democracy to criticisms from the opposition which foretold of a legitimacy crisis if democratic reforms were not put in place. There were also discussions on the presidential elections and their meaning for democracy. In 1993, Minister Rudini had taken pains to clarify that the fact that President Suharto was the sole candidate for the elections in no way meant that democracy was being undermined. According to Rudini, what was important was not who was nominated but the procedures of nomination that were adhered to by the Organization of Election Participants (OPP). In this case, the decision to nominate Mr Suharto reflected the aspirations of the vast majority of Indonesians, including those in the rural areas.

Nevertheless, openness in Indonesia has been, for the most part, very much dependent on how far President Suharto and his technocrats can tolerate it. Only days before Information Minister Harmoko announced the press ban, Indonesian State Secretary Murdiono addressed a seminar organized by the Indonesian Institute of Sciences where he said that the time had come for the Indonesian political system to be more open. But he stressed the need to guard against openness leading to anarchy. He had hardly spoken when on June 21st, 1994, the nation saw Harmoko's televized statement to the effect that the publishing permits of the three weeklies, *Tempo, Editor* and *Detik* were cancelled on the grounds that they had jeopardized national stability. And as if that was not enough, the government had threatened action against another leading magazine, *Forum Keadilan* (Justice Forum) over its coverage of the ban.

In spite of the fact that the Indonesian government gave assurances that the policy of openness would continue, many see the ban as another bout in the authoritarian challenge being faced by journalists, academicians and other members of the intelligentsia. A petition issued by protestors who marched on Harmoko's ministry the day after the ban was announced said that the ban was a 'disaster for the democratization process, which carried with it the right to express oral or written opinions freely'. Weeks later students demonstrating outside parliament, demanding the release of the publishers of *Independen,* shouted, 'we want a press which does not tell lies to the people'.[15]

More recently, after potential presidential candidate, Megawati Sukarnoputri, daughter of late founding president Sukarno, was ousted from the leadership of the Indonesian Democratic Party (PDI) by a government-backed rival faction during a congress in Medan, North Sumatra in June 1996, weeks of political unrest culminated in violent protests in late July. The riots were put down by the military, but only after three people had been killed and more than 90 injured.[16] Damage control in the aftermath of the protests included plans by the government to expand the police force and the introduction of a new Bill on internal security.[17]

The challenges to democracy in Indonesia are onerous in view of the fact that it is precisely under authoritarian conditions that giant strides in economic development have taken place. For example, the rate of poverty in Suharto's Indonesia had been reduced from 60 per cent in the early 1970s to 15 per cent today. Infant mortality rates have been lowered and roads, schools and hospitals in rural areas have been built. At the level of public discourse it is hard to score points against authoritarianism in the context of such progress.

Nevertheless, it is precisely when a country achieves high rates of economic growth that the middle classes gain some self-confidence and will themselves into moving against the state, as happened in Thailand in 1992 when pro-democracy demonstrators toppled the military government of Suchinda. In Indonesia, some journalists may have misread the apparent atmosphere of openness and gone too far in exercising their rights to free speech. It appears that they had taken literally Mr Suharto's promise of greater openness and felt free to publish critical articles on government policies.

According to some observers, Indonesia has actually been moving in the direction of greater authoritarianism. One reason for this is that the state is economically powerful, not only from its control of major resources but from its position as patron of the largely Chinese-owned and controlled private businesses. Therefore, the urge for democracy is unlikely to come from the Chinese conglomerates, seeing how vulnerable they are politically. Neither is much to be expected from the indigenous middle class which tends to be depoliticized and caught up in a form of consumerism that seems oblivious or despairingly tolerant of political licence and extremism.

In the end, what it comes down to is the outlook for democratization. The call for democracy in Indonesia can better be understood as one for greater political liberalization. The thirst for the freedom of speech and political association had been partially quenched by government overtures, but it was always clear that these rights had to be exercised within the framework of the national ideology of Pancasila. Furthermore, the government's view was that liberalization or openness had to support development and not subvert it. In the case of the three banned publications, the government's position was that they had published stories which threatened national stability. For example, *Detik* reported that vice-president Try Sutrisno would be the next president, even though the constitution requires the convening of a consultative assembly which had not yet taken place. This allegedly had the effect of pitting one government official against the other.

Nevertheless, Indonesian activists view the ban and the action against AJI as a reaction to the unprecedented coverage that the three publications along with *Independen* gave to controversial activities of the state elite, including Technology Minister Jusuf Habibie's US$1.1 billion purchase of 39 ex-East German warships, a corruption scandal involving one of Suharto's senior aides, and other issues.[18] As Suharto himself has said, openness does not mean total freedom. Unlimited freedom would get in the way of attempts to implement policies to achieve Indonesia's long-term development goals. Freedom of the press can only be allowed if there is responsibility. From the state's point of view, a 'free and responsible' press means that the media ought to consider the interests of the state and the rule of law.[19] The late Dr Alfian, an Indonesian political scientist, said that the Indonesian government was implementing a 'rubber band' policy of openness. Through this policy liberties are granted to the public to the extent that the interests of the government are not jeopardized. These liberties could always be revoked when necessary. Democracy, therefore, is interpreted by the state in line with the interests of the ruling elite.[20]

Turning to the case of Malaysia, in spite of the characterization of this state as a statist or semi-democracy,[21] some observers suggest that authoritarianism is in the ascendant. Applying O'Donnell's concept of the bureaucratic–authoritarian state, Saravanamuttu notes that political exclusion, suppression of popular mobilization and depoliticization are evident in Malaysia. Examples are the use of the Internal Security Act (ISA) to detain 106 political opponents and critics, amendments to the Sedition Act (1970) and Official Secrets Act (1986), gerrymandering in general elections,[22] and the suspension of the Lord President Tun Mohamed Salleh Abas on May 31st, 1988.[23] There was also reaction to what was perceived as draconian measures taken by the government in terms of signature campaigns and the holding of public forums to denounce such amendments.

Table 7.1   Measures of democracy for Indonesia and Malaysia

	Indonesia		Malaysia	
Year	1960	1965	1960	1965
Bollen[1]	20.3	9.8	83.5	80.3
Year	1978	1988	1978	1988
Gastil[2]	5	5	3	4
Year	1978	1988	1978	1988
Gastil[3]	5	5	3	5
Year	1980	1988	1980	1988
Vanhanen[4]	1.1	0.8	11.5	12.3

Notes:

[1] Kenneth A. Bollen, 'Political Democracy: Conceptual and Measurement Traps', in Alex Inkeles, ed., *On Measuring Democracy: Its Consequences and Concomitants*, New Brunswick: Transaction Publishers, 1991, pp. 3–20. Political democracy index range from 0 to 100 with 0 offering lowest level of political democracy and 100 highest.

[2] Raymond Duncan Gastil, 'The Comparative Survey of Freedom: Experiences and Suggestions', in Inkeles, ed., *On Measuring Democracy*, pp. 21–46. Scales use numbers 1 to 7, 1 referring to highest level of political democracy and 7 referring to lowest.

[3] Gastil, 'The Comparative Survey of Freedom'. Scales use numbers 1 to 7, 1 referring to highest level of civil liberties and 7 referring to lowest.

[4] Tatu Vanhanen, *The Process of Democratization: A Comparative Study of 147 States, 1980–1988*, New York: Crane Russak. Index of democratization range from 0 to 40.1 Index points in order of increasing democratization.

Opposition to the state has resulted in a few anti-democratic moves on the part of the state. The opposition was mainly of the legal type, that is, in the form of legal suits against the government or the ruling UMNO party. Such opposition led to an attack on the judiciary that has been interpreted as the curtailment of democratic rights in Malaysia.[24]

PROSPECTS FOR DEMOCRATIZATION: THE STATE AND CIVIL SOCIETY

While it would seem to be the case that democratization in Indonesia and an ascendant authoritarianism in Malaysia are resulting in the convergence of regime types, a number of rating systems do not seem to resonate with this statement (Table 7.1). It can be seen that Indonesia and Malaysia have generally not been evolving in a common direction as far as political democracy, civil rights and openness are concerned. In fact, in terms of the three conditions of democracy that have been the focus of the present work, that is, armed resistance against the state, elite consensus and internal state strength, this is a reasonable conclusion.

In Indonesia, since independence to the beginnings of the New Order period, the state was faced with armed resistance, was characterized by a low degree of elite consensus and was internally weak. Today, the New Order regime refers to the threat of separatist movements to justify authoritarianism.[25] Nevertheless, it is unlikely that separatism is or will be a serious issue as it was in the past, beyond the three regions of East Timor, Irian Jaya and Aceh.[26]

On the question of elite consensus, two scenarios are presented by Crouch. One is that the current rivalry between the government and the military elite may lead to a higher intensity conflict between Suharto and the military.[27] Crouch looks at how patrimonial politics takes the form of struggle for influence within the elite in the New Order period. As the elite during this period comprised both army officers and Western-trained technocrats, it was necessary for Suharto to have a hold over the armed forces by rewarding them through the distribution of patronage, which included appointments to lucrative civilian posts, or licences, credit and contracts for those officers who went into business.[28] One factor promoting the stability of the patrimonial regime is an ideologically homogeneous elite, but Crouch notes that basic conflicts over policy issues and the nature of the regime were becoming increasingly important.[29] However, elite factionalism is unlikely as Suharto had appointed General Try Sutrisno as vice-president, a man very much acceptable to the military.[30] The second scenario offered by Crouch suggests that rivalry within the military elite gives some space to civilian parties to consolidate themselves and eventually form the government.[31] This is not necessarily unlikely in the foreseeable future. Although there have been earlier attempts to read a lack of cohesion in the military[32] some observers say that by now the unity of ABRI is no longer in question.[33] Occasionally, however, some indications of the lack of unity surface as, for example, in March 1996 when Indonesian army chief R. Hartono donned Golkar's yellow jacket, declared military personnel to be party cadres and caused discomfort on the part of other senior generals.[34] Whereas in the early post-colonial period, armed resistance against the state, the lack of elite consensus and an internally weak state were factors behind the rise of authoritarianism, in

Table 7.2   Central government revenue (% GDP)

	1965	1973	1976	1980	1984	1988	1993
Indonesia	3.9	14.8	18.15	21.40	20.43	16.23	–
Malaysia	20.6	24.0	21.82	26.35	25.78	25.73	27.54

Source: International Monetary Fund, *Government Finance Statistics Yearbook*, 1994.

the New Order period an internally strong state and elite cohesion emerged, in the absence of widespread armed resistance, in the context of an authoritarian regime, supported by an army that will in all likelihood stick to constitutional politics.[35]

In Malaysia, the same conditions that account for democratic stability in the early post-colonial period obtain today. This is not to say that there has been no significant movement away from its semi-democratic status. There has been a decline in democracy during the last 15 years. In general however, internal state strength and elite cohesion, in both Indonesia and Malaysia, serve to preserve the status quo. Looking at a measure of state strength, both states are in comparatively strong positions vis-à-vis their respective societies, while the rate of increase in state strength has been greater in Indonesia (Table 7.2).

In fact, if there is to be any force for democratic change in Malaysia and Indonesia, it will in all likelihood come from extra-bureaucratic forces rather than from within the state. A central feature of a democracy is the prominence of civil society, this intermediate sphere of society between the private realm of the family and the political relations of the state. It consists of a whole set of NGOs engaged in a wide variety of activities as interest and pressure groups seeking to influence public policy.

It is necessary to understand the political and social contexts in which NGOs ideally work in order to appreciate the importance of their tasks and the oftentimes great constraints under which they operate. The NGO is a vital feature of democracies or polities struggling to make the transition to more representational forms of government, and operates within that sphere known as civil society.

Democracy is more than just the right to elect leaders. If voting was all there was to democracy, then citizens would only be exercising their rights once every few years. But democracy also includes an impressive list of rights which makes government accountable and participatory. Such rights include free speech, freedom of the press, access to information, and freedom of association in, for example, pressure groups, trade unions or other voluntary organizations or NGOs. The freedom of association allows like-minded men and women to come together to urge the rulers whom they elected to bring about changes deemed necessary.

A distinctive feature of democracies is citizenship. While all types of political systems have rulers and the ruled, it is only democracies which have citizens. The concept of citizenship dates back to classical Greece but acquired its modern understanding after the French and American revolutions. Development is meaningful only when there are opportunities for the full participation of citizens in public affairs, whether this refers to NGOs, professional associations, the mass media, trade unions or others. This public realm, which lies beyond the private sphere of the individual and household, is referred to as civil society. Civil society can be said to be the participatory and dynamic side of citizenship.

Although the role of NGOs has become increasingly important in Indonesia and Malaysia in recent years, their activities have generally been confined to developmental rather than political issues. In Indonesia, despite the existence of radical NGOs that are willing to push for political changes,[36] the government has been quite successful in coopting NGOs into national development programmes as well as resorting to 'carrot and stick' tactics to keep them within the sphere of their influence.[37] In Malaysia, NGO activities are limited, ostensibly because national security is under threat.[38] NGOs have been on the increase in Malaysia and the government plans to tighten regulations to 'prevent them from tarnishing the image of the country'.[39]

If NGOs are not expected to be a force for democratic change, this is even less the case with the middle class in Indonesia and Malaysia. What characterizes this middle class is 'narrow specialism, group conformity, a lack of interest in wider political issues, and respect for their own and other's expert knowledge', the illiberal political implications of which are obvious.[40] A further obstacle to the development of civil society and democratization is the phenomenon of bureaucratic–business collusions[41] which tends to have a non-liberalizing effect on the middle classes.

But Indonesia and Malaysia, like many other states in East Asia, are development-oriented states. The characteristics of such states include a great deal of state autonomy, a politically powerful bureaucracy, tight labour controls, and minimum interference from the public. Of course, it is by no means evident that such authoritarianism, hard or soft, is a necessary condition for development. The development-oriented state may incline either towards democracy or authoritarianism. The high correlation between East Asian development and soft authoritarianism does not warrant the claim that there is a necessary relationship between the two. Furthermore, it does not necessarily mean that democracy will prevent the successful workings of a development-oriented state. The experience of countries such as South Korea, Taiwan and Singapore point to peculiar economic and geopolitical circumstances as well as extraordinary internal features, many of which have nothing to do with authoritarianism. Democratization in Indonesia and Malaysia must always be in a state of flux and uncertainty. But, if rapid development increases the stakes for the government, it also strengthens the resolve of extra-bureaucratic forces to press on for democratic reforms.

Notes

Chapter 1

1. Fred Riggs, *Thailand: The Modernization of a Bureaucratic Polity,* Honolulu: East-West Center Press, 1960; John L. S. Girling, *The Bureaucratic Polity in Modernizing Societies: Similarities, Differences, and Prospects in the ASEAN Region,* Singapore: Institute of Southeast Asian Studies, 1986; Guillermo O'Donnell, *Modernization and Bureaucratic Authoritarianism,* 2nd edn, Berkeley: University of California, Institute of International Studies, 1979; Arief Budiman, 'The Emergence of the Bureaucratic–Capitalist State in Indonesia,' in Lim Teck Ghee, ed., *Reflections on Development in Southeast Asia,* Singapore: Institute of Southeast Asian Studies, 1988, pp. 110–28.
2. Guillermo O'Donnell, 'Delegative Democracy', *Journal of Democracy* 5, 1, 1994, 55–69: p. 56.
3. Raymond Aron, *Democracy and Totalitarianism,* London: Weidenfeld & Nicholson, 1968, p. 83.
4. K. G. Tregonning, 'The Failure of Economic Development and Political Democracy in Southeast Asia', *Asian Studies* 5, 2, 1967, 323–31.
5. NSTP, *Elections in Malaysia: Facts and Figures,* Kuala Lumpur: NSTP Research and Informations Services, 1994; Ahmad Fawzi Mohd Basri, 'Pilihan Raya Umum 1995: Mandat Baru Menjelang 2000', *Dewan Masyarakat* May 1995.
6. Diane K. Mauzy, 'Malaysia in 1987: Decline of the "Malay Way"' *Asian Survey* 28, 2, 1988, 213–22: p. 217.
7. For a brief account on Mahathir and the judiciary see K. S. Nathan, 'Malaysia in 1988: The Politics of Survival', *Asian Survey* 29, 2, 1989, 129–39.
8. James V. Jesudason, 'Statist Democracy and the Limits to Civil Society in Malaysia', *Journal of Commonwealth and Comparative Politics* 33, 3, 1995, 335–56.
9. *The Process and Progress of Pancasila Democracy,* Jakarta: Department of Information, Republic of Indonesia, 1991/1992.
10. Goh Cheng Teik, 'Why Indonesia's Attempt at Democracy in the Mid-1950s Failed', *Modern Asian Studies* 6, 2, 1972, 225–44: pp. 225–6.
11. Ulf Sundhaussen, 'Indonesia: Past and Present Encounters with Democracy,' in Larry Diamond, Juan J. Linz, and Seymour Martin Lipset, eds., *Volume 3, Democracy in Developing Countries: Asia,* Boulder, CO: Lynne Rienner Publishers; London: Adamantine Press, Ltd., 1989 *Countries,* pp. 423–74: p. 431.
12. Ibid., pp. 431–2.
13. Ibid., pp. 435–6.
14. For a review of the party system see Daniel Dhakidae, 'Partai Politik dan Sistem Kepartaian di Indonesia', *Prisma* 10, 12, 1981, 3–23.
15. C. van Dijk, 'The Indonesian General Elections 1971–92,' *Indonesia Circle* 58, 1992, 48–66.

16. 'There is no need for an opposition, says Suharto', *Straits Times* 9 September 1995.
17. R. William Liddle, 'Indonesia in 1987: The New Order at the Height of its Power,' *Asian Survey* 28, 2, 1988, 180–91: p. 181.
18. Ibid., p. 184.
19. Ibid.
20. Tan Chee Leng, 'Indonesia in 1992: Anticipating Another Soeharto Term', *Southeast Asian Affairs* 1993, 147–60: p. 148.
21. Liddle, op. cit.
22. Ulf Sundhaussen, 'The Military: Structure, Procedures, and Effects on Indonesian Society,' in Karl D. Jackson & Lucian W. Pye, eds., *Political Power and Communications in Indonesia,* Berkeley, Los Angeles, & London: University of California Press, 1978, pp. 45–81, p. 51.
23. Robert C. Johansen, 'Military Policies and the State System as Impediments to Democracy,' *Political Studies* 40, special issue, 1992, 99–115.
24. For some general works see Samuel P. Huntington, 'Will More Countries Become Democratic', *Political Science Quarterly* 99, 2, 1984, 193–218; Huntington, *The Third Wave: Democratization in the Late Twentieth Century,* Norman: University of Oklahoma Press, 1991; Huntington, 'Democracy's Third Wave', *Journal of Democracy* 2, 2, 1991, 12–34; Huntington, 'How Countries Democratize', *Political Science Quarterly* 106, 4, 1991–2, 579–616; Chan Heng Chee, 'Democracy: Evolution and Implementation – An Asian Perspective', in Robert Bartley, Chan Heng Chee, Samuel P. Huntington and Shijuro Ogata, *Democracy and Capitalism: Asian and American Perspectives,* Singapore: Institute of Southeast Asian Studies, 1993, pp. 1–26; James Cotton, 'The Limits to Liberalization in Industrializing Asia: Three Views of the State', *Pacific Affairs* 64, 3, 1991, 311–27; Grzegorz Ekiert, 'Democratization Processes in East Central Europe: A Theoretical Reconsideration', *British Journal of Political Science* 21, 3, 1991, 285–313; Diane Ethier, ed., *Democratic Transition and Consolidation in Southern Europe, Latin America and Southeast Asia,* Basingstoke: Macmillan, 1990; Ethier, 'Democratic Consolidation in Southern Europe, Latin America and Southeast Asia: Comparative Perspectives', *Journal of Developing Societies* 7, 1991, 195–217; Edward Friedman, ed., *The Politics of Democratization: Generalising East Asian Experiences,* Boulder: Westview, 1994; Kanishka Jayasuriya, 'Political Economy of Democratisation in East Asia', *Asian Perspective* 18, 2, 1994, 141–80; Stephanie Lawson, 'Conceptual Issues in the Comparative Study of Regime Change and Democratization', *Comparative Politics* 25, 2, 1993, 183–205; James Petras, 'State, Regime and the Democratization Muddle', *Journal of Contemporary Asia* 19, 1, 1989, 26–33; Doh Chull Shin, 'On the Third Wave of Democratization: A Synthesis and Evaluation of Recent Theory and Research', *World Politics* 47, 1994, 135–70; Francisco C. Weffort, 'What is a "New Democracy"', *International Social Science Journal* 136, 1993, 245–56.
25. James V. Jesudason, 'The Limits to Civil Society and Democracy in Malaysia.' Paper presented at a conference on Transition to Democracy, organized by the Friederich–Naumann Stiftung, Phuket 28 May – 1 June 1993; Johan Saravanamuttu, 'The State and Democratisation: Reflections on the Malaysian Case.' Paper presented at the Joint Annual Convention

of the British International Studies Association and the International Studies Association, London, 28 March – 1 April 1989.

26. See, for example, Chandra Muzaffar, *Freedom in Fetters: An Analysis of the State of Democracy in Malaysia*, Penang: Aliran, 1984; Johan Saravanamuttu, 'Authoritarian Statism and Strategies for Democratisation: Malaysia in the 1980s,' in Peter Limqueco, ed., *Partisan Scholarship: Essays in Honour of Renato Constantino*, Manila & Wollongong: Journal of Contemporary Asia Publishers, 1989, pp. 223–51.

27. Ian Chalmers, 'Indonesia 1990: Democratization and Social Forces,' *Southeast Asian Affairs 1991*, Singapore: Institute of Southeast Asian Studies, pp. 107–21; Chua Beng Huat, 'Looking for Democratization in Post-Soeharto Indonesia', *Contemporary Southeast Asia* 15, 2, 1993, 131–60; J. Soedjati Djiwandono, 'Democratic Experiment in Indonesia: Between Achievements and Expectations,' *Indonesian Quarterly* 15, 4, 1987, 661–9; Djiwandono, 'Indonesia in 1988: Progress in Democratic Experiment?' *Indonesian Quarterly* 17, 4, 1989, 335–49; Max Lane, '"Openness", Political Discontent and Succession in Indonesia: Political Developments in Indonesia 1989–91', Australia–Asia Papers no 56, Centre for the Study of Australia–Asia Relations, Division of Asian and International Studies, Griffith University, Nathan, Qld, 1991; Riwanto Tirtosudarmo, 'Indonesia 1991: Quest for Democracy in a Turbulent Year,' *Southeast Asian Affairs 1992*, Singapore: Institute of Southeast Asian Studies, pp. 123–39; Anders Uhlin, 'Indonesian Democracy Discourse in a Global Context: The Transnational Diffusion of Democratic Ideas', Working Paper no. 83, Centre of Southeast Asian Studies, Monash University, Clayton, Vic., 1993.

28. Amir Santoso, 'Democracy and Parliament: Future Agenda,' *Indonesian Quarterly* 20, 1, 1992, 84–93; R. Eep Saefullah Fatah, 'Dwi Fungsi ABRI dan Demokratisasi: Retrospeksi dan Prospeksi Peranan Politik Militer di Masa Orde Baru,' *Cendekia Muda* 1, 1, 1993, 5–20; Kartjono, 'Demokratisasi di Tingkat "Grassroots": Peranan Lembaga Swadaya Masyarakat,' *Prisma* 17, 6, 1988, 28–40; David Reeve, 'Sukarnoism and Indonesia's "Functional Group" State – Part One: Developing "Indonesian Democracy",' *Review of Indonesian and Malaysian Affairs* 12, 2, 1978, 43–94; Reeve, 'Sukarnoism and Indonesia's "Functional Group" State – Part Two: Implementing "Indonesian Democracy",' *Review of Indonesian and Malaysian Affairs* 13, 1, 1979, 52–115; Olle Tornquist, *Struggle for Democracy – A New Option in Indonesia?*, Uppsala: The AKUT series no. 33, University of Uppsala, 1984, ch. 2.

29. For general works encompassing a wide range of theoretical perspectives see Syed Farid Alatas, 'Theoretical Perspectives on the Role of State Elites in Southeast Asian Development', *Contemporary Southeast Asia* 14, 4, 1993, 368–95; Richard P. Appelbaum & Jeffry Henderson, eds, *States and Development in the Asian Pacific Rim*, Newbury Park: Sage, 1992; Fred Block, 'The Roles of the State in the Economy', in Neil J. Smelser & Richard Swedberg, eds, *The Handbook of Economic Sociology*, Princeton: Princeton University Press, 1994, pp. 691–710; Richard H. Brown & William T. Lin, eds, *Modernization in East Asia: Political, Economic and Social Perspectives*, Westport, CT: Praeger, 1992; William L. Canak, 'The Peripheral State Debate: State Capitalist and Bureaucratic–Authoritarian

Regimes in Latin America', *Latin American Research Review* 19, 1, 1984, 3–36; James Cotton, 'The State in the Asian NICs', *Asian Perspective* 18, 1, 1994, 39–56; Frederic C. Deyo, ed., *The Political Economy of the New Asian Industrialism*, Ithaca: Cornell University Press, 1987; Peter B. Evans, Dietrich Rueschemeyer & Theda Skocpol, eds, *Bringing the State Back In*, Cambridge: Cambridge University Press, 1985; Ziya Onis, 'The Logic of the Developmental State', *Comparative Politics* 24, 1, 1991, 109–26; Robert Wade, *Governing the Market: Economic Theory and the Role of Government in East Asian Industrialization*, Princeton: Princeton University Press, 1990; Ding-xin Zhao & John A. Hall, 'State Power and Patterns of Late Development: Resolving the Crisis of the Sociology of Development', *Sociology* 28, 1, 1994, 211–29.

30. On the regulation of the economy and direct involvement in capital accumulation in Indonesia see M. Bosch, 'Rol van de Staat in Indonesies Industrialisaties: Huidige Industriepolitiek Vol Tegenstrijdigheden,' *Indonesia Feiten en Meningen* 11, 5, 1986, 24–30; Olle Tornquist, 'Rent Capitalism, State, and Democracy: A Theoretical Proposition,' in Arief Budiman, ed., *State and Civil Society in Indonesia*, Clayton, Vic.: Centre of Southeast Asian Studies, Monash University, 1990, pp. 29–49; Bruce Glassburner, 'Political Economy and the Soeharto Regime,' *Bulletin of Indonesian Economic Studies* 14, 3, 1978, 24–51; Andrew Macintyre, *Business and Politics in Indonesia*, Sydney: Allen & Unwin, 1990; Yahya Muhaimin, *Bisnis dan Politik: Kebijaksanaan Ekonomi Indonesia 1950–1980*, Jakarta: LP3ES, 1990; Richard Robison, *Indonesia: The Rise of Capital*, Sydney: Allen and Unwin, 1986; Robison, 'Towards a Class Analysis of the Indonesian Military Bureaucratic State,' *Indonesia* 25, 1978, 17–39; Robison, 'Culture, Politics, and Economy in the Political History of the New Order,' *Indonesia* 31, 1981, 1–29; Hans van der Veen, 'Staats Obstakel voor Industrialisering,' *Indonesia Feiten en Meningen* 11, 5, 1986, 8–9.

On the same in Malaysia see Fatimah Halim, 'Capital, Labour and the State: The West Malaysian Case,' *Journal of Contemporary Asia* 12, 3, 1982, 259–80; Fatimah Halim, 'The State in West Malaysia,' *Race and Class* 24, 1, 1982, 33–45; Edmund Terence Gomez, *Politics in Business: UMNO's Corporate Investments*, Kuala Lumpur: Forum, 1990; Halim Salleh, 'State Capitalism in Malaysian Agriculture', *Journal of Contemporary Asia* 21, 3, 1991, 327–43; James V. Jesudason, *Ethnicity and the Economy: The State, Chinese Business, and Multinationals in Malaysia*, Singapore: Oxford University Press, 1989; Johan Saravanamuttu, 'The State, Authoritarianism and Industrialization: Reflections on the Malaysian Case,' *Kajian Malaysia* 5, 2, 1987, 43–75; Jomo Kwame Sundaram, *A Question of Class: Capital, the State, and Uneven Development in Malaya*, Singapore: Oxford University Press, 1986; Lim Mah Hui, 'Contradictions in the Development of Malay Capital: State, Accumulation and Legitimation,' in John G. Taylor & Andrew Turton, eds, *Sociology of Developing Societies: Southeast Asia*, Basingstoke: Macmillan, 1988, pp. 19–32; Lim Mah Hui & William Canak, 'The Political Economy of State Policies in Malaysia,' *Journal of Contemporary Asia* 11, 2, 1981, 208–24; Mohamad Abdad Mohamad Zain, 'Ekonomi Politik Kabinet: Satu Peralihan Kelas di Kalangan Elit Kuasa dan Hala Himpunan Lebihan di Malaysia Kini,' *Kajian Malaysia*

7, 1/2, 1989, 38–57; Loong Wong, 'The State and Organised Labour in West Malaysia, 1967–1980', *Journal of Contemporary Asia* 23, 2, 1993, 214–37.

31. Syed Hussein Alatas, *Corruption: Its Nature, Causes and Functions*, Aldershot: Avebury, 1990; A Hamzah, *Korupsi dalam Pengelolaan Proyek Pembangunan*, Jakarta: Penerbit Akademika Pressindo, 1985; Hamzah, *Korupsi di Indonesia: Masalah dan Pemecahannya*, Jakarta: Gramedia, 1991; L. V. Cariño, *Bureaucratic Corruption in Asia: Causes, Consequences and Controls*, Quezon City: JMC Press & Manila: College of Public Administration, University of the Philippines, 1986; Nor Azizan Idris, 'Nepotisme dalam Politik Malaysia,' *Ilmu Masyarakat* 20, 1991, 16–43.

32. Arend Lijphart, 'Consociational Democracy', *World Politics* 21, 2, 1969, 207–25; Anek Laothamatas, *Business Associations and the New political Economy of Thailand: From Bureaucratic Polity to Liberal Corporatism*, Boulder: Westview, 1992; Beng-Huat Chua, *Communitarian Ideology and Democracy in Singapore*, London: Routledge, 1995.

33. Atilio Boron, 'New Forms of Capitalist State in Latin America: An Exploration', *Race and Class* 20, 3, 1979, 263–76; Robin Luckham, 'Militarism: Force, Class and International Conflict', *IDS Bulletin* 9, 1, 1978, 19–32; James Petras, 'State Capitalism and the Third World', *Development and Change* 8, 1, 1977, 1–17; Petras, 'The "Peripheral State": Continuity and Change in the International Division of Labour', *Journal of Contemporary Asia* 12, 4, 1982, 415–31; W. Ziemann & M. Lanzendorfer, 'The State in Peripheral Societies', in Ralph Miliband & John Saville, eds, *The Socialist Register*, London: Merlin Press, 1977, pp. 143–77.

34. Riggs, *Bureaucratic Polity*; Girling, *The Bureaucratic Polity in Modernizing Societies*.

35. O'Donnell, *Modernization and Bureaucratic–Authoritarianism*; O'Donnell, 'Reflection on the Patterns of Change in the Bureaucratic–Authoritarian State', *Latin American Research Review* 13, 1, 1978, 3–38.

36. Hamza Alavi, 'The State in Post-Colonial Societies: Pakistan and Bangladesh', *New Left Review* 74, 1972, 59–81; Colin Leys, 'The "Overdeveloped" Post-Colonial State: A Re-Evaluation', *Review of African Political Economy* 5, 1976, 40–8; John Saul, 'The State in Post-Colonial Societies: Tanzania', in Saul, *The State and Revolution in Eastern Africa*, New York & London: Monthly Review Press, 1979, pp. 167–99; S. Andreski, *Parasitism and Subversion: The Case of Latin America*, London: Weidenfeld & Nicolson, 1966; Andreski, 'Kleptocracy as a System of Government in Africa', in Arnold J. Heidenheimer, ed., *Political Corruption: Readings in Comparative Analysis*, New York: Reinhart & Winston, 1970, pp. 346–57.

37. Alfian, *Masalah dan Prospek Pembangunan Politik di Indonesia: Kumpulan Karangan*, Jakarta: Gramedia, 1990, chap 21; Miriam Budiardjo, *Dasar-Dasar Ilmu Politik*, Jakarta: Gramedia, 1992, pp. 73–6; R. William Liddle, 'The Politics of *Ekonomi Pancasila*: Some Reflections on a Recent Debate', *Bulletin of Indonesian Economic Studies* 18, 1, 1982, 96–101; Mashuri, 'Pancasila Democracy', *Indonesian Quarterly* 5, 4, 1977, 32–43; M. Taopan, *Demokrasi Pancasila: Analisa Konsepsional Aplikatif*, np: Sinar Grafika, 1989.

38. Benedict R. O'G. Anderson, 'Old State, New Society: Indonesia's New

Order in Comparative Historical Perspective', *Journal of Asian Studies* 42, 3, 1983, 477–96; Benedict Anderson & Audrey Kahin, eds., *Interpreting Indonesian Politics: Thirteen Contributions to the Debate*, Ithaca, NY: Cornell Modern Indonesia Project, Southeast Asia Program, Cornell University, 1982; Arief Budiman, 'The Emergence of the Bureaucratic Capitalist State in Indonesia,' in Lim Teck Ghee, ed., *Reflections on Development in Southeast Asia*, Singapore: Institute of Southeast Asian Studies, 1988, pp. 110–28; Farchan Bulkin, 'Negara, Masyarakat dan Ekonomi', *Prisma* 8, 1984, 3–17; Heri Akhmadi, 'Military–Bureaucratic Political Machinery in Indonesia,' *New Asian Visions* 5, 1, 1988, 64–73; Alec Gordon, 'Imaginary Histories and the Real Thing: A Critique of Anderson and Benda on the "Autonomous State" in Indonesia', *Journal of Contemporary Asia* 23, 4, 1993, 444–65; Vedi R. Hadiz, 'Politik, Budaya, dan Perubahan Sosial: Sebuah Rekonstruksi dan Kritik Terhadap Pemikiran Ben Anderson', *Prisma* 18, 2, 1989, 29–49; John A. MacDougall, 'Patterns of Military Control in the Indonesian Higher Central Bureaucracy,' *Indonesia* 33, 1982, 89–121; Aswab Mahasin, 'State, People, and Problems of Legitimacy', *Prisma: The Indonesian Indicator*, 34, 1984, 3–12; Richard Robison, 'Authoritarian States, Capital-Owning Classes, and the Politics of Newly Industrializing Countries: The Case of Indonesia', *World Politics* 41, 1, 1988, 52–74; Marvin L. Rogers, 'Depoliticization of Indonesia's Political Parties: Attaining Military Stability', *Armed Forces and Society* 14, 2, 1988, 247–72; S. M. Amin, *Indonesia di Bawah Rezim Demokrasi Terpimpin*, Jakarta: Bulan Bintang, 1967; Fridus Steylen, 'Bureaukratie Verlamt Emancipatie,' *Indonesia Feiten en Meningen* 11, 5, 1986, 20–1; Hans van der Veen, 'Militarisering en Bureaukratisering Versterken Totalitair Karakter Indonesische Natie,' *Indonesia Feiten en Meningen* 11, 5, 1986, 16–18.

39. Afan Gaffar, *Javanese Voters: A Case Study of Election Under a Hegemonic Party System*, Yogyakarta: Gadjah Mada University Press, 1992, pp. 37–8.

40. Karl von Vorys, *Democracy Without Consensus: Communalism and Political Stability in Malaysia*, Princeton: Princeton University Press, 1975, pp. 4, 122ff.

41. As far as I know, the term quasi-democracy was first used in Frank C. Darling, *The Westernization of Asia: A Comparative Political Analysis*, Boston: G. K. Hall & Co. & Cambridge: Schenkman Publishing Co., 1979, p. 259. The term has also been used by Zakaria Haji Ahmad in 'Malaysia: Quasi Democracy in a Divided Society,' in Larry Diamond, Juan J. Linz, and Seymour Martin Lipset, eds, *Volume 3, Democracy in Developing Countries*, pp. 347–81: p. 349. Other works which refer to the modified or hybrid nature of Malaysian democracy are S. S. Bedlington, *Malaysia and Singapore: The Building of New States*, Ithaca: Cornell University Press, 1978; Gordon P. Means, *Malaysian Politics*, London: Hodder & Stoughton, 1976; R. S. Milne & D. K. Mauzy, *Politics and Government in Malaysia*, Singapore: Federal Publications, 1977.

42. Hua Wu Yin. *Class and Communalism in Malaysia: Politics in a Dependent State*, London: Zed Books, 1983, pp. 2, 108.

43. Harold Crouch, 'Authoritarian Trends, the UMNO Split and the Limits to State Power,' in Joel Kahn & Francis Loh, eds, *Fragmented Vision: Culture and Politics in Contemporary Malaysia*, Sydney: Allen & Unwin, 1992,

pp. 21–43: 26–7. See also Simon Tan, 'The Rise of State Authoritarianism in Malaysia', *Bulletin of Concerned Asian Scholars* 22, 3, 1990, 32–42: p. 42, where the term benign authoritarianism is used.
44. Harold Crouch, 'Malaysia: Neither Authoritarian Nor Democratic,' in Kevin Hewison, Richard Robison, & Garry Rodan, ed., *Southeast Asia in the 1990s: Authoritarianism, Democracy and Capitalism*, St. Leonard, NSW: Allen & Unwin, 1993, pp. 135–57.

Chapter 2

1. For more on psychological theories of regime type see Zevedei Barbu, *Democracy and Dictatorship: Their Psychology and Patterns of Life*, London: Routledge & Kegan Paul, 1956; Lawrence E. Grinter, 'The Social Psychology of Political Development', *Southeast Asian Spectrum* 2, 1, 1973, 1–10; Everett E. Hagen, *On the Theory of Social Change*, Homewood, IL: The Dorsey Press, 1962; Robert D. Hess, 'The Socialization of Attitudes toward Political Authority,' *International Social Science Journal* 15, 1963, 542–59; Lucian Pye, *Politics, Personality, and Nation Building*, New Haven: Yale University Press, 1962.
2. Samuel Huntington, 'Will More Countries Become Democratic', *Political Science Quarterly* 99, 2, 1984, 193–218: p. 216.
3. Darling, *The Westernization of Asia*, pp. 259–60.
4. Gabriel Almond and G. Bingham Powell, *Comparative Politics: A Developmental Approach*, Boston: Little Brown, 1966.
5. Alvin A. Rabushka & Kenneth A. Shepsle, *Politics in Plural Societies: A Theory of Democratic Instability*, Columbus, OH: Merril, 1972.
6. Robert A. Dahl, *A Preface to Democratic Theory*, Chicago: University of Chicago Press, 1956; Lipset, 'The Social Requisites of Democracy Revisited: 1993 Presidential Address', *American Sociological Review* 59, 1, 1994, 1–22.
7. Miriam Budiardjo, *Dasar-Dasar Ilmu Politik*, Jakarta: Gramedia, 1992, pp. 69–72.
8. Charles Taylor & Michael C. Hudson, *World Handbook of Political and Social Indicators*, 2nd ed, New Haven, CT: Yale University Press, 1972; Volker Bornschier & Peter Heintz, eds, *Compendium of Data for World-System Analysis: A Sourcebook of Data Based on the Study of MNCs, Economic Policy and National Development*, Zurich: Soziologisches Institut der Universitat Zurich, n.d.
9. Taylor & Hudson, *World Handbook*, p. 271.
10. This difference is slight in light of the fact that for 129 countries, the index of ethnolinguistic fractionalization ranges from a low of 0.01 to a high of 0.93, with the mean at 0.4 and the median at 0.36.
11. Rabushka & Shepsle, *Politics in Plural Societies*, p. 92.
12. Richard Robison, 'Culture, Politics, and Economy in the Political History of the New Order', *Indonesia* 31, 1981, 1–29. This article is a critique of the so-called 'cultural politics' approach in the following: Donald Emmerson, *Indonesia's Elite: Political Culture and Cultural Politics*, Ithaca: Cornell University Press, 1976; R. W. Liddle, 'Models of Indonesian Politics', Paper presented to the Department of Politics Seminar, Monash University, 1977; Karl Jackson, 'Bureaucratic Polity: A Theoretical Framework

for the Analysis of Power and Communications in Indonesia', in Karl D. Jackson & Lucian W. Pye, eds, *Political Power and Communication in Indonesia*, Berkeley: University of California Press, 1978, pp. 82–136. See also Burhan D. Magenda, 'Ethnicity and State-Building in Indonesia: the Cultural Base of the New Order', in Remo Guidieri, Francesco Pellizi & Stanley J. Tambiah, eds, *Ethnicities and Nations: Process of Interethnic Relations in Latin America, Southeast Asia, and the Pacific*, Houston: Rothko Chapel, 1988, pp. 345–61.

13. On another aspect of the relationship between culture and democracy see Ingrid Creppell, 'Democracy and Literacy: The Role of Culture in Political Life', *European Journal of Sociology* 30, 1989, 22–47.

14. David E. Apter & Charles Andrain, 'Comparative Government: Developing New Nations,' *Journal of Politics* 30, 2, 1968, 372–416: p. 390.

15. Rupert Emerson, *From Empire to Nation: The Rise to Self-Assertion of Asian and African Peoples*, Cambridge: Harvard University Press, 1960.

16. Lucian Pye, 'The Politics of Southeast Asia,' in Gabriel A. Almond & James S. Coleman, eds, *The Politics of Developing Areas*, Princeton: Princeton University Press, 1960, pp. 65–152: p. 91.

17. Ibid.

18. Ibid., p. 93.

19. Richard Butwell, *Southeast Asia: A Political Introduction*, New York: Praeger, 1975, pp. 57, 62.

20. See Rupert Emerson, *Representative Government in Southeast Asia*, Cambridge, MA: Harvard University Press, 1955, pp. 20–3, 64–77, for accounts of pre-independence experiences with democratic procedures in the Netherlands Indies and British Malaya.

21. J.S. Furnivall, *Colonial Policy and Practice: A Comparative Study of Burma and Netherlands India*, New York: New York University, 1956, pp. 238–9.

22. Rupert Emerson, *Malaysia: A Study in Direct and Indirect Rule*, New York: The Macmillan Company, 1937, p. 423.

23. Amry Vandenbosch, *The Dutch East Indies: Its Government, Problems, and Politics*, Berkeley & Los Angeles: University of California Press, 1941, p. 114.

24. Ibid., p. 118.

25. Karl Marx, *Manifesto of the Communist Party*, Peking: Foreign Languages Press, 1965, p. 35.

26. Karl Marx, *The German Ideology,* New York: International Publishers, 1970, pp. 79–80.

27. Barrington Moore, Jr., *Social Origins of Dictatorship and Democracy*, Boston: Beacon Press, 1966, p. xv.

28. Ibid., pp. xv–xvi.

29. Ibid., p. xvi.

30. Ibid.

31. Christopher Chase-Dunn, *Global Formation: Structures of the World-Economy*, New York: Basil Blackwell, 1989, p. 125.

32. Karl Marx, 'The Class Struggles in France,' pt. 2, in Karl Marx & Frederick Engels, *Collected Works: Volume 10, Marx & Engels, 1849–1851*, Moscow: Progress Publishers, 1978, pp. 45–145: p. 79.

33. For a test of Moore's theory see John D. Stephens, 'Democratic Transition

and Breakdown in Western Europe, 1870–1939: A Test of the Moore Thesis', *American Journal of Sociology* 94, 5, 1989, 1019–77.

34. Vilfredo Pareto, *The Mind and Society*, 4 vols, New York: Harcourt Brace Jovanovich 1935; Gaetano Mosca, *The Ruling Class*, New York: McGraw-Hill, 1939; Robert Michels, *Political Parties*, New York: Free Press, 1962.
35. Eva Etzioni-Halevy, 'Democratic–Elite Theory: Stabilization versus Breakdown of Democracy', *European Journal of Sociology* 31, 2, 1990, 317–50; L. G. Field & J. Higley, *Elites and Non-Elites: The Possibilities and Their Side Effects*, Andover, MA: Warner Modular Publications, 1973; J. Higley K. & M. G. Burton, 'The Elite Variable in Democratic Transitions and Breakdowns', *American Sociological Review* 54, 1989, 17–32; J. Higley, Ursula Hoffman-Lange, Charles Kadushin & Gwen Moore, 'Elite Integration in Stable Democracies: A Reconsideration', *European Sociological Review* 7, 1, 1991, 35–53; A. Lijphart, 'Consociational Democracy', *World Politics* 21, 1969, 207–25; K. Prewitt & A. Stone, *The Ruling Elites: Elite Theory, Power, and American Democracy*, New York: Harper & Row, 1973.
36. Magnus Blomstrom & Bjorn Hettne, *Development Theory in Transition – The Dependency Debate and Beyond: Third World Responses*, London: Zed, 1985, p. 20.
37. For a critical discussion see Joseph R. Gusfield, 'Tradition and Modernity: Misplaced Polarities in the Study of Social Change', *American Journal of Sociology* 72, 4, 1967, 351–62.
38. Bert Hoselitz et al, *Theories of Economic Growth*, Glencoe, IL: Free Press, 1960.
39. Walter W. Rostow, *The Stages of Economic Growth: A Non-Communist Manifesto*, Cambridge: Cambridge University Press, 1961.
40. Gabriel A. Almond, 'Introduction: A Functional Approach to Comparative Politics', in Almond & James S. Coleman, eds, *The Politics of Developing Areas*, Princeton: Princeton University Press, 1960, pp. 3–64; Almond, 'A Developmental Approach to Political System', *World Politics* 17, 1965, 183–214; Almond & G. Bingham Powell, Jr., *Comparative Politics: A Developmental Approach*, Boston: Little Brown, 1966.
41. Almond, 'Comparative Political Systems', *Journal of Politics* 18, 1956, 391–409; Almond & Powell, *Comparative Politics*.
42. David E. Apter, *The Politics of Modernization*, Chicago: University of Chicago Press, 1965.
43. A. F. K. Organski, *The Stages of Political Development*, New York: Alfred A. Knopf, 1965.
44. Samuel Huntington, *Political Order in Changing Societies*, New Haven: Yale University Press, 1968.
45. Karl Marx, *The Eighteenth Brumaire of Louis Bonaparte*, New York: International Publishers, 1963, p. 122.
46. Ibid., pp. 131–2.
47. Ibid., p. 132.
48. For a discussion of the two conceptions of the state in Marx, see Ralph Miliband, 'Marx and the State,' *Socialist Register*, London: Merlin Press, 1965, pp. 278–96.
49. See, for example, S. M. Lipset, 'Some Social Requisites of Democracy:

Economic Development and Political Legitimacy,' *American Political Science Review* 53, 1, 1959, 69–105; Lipset, 'The Social Requisites of Democracy Revisited: 1993 Presidential Address', *American Sociological Review* 59, 1, 1994, 1–22; S. M. Lipset, Kyong-Ryung Seong & John Charles Torres, 'A Comparative Analysis of the Social Requisites of Democracy', *International Social Science Journal* 136, 1993, 155–75; Karl W. Deutsch, 'Social Mobilization and Political Development,' *American Political Science Review* 55, 3, 1961, 473–514.

50. Georg P. Muller (with the collaboration of Volker Bornschier), *Comparative World Data: A Statistical Handbook for the Social Sciences*, Baltimore & London: The Johns Hopkins University Press, 1988, pp. 240, 304.

51. See, for example, Kenneth Bollen, 'World System Position, Dependency, and Democracy: The Cross-National Evidence,' *American Sociological Review* 48, 4, 1983, 468–79.

52. Kenneth A. Bollen & Robert W. Jackman, 'Economic and Noneconomic Determinants of Political Democracy in the 1960s,' *Research in Political Sociology* 1, 1985, 27–48: pp. 38–9. Earlier studies with similar results are Lipset, 'Some Social Requisites of Democracy,'; Phillip Cutright, 'National Political Development: Measurement and Analysis,' *American Sociological Review* 28, 2, 1963, 253–64; Deane Neubauer, 'Some Conditions of Democracy,' *American Political Science Review* 61, 4, 1967, 1002–9; Robert W. Jackman, 'On the Relation of Economic Development to Democratic Performance,' *American Journal of Political Science* 17, 3, 1973, 611–21.

53. Bollen, 'World System Position, Dependency, and Democracy,' p. 477.

54. Christopher Chase-Dunn, 'The Effects of International Economic Dependence on Development and Inequality: A Cross-National Study,' *American Sociological Review* 40, 6, 1975, 720–38; Volker Bornschier, Christopher Chase-Dunn, & Richard Rubinson, 'Cross-National Evidence of the Effects of Foreign Investment and Aid on Economic Growth and Inequality: A Survey of Findings and a Reanalysis,' *American Journal of Sociology* 84, 3, 1978, 651–83.

55. Michael Timberlake & Kirk R. Williams, 'Dependence, Political Exclusion, and Government Repression: Some Cross-National Evidence,' *American Sociological Review* 49, 1, 1984, 141–6.

56. Richard Rubinson, 'Dependence, Government Revenue, and Economic Growth, 1955–1970,' *Studies in Comparative International Development* 12, 2, 1977, 3–28.

57. See Chase-Dunn, 'The Effects of International Economic Dependence,' for the conceptualization and operationalization of investment and debt dependence.

58. Richard Rubinson, 'The World-Economy and the Distribution of Income Within States: A Cross-National Study,' *American Sociological Review* 41, 4, 1976, 638–59: p. 641.

59. Bollen, 'World System Position, Dependency, and Democracy: The Cross-National Evidence,' *American Sociological Review* 48, 4, 1983, 468–79: p. 470.

60. Chase-Dunn, 'The Effects of International Economic Dependence', p. 723.

61. Bollen, 'World System Position,' p. 470.

62. Chase-Dunn, *Global Formation*, pp. 111–14.
63. Ibid., p. 112.
64. Ibid., p. 111.
65. Ibid., p. 126.
66. Ibid.
67. Guillermo O'Donnell, *Modernization and Bureaucratic Authoritarianism: Studies in South American Politics*, Berkeley: Institute of International Studies, University of California, 1973. See also David Collier, 'Overview of the Bureaucratic–Authoritarian Model,' in David Collier, ed., *The New Authoritarianism in Latin America*, Princeton: Princeton University Press, pp. 19–32.
68. Guillermo O'Donnell & P. C. Schmitter, *Transitions from Authoritarian Rule: Tentative Conclusions About Uncertain Democracies*, Baltimore: Johns Hopkins University Press, 1986. See also James Cotton, 'From Authoritarianism to Democracy in South Korea', *Political Studies* 37, 1989, 244–59.
69. See, for example, Hooshang Amirahmadi, 'The Non-Capitalist Way of Development,' *Review of Radical Political Economics* 19, 1, 1987, 22–46; Clive Y. Thomas, 'The "Non-Capitalist Path" as Theory and Practice of Decolonisation and Socialist Transformation,' *Latin American Perspectives* 5, 2, 1978, 10–28.
70. Hamza Alavi, 'The State in Post-Colonial Societies: Pakistan & Bangladesh,' *New Left Review* 74, 1972, 59–81: p. 62; Idem., 'State and Class Under Peripheral Capitalism,' in Hamza Alavi & Teodor Shanin, eds, *Introduction to the Sociology of Developing Societies*, London: Macmillan Educational Ltd., 1982, pp. 289–307: p. 298.
71. Alavi, 'The State in Post-Colonial Societies,' p. 62.
72. Alavi, 'The State and Class,' p. 302.
73. Hamza Alavi, 'India and the Colonial Mode of Production,' *Economic and Political Weekly* 10, 33–5 (special issue), 1975, 1235–62: p. 1235.
74. Alavi, 'The State in Post-Colonial Societies,' p. 62.
75. Ibid., pp. 59, 61.
76. Ibid., p. 62.
77. O'Donnell, *Modernization*.
78. Alavi, 'The State in Post-Colonial Societies,' p. 60.
79. See, for example, Hamza Alavi, 'Peasants and Revolution,' *The Socialist Register*, London: Merlin Press, 1975, pp. 241–77; Idem., 'India and the Colonial Mode of Production.'
80. Thomas, *The Rise of the Authoritarian State*, pp. 71–9.
81. Nicos Poulantzas, 'Capitalism and the State,' *New Left Review* 58, 1969, p. 74.
82. Alavi, 'The State in Post-Colonial Societies,' p. 72.
83. Thomas, *The Rise of the Authoritarian State*, p. 71.
84. Alavi, 'The State in Post-Colonial Societies,' p. 61; Idem., 'State and Class,' pp. 299–301.
85. Alavi, 'The State in Post-Colonial Societies,' p. 61.
86. John Saul, 'The State in Post-Colonial Societies: Tanzania,' in idem, *The State and Revolution in Eastern Africa*, New York & London: Monthly Review Press, 1979, pp. 167–99.

87. Colin Leys, 'The "Overdeveloped" Post-Colonial State: A Re-Evaluation,' *Review of African Political Economy* no. 5, 1976, 40–8: p. 42.
88. Ibid., p. 41.
89. These conditions of democracy are defined in Chapter 2.
90. See Neil J. Smelser, *Comparative Methods in the Social Sciences*, Englewood Cliffs, New Jersey: Prentice-Hall, 1976, pp. 215–20.
91. Chase-Dunn, *Global Formation*, p. 113.

Chapter 3

1. Harry J. Benda, 'The Structure of Southeast Asian History,' in idem., *Continuity and Change in Southeast Asia: Collected Journal Articles of Harry J. Benda*, New Haven: Yale University Southeast Asia Studies, 1972, pp. 121–53: p. 127.
2. S. H. Alatas, *The Myth of the Lazy Native*, London: Frank Cass, 1977, p. 190.
3. Syed Farid Alatas, 'Notes on Various Theories Regarding the Islamization of the Malay Archipelago," *Muslim World* 75, 3–4, 1985, 162–75: p. 174.
4. Syed M. Naguib Al-Attas, *Islam dalam Sejarah dan Kebudayaan Melayu*, Kuala Lumpur: Penerbit Universiti Kebangsaan Malaysia, 1972, p. 21.
5. Syed M. Naguib Al-Attas, *Preliminary Statement on a General Theory of the Islamization of the Malay–Indonesian Archipelago*, Kuala Lumpur: Dewan Bahasa dan Pustaka, 1969, p. 28.
6. For more on the influence of Islam on Malay–Indonesian kingship see A. C. Milner, 'Islam and Malay Kingship,' *Journal of the Royal Asiatic Society of Great Britain and Ireland* 1, 1981, 46–70; Milner, 'Islam and the Muslim State,' in M. B. Hooker, ed., *Islam in Southeast Asia*, Leiden: Brill, 1983, pp. 23–49.
7. J. C. van Leur, *Indonesian Trade and Society*, The Hague: W. van Hoeve, 1955, pp. 104–5; W. F. Wertheim, *Indonesian Society in Transition: A Study of Social Change*, The Hague & Bandung: W. van Hoeve, 1959, p. 53.
8. Bennet Bronson, 'Exchange at the Upstream and Downstream Ends: Notes Toward a Functional Model of the Coastal State in Southeast Asia,' in Karl L. Hutterer, ed., *Economic Exchange and Social Interaction in Southeast Asia: Perspectives from Prehistory, History, and Ethnography*, Ann Arbor: University of Michigan Center for South and Southeast Asian Studies, 1978, pp. 39–52: p. 43.
9. Ibid.
10. Kenneth R. Hall, *Maritime Trade and State Development in Early Southeast Asia*, Honolulu: University of Hawaii Press, 1985, pp. 15–18.
11. Karl Marx, *Contribution to the Critique of Political Economy*, Moscow: Progress Publishers, 1970, p. 20.
12. Tom Bottomore, *Dictionary of Marxist Thought*, Cambridge, MA: Harvard University Press, 1983, p. 178; Barry Hindess & Paul Q. Hirst, *Pre-Capitalist Modes of Production*, London & Boston: Routledge & Kegan Paul, 1975, pp. 9–10.
13. Hindess & Hirst, *Pre-Capitalist Modes of Production*, pp. 10–11; Eric R. Wolf, *Europe and the People Without History*, Berkeley, Los Angeles,

& London: University of California Press, 1982, p. 75.
14. J. M. Gullick, *Indigenous Political Systems of Western Malaya*, London: The Athlone Press, 1958, p. 21.
15. Ibid.
16. Ibid.
17. Ibid.
18. Ibid., p. 21.
19. Ibid.
20. Ibid., pp. 21–2.
21. Ibid., p. 22.
22. Ibid., pp. 31, 98, 104.
23. Ibid., pp. 97–8.
24. Ibid., p. 127.
25. Ibid., pp. 44, 95, 127.
26. Ibid., p. 44.
27. Ibid., p. 126.
28. P. L. Burns, 'Capitalism and the Malay States,' in Hamza Alavi, P. L. Burns, G. R. Knight, P. B. Mayer, and Doug McEachern, *Capitalism and Colonial Production*, London & Sydney: Croom Helm, 1982, pp. 159–78: p. 165.
29. Ibid., p. 166.
30. Gullick, *Indigenous Political Systems*, p. 31.
31. Soemarsaid Moertono, *State and Statecraft in Old Java: A Study of the Late Mataram Period, 16th to 19th Century*, Ithaca: Modern Indonesia Project, Southeast Asia Program, Department of Asian Studies, Cornell University, 1968, p. 26.
32. Ibid., pp. 101, 112.
33. Ibid., pp. 93, 95.
34. Ibid., p. 117.
35. Ibid., p. 117.
36. Ibid., p. 15.
37. Ibid., p. 115.
38. Ibid., pp. 138, 146–50.
39. G. P. Rouffaer, 'Vorstenlanden,' *Adatrechtbundel* 34, 81, serie D, The Hague: K. Instituut voor de Taal-, Land-, en Volkenkunde van Nederlandsch-Indies, 1931, p. 73.
40. Moertono, *State and Statecraft in Old Java*, p. 116.
41. Moertono, *State and Statecraft in Old Java*, pp. 83–4.
42. Ibid., pp. 116–17.
43. Ibid., pp. 136–7.
44. Jomo Kwame Sundram, *A Question of Class: Capitalism, the State, and Uneven Development*, Singapore: Oxford University Press, 1986, p. 10.
45. William E. Maxwell, 'Labour and Custom of the Malays with Reference to the Tenure of Land,' *Journal of the Straits Branch, Royal Asiatic Society* 13, 1884, 75–220; Maxwell, 'The Law Relating to Slavery Among the Malays,' *Journal of the Straits Branch, Royal Asiatic Society* 19, 1890, 247–96.
46. Frank Swettenham, *British Malaya: An Account of the Origin and Progress of British Influence in British Malaya*, London: Allen & Unwin, 1948.

47. Jomo, *A Question of Class*; Lim Teck Ghee, *Origins of a Colonial Economy: Land and Agriculture in Perak, 1874–1897*, Penang: Penerbit Universiti Sains Malaysia, 1976; David Wong, *Land Tenure and Land Dealings in the Malay States*, Singapore: Singapore University Press, 1975.
48. Max Weber, *Economy and Society: An Outline of Interpretive Sociology*, Guenther Roth & Claus Wittich, eds, Berkeley, Los Angeles, & London: University of California Press, 1978, p. 255; Gianfranco Poggi, *The Development of the Modern State: A Sociological Introduction*, Stanford, California: Stanford University Press, 1978, pp. 21–2.
49. Weber, *Economy and Society*, p. 255.
50. Poggi, *The Development of the Modern State*, p. 23.
51. Wolf, *Europe and the People Without History*, pp. 79–82.
52. Wolf, *Europe*, pp. 79–80.
53. Ibid., p. 80.
54. F. Tichelman, *The Social Evolution of Indonesia: The Asiatic Mode of Production and its Legacy*, The Hague: Martinus Nijhoff, 1980; J. I. Bakker, 'Class Relations in Java in the Nineteenth Century: A Weberian Perspective,' *Canadian Journal of Development Studies* 8, 1, 1987, 137–56; Idem, 'Patrimonialism, Involution, and the Agrarian Question in Java: A Weberian Analysis of Class Relations and Servile Labour,' in John Gledhill, Barbara Bender, and Mogens Trolle Larsen, eds, *State and Society: The Emergence and Development of Social Hierarchy and Political Centralization*, London: Unwin Hyman, 1988, pp. 279–99.
55. Karl Marx, *Capital, Vol. 3*, London: Lawrence & Wishart, 1970, p. 791; Marx, 'India,' in Karl Marx & Frederick Engels, *On Colonialism*, Moscow: Progress Publishers, 1974, pp. 77–80: p. 79; Asaf Savas Akat, 'Proposal for a Radical Reinterpretation of the Asiatic Versus the European Social Formation,' in Anouar Abdel Malek, ed., *The Civilizational Project: The Visions of the Orient*, Mexico City: El Colegio de Mexico, 1981, pp. 69–79: p. 70; Ferenc Tokei, 'Le Mode de Production Asiatique dans l'Oeuvre de K. Marx et F. Engels,' *La Pensée* no. 114, 1964, 7–32.
56. Wolf, *Europe and the People Without History*, p. 80.
57. Karl Marx, *Pre-Capitalist Economic Formations*, E. J. Hobsbawm, trans., London: Lawrence & Wishart, 1964, p. 82.
58. Ibid., p. 70.
59. Marx, 'India,' p. 81.
60. Ervand Abrahamian, 'Oriental Despotism: The Case of Qajar Iran,' *International Journal of Middle East Studies* 5, 1974, 3–31: p. 6.
61. Ibid., pp. 6–7.
62. Bryan S. Turner, *Marx and the End of Orientalism*, London: George Allen & Unwin, 1978, pp. 45–6.
63. Moertono, *State and Statecraft in Old Java*, pp. 116–17.
64. Ibid., p. 117.
65. C. van Vollenhoven, *Javaansch Adatrecht*, Leiden: E. J. Brill, 1923.
66. Weber, *Economy and Society*, pp. 259–61.
67. Bakker, 'Patrimonialism and Involution,' p. 281.
68. Moertono, *State and Statecraft in Old Java*, pp. 104–5, 116–17.
69. Samir Amin, *Unequal Development: An Essay on the Social Formations of Peripheral Capitalism*, Sussex: Harvester Press, 1976, p. 17.

70. See Chapter 12, Syed Hussein Alatas, *The Myth of the Lazy Native: A study of the Image of the Malays, Filipinos and Javanese from the 16th to the 20th Century and its Function in the Ideology of Colonial Capitalism*, London: Frank Cass, 1977.
71. W. F. Wertheim, *Evolution and Revolution: The Rising Waves of Emancipation*, Harmondsworth: Penguin, 1974.
72. Barbara Watson Andaya & Leonard Y. Andaya, *A History of Malaysia*, New York: St. Martin's Press, 1982, p. 69.
73. Ibid., pp. 107–8.
74. Ibid., p. 122; M. C. Ricklefs, *A History of Modern Indonesia, c. 1300 to the Present*, Bloomington, IN: Indiana University Press, 1981, p. 135.
75. Rupert Emerson, *Malaysia: A Study in Direct and Indirect Rule*, New York: The Macmillan Company, 1937, p. 3.
76. Ibid., p. 7.
77. J. S. Furnivall, *Colonial Policy and Practice: A Comparative Study of Burma and Netherlands India*, New York: New York University Press, 1956, p. 277.
78. Ibid.
79. Emerson, *Malaysia*, pp. 389–90.
80. Andaya & Andaya, *A History of Malaysia*, p. 122.
81. Ibid., p. 183.
82. For more on the Unfederated Malay States see J. Chandran 'The British Foreign Office and the Siamese Malay States, 1890–97,' *Modern Asian Studies* 5, 1971, 143–59; Emerson, *Malaysia*, chap. 5; Eunice Thio, 'Britain's Search for Security in North Malaya,' *Journal of Southeast Asian History* 10, 2, 1969, 279–303.
83. Andaya & Andaya, *A History of Malaysia*, p. 200.
84. Emerson, *Malaysia*, p. 55.
85. Ibid. See also A. D. A. de Kat Angelino, *Colonial Policy, Vol. 2: The Dutch East Indies*, Chicago: University of Chicago Press, 1931, pp. 80–97.
86. de Kat Angelino, *Colonial Policy, Vol. 2*, pp. 102–3.
87. J. S. Furnivall, *Netherlands India: A Study of Plural Economy*, Cambridge: Cambridge University Press, 1944, p. 292; De Kat Angelino, *Colonial Policy, Vol. 2*, pp. 68–9.
88. Furnivall, *Netherlands India*, p. 88.
89. For more on the British Residential System see Chai Hon-Chan, *The Development of British Malaya, 1896–1909*, Kuala Lumpur: Oxford University Press, 1964; C. D. Cowan, *Nineteenth-Century Malaya: The Origins of British Political Control*, London: Oxford University Press, 1961; Emily Sadka, *The Protected Malay States, 1874–1895*, Kuala Lumpur: University of Malaya Press, 1968.
90. Amry Vandenbosch, *The Dutch East Indies: Its Government, Problems, and Politics*, Berkeley & Los Angeles: University of California Press, 1941, p. 58.
91. G. C. Allen & A. G. Donnithorne, *Western Enterprise in Indonesia and Malaya: A Study in Economic Development*, New York: The Macmillan Company, p. 23.
92. For an analysis of Javanese village life under the *cutuurstelsel* see R. E. Elson, *Village Java under the Cultivation System, 1830–1870*, Asian Studies

Association of Australia Publication Series #25, 1994.
93. Furnivall, *Netherlands India*, p. 134.
94. C. Fasseur, 'Some Remarks on the Cultivation System in Java', *Acta Historiae Neerlandicae* 10, 1976, 143–62: p. 157; Fasseur, 'Purse or Principle: Dutch Colonial Policy in the 1860s and the Decline of the Cultivation System', *Modern Asian Studies* 25, 1, 1991, 33–52.
95. Furnivall, *Colonial Policy*, p. 223.
96. Allen & Donnithorne, *Western Enterprise*, p. 24.
97. Ibid., p. 25.
98. Ibid., p. 70.
99. Ibid., p. 71.
100. Ibid., pp. 80–1.
101. Ibid., p. 81.
102. Ibid., p. 81.
103. Ibid., p. 31.
104. Ibid., p. 168.
105. Ibid., pp. 257–8.
106. Ibid., p. 259.
107. Ibid., p. 41.
108. Ibid., pp. 152–3.
109. Ibid., p. 153.
110. Ibid., p. 41.
111. Ibid., pp. 41–2.
112. Ibid., p. 42.
113. Lim Chong-Yah, *Economic Development of Modern Malaya*, Kuala Lumpur: Oxford University Press, 1967, p. 120.
114. Allen & Donnithorne, *Western Enterprise*, pp. 43–4.
115. J. A. Hobson, *Imperialism*, Ann Arbor: University of Michigan Press, 1971.
116. N. Bukharin, *Imperialism and World-Economy*, London: Merlin, 1972, pp. 17, 20, 21.
117. V. I. Lenin, *Imperialism, the Highest Stage of Capitalism*, Peking: Foreign Languages Press, 1975, p. 104.
118. J. H. Boeke, *The Structure of Netherlands Indian Economy*, New York: Institute of Pacific Relations, 1942; Boeke, *The Evolution of the Netherlands Indian Economy*, New York: Institute of Pacific Relations, 1946; Boeke, *Economics and Economic Policy of Dual Societies: As Exemplified by Indonesia*, New York: Institute of Pacific Relations, 1953. For a critical appraisal of Boeke see M. Sadli, 'Some Remarks on Prof. Boeke's Theory of Dualistic Economies', *Ekonomi dan Kewangan Indonesia* 10, 6, 1957, 363–384.
119. Boeke, *Economics and Economic Policy*, p. 4.
120. A. G. Frank, *Capitalism and Underdevelopment in Latin America*, New York: Monthly Review Press, 1967.
121. Ernesto Laclau, 'Feudalism and Capitalism in Latin America,' *New Left Review* no. 67, 1971, 19–38: p. 25.
122. Ibid.
123. Ibid., p. 31.
124. See for example, Talal Asad & Harold Wolpe, 'Concepts of Modes of

Production,' *Economy and Society* 5, 4, 1976, 470–506; Aidan Forster-Carter, 'The Modes of Production Controversy,' *New Left Review* no. 107, 1978, 47–77.

125. Laclau, 'Feudalism and Capitalism,' pp. 22, 31.
126. Christopher Chase-Dunn, *Global Formation: Structures of the World Economy*, Cambridge, MA: Basil Blackwell, 1989, p. 39.
127. Ibid., p. 43.
128. Ibid., p. 221.
129. Ibid., pp. 39–40.
130. Ibid., p. 41.
131. Ibid., p. 46.
132. A Portes & J. Walton, *Labor, Class and the International System*, Orlando: Academic Press, 1981, p. 7.
133. A. Emmanuel, *Unequal Exchange Revisited*, Brighton: IDS, 1975.
134. Hamza Alavi, 'India and the Colonial Mode of Production,' *Economic and Political Weekly* 10, 33–35 (special issue), 1975, 1235–62: p. 1247.
135. Ibid.
136. Ibid., pp. 1253, 1257.
137. S. B. D. de Silva, *The Political Economy of Underdevelopment*, London: Routledge & Kegan Paul, 1982, p. 445.
138. Ibid., pp. 445, 448–50.
139. Ibid., p. 446.
140. Ibid., pp. 456–60.
141. Ibid., p. 461.
142. Ibid., pp. 464–5.
143. Ibid., p. 468.
144. Boeke, *Economics and Economic Policy*, p. 4.
145. Ibid., p. 29.
146. Ibid., pp. 68–70. There will be more references to Boeke on the immiseration of the peasantry in Chapter 4.
147. Alavi, 'India and the Colonial Mode of Production,' p. 1247.
148. G. R. Knight, 'Capitalism and Commodity Production in Java,' in Hamza Alavi, P. L. Burns, G. R. Knight, P. B. Mayer, and Doug McEachern, *Capitalism and Colonial Production*, London & Sydney: Croom Helm, 1982, pp. 119–58. p. 146.
149. Chase-Dunn, *Global Formation*, p. 30.
150. Tichelman, *The Social Evolution of Indonesia*, p. 42.
151. See the old Javanese text of 1365, the Nagarakertagama, in Th. G. Th. Pigeaud, *Java in the Fourteenth Century: A Study in Cultural History*, 5 Vols., The Hague: Martinus Nijhoff, 1960–3.
152. M. C. Ricklefs, *A History of Modern Indonesia, c. 1300 to the present*, Basingstoke: Macmillan Education Ltd., 1981, p. 17.

Chapter 4

1. Karl Marx, *The Class Struggle in France, 1848–1850*, Moscow: Progress Publishers, 1972, p. 112.
2. Friedrich Engels, *The Peasant War in Germany*, Chicago: University of Chicago Press, 1967, p. 10.

3. See, for example, Karl Marx, *Manifesto of the Communist Party*, Peking: Foreign Languages Press, 1965, p. 42.
4. V. I. Lenin, 'The Development of Capitalism in Russia,' in idem., *Collected Works, Vol. 3*, Moscow: Progress Publishers, 1972, p. 33.
5. Mao Tse-Tung, 'Report on an Investigation of the Peasant Movement in Hunan,' in Mao, *Selected Works, Vol. 1*, Peking: Foreign Languages Press, 1967, p. 24.
6. Mao Tse-Tung, 'A Report of the Front Committee to the Central Committee of the Party,' in Stuart Schram, *The Political Thought of Mao Tse-Tung*, New York: Praeger, 1976, p. 259.
7. For an account of the views of Marx, Engels, Lenin and Mao on the peasantry see Anne E. Lucas-Rouffignas, *The Contemporary Peasantry in Mexico: A Class Analysis*, New York: Praeger, 1985, pp. 1–16.
8. Barrington Moore, Jr., *Social Origins of Dictatorship and Democracy*, Boston: Beacon Press, 1966.
9. Hamza Alavi, 'Peasants and Revolution,' *The Socialist Register*, London: Merlin, 1965, pp. 241–77: p. 244.
10. Ibid.
11. Ibid.
12. James C. Scott, 'Hegemony and the Peasantry,' *Politics and Society* 7, 3, 1977, 267–96: p. 289.
13. Eric R. Wolf, *Peasant Wars of the Twentieth Century*, New York: Harper & Row, 1969, p. 290.
14. Theda Skocpol, 'What Makes Peasants Revolutionary,' *Comparative Politics* 14, 3, 1982, 351–75: p. 363.
15. Ibid.
16. Ibid., p. 364.
17. Jeffery M. Paige, *Agrarian Revolution: Social Movements and Export Agriculture In the Underdeveloped World*, New York: The Free Press, 1975.
18. Ibid., p. 70.
19. Ibid., p. 49.
20. Ibid., pp. 50–8.
21. Ibid., p. 45.
22. Ibid., pp. 58–9.
23. Ibid., p. 70.
24. Lim, *Peasants and Their Agricultural Economy*, p. 226.
25. Ibid., pp. 229–30.
26. Ibid., p. 230.
27. Ibid., pp. 230–1.
28. Ibid., p. 233.
29. Ibid., p. 155.
30. Ibid., p. 156.
31. Ibid.
32. Ibid., p. 161.
33. Ibid., p. 200.
34. Furnivall, *Colonial Policy and Practice*, p. 337.
35. Boeke, *Economics and Economic Policy*, pp. 81–2.
36. Ibid., pp. 82–3.

37. Ibid., p. 70.
38. Ibid., p. 76.
39. Ibid. For more on this see D. H. Burger, 'Structuurveranderingen in de Javaanse Samenleving,' *Indonesie* 2 & 3, 1949/49 & 1949/50, 381–98 & 1–18, 101–23, 225–50, 347–50, 381–9, 512–34.
40. Shahril Talib, *After Its Own Image: The Trengganu Experience*, 1881–1941, Kuala Lumpur: Oxford University Press, 1984. According to Kershaw, however, 'the idea of the 1928 revolt as a would-be precursor of peasant liberation movements begins to feel a little brittle', citing lack of evidence and other points as reasons. See Roger Kershaw, 'Difficult Synthesis: Recent Trends in Malay Political Sociology and History', *Southeast Asian Journal of Social Science* 16, 1, 1988, 134–58: p. 144.
41. Tan Ban Teik, 'The Tok Janggut Rebellion of 1915 in Kelantan: A Reinterpretation,' in Cheah Boon Kheng, ed., *Tokoh-tokoh Tempatan*, Pulau Pinang: Universiti Sains Malaysia, 1982, pp. 97–113.
42. For case studies see Sartono Kartodirdjo, *Protest Movements in Rural Java: A Study of Agrarian Unrest in the Nineteenth and Early Twentieth Centuries*, Singapore: Oxford University Press, 1973.
43. Virginia Thompson, *Labour Problems in Southeast Asia*, New Haven: Yale University Press, 1947, p. 103.
44. Ibid., p. 104.
45. Ibid.
46. Ibid., p. 105. See also J. Norman Parmer, 'Chinese Estate Workers' Strikes in Malaya in March 1937,' in C. D. Cowan, ed., *The Economic Development of Southeast Asia: Studies in Economic History and Political Economy*, London: George Allen & Unwin, 1964, pp. 154–73.
47. Thompson, *Labour Problems*, p. 112.
48. Kamaruddin M. Said, 'Mogok dan Konflik Industri di Malaysia: Suatu Pembicaraan Awal,' *Jurnal Antropologi dan Sosiologi* 7, 1979, 75–108: p. 95.
49. Ibid., p. 100.
50. Lucian Pye, *Guerilla Communism in Malaya: Its Social and Political Meaning*, Princeton: Princeton University Press, 1956.
51. Kamaruddin, 'Mogok dan Konflik,' p. 101.
52. Thompson, *Labour Problems*, p. 158.
53. Ibid.
54. Ibid., p. 159.
55. George M. Kahin, *Nationalism and Revolution in Indonesia*, Ithaca: Cornell University Press, 1952, p. 86. See J. Th. Blumberger, *De Communistische Beweging in Nederlandsch-Indie*, Haarlem: Tjeen Willink, 1935, and Shelton Stromquist, 'The Communist Uprisings of 1926–1927 in Indonesia: A Re-Interpretation', *Journal of Southeast Asian History* 8, 2, 1967, 189–200.
56. For more on union activities see J. Ingleson, *In Search of Justice: Workers and Unions in Colonial Java*, Singapore: Oxford University Press, 1986.
57. Thompson, *Labour Problems*, p. 160.
58. Theda Skocpol, *States and Social Revolution: A Comparative Analysis of France, Russia, and China*, Cambridge: Cambridge University Press, 1979.

59. I realize that Malaysia did not go through a revolution to obtain formal independence. Nevertheless, what is crucial here is what we mean by the impact of peasants on state formation, whether this took place through a revolution or not.
60. Skocpol, *States and Social Revolutions*, pp. 66–7.
61. Ibid., p. 98.
62. Ibid., p. 114.
63. Ibid., p. 122.
64. Ibid., p. 137.
65. Ibid., p. 118.
66. Ibid., p. 203.
67. Ibid., p. 253.
68. Ibid., p. 264.
69. Ibid., p. 269.
70. Kahin, *Nationalism and Revolution*, pp. 300–1.
71. Ibid., p. 301.
72. B. Gunawan, 'Political Mobilization in Indonesia: Nationalists Against Communists', *Modern Asian Studies* 7, 4, 1973, 707–15: pp. 709–710.
73. Ibid., p. 712.
74. Ibid.
75. Ibid.
76. The reasons for this are explained later in the chapter, when the impact of capitalism on the peasantry is discussed.
77. Michael Adas, 'From Avoidance to Confrontation: Peasant Protest in Precolonial and Colonial Southeast Asia,' *Comparative Studies in Society and History* 23, 2, 1981, 217–47: p. 217. See also James C. Scott, *Weapons of the Weak: Everyday Forms of Peasant Resistance*, New Haven: Yale University Press, 1986; James C. Scott & Benedict J. Tria Kerkvliet, eds, *Everyday Forms of Peasant Resistance in Southeast Asia*, London: Frank Cass, 1986.
78. Mohd. Noordin Sopiee, 'The Penang Secession Movement, 1948–1951', *Journal of Southeast Asian Studies* 4, 1, 1973, 52–71.
79. Chandran Jeshurun, 'Government Responses to Armed Insurgency in Malaysia, 1957–82,' in idem, ed., *Governments and Rebellions in Southeast Asia*, Singapore: Institute of Southeast Asian Studies 1985, pp. 134–65: p. 136.
80. Ibid., p. 137.
81. For example, the Samin and Samat movements in Java. See The Siauw Giap, 'The Samin Movement in Java: Complementary Remarks', *Revue du Sud-est Asiatique* 1, 1961, 63–78; The, 'The Samin and Samat Movements in Java: Two examples of Peasant Resistance', *Revue du Sud-est Asiatique* 1, 1968, 107–14.
82. Justus M. van der Kroef, 'Separatist Movements in Indonesia', *Southeast Asian Spectrum* 4, 4, 1976, 9–19; Abdurrahman Wahid & Dorodjatun Kuntjoro-Jakti, 'Government Responses to Armed Communist and Separatist Movements in Indonesia: Islamic and Military Perspectives,' in Jeshurun, ed., *Governments and Rebellions*, pp. 166–79; S. Soebadi, 'Kartosuwiryo and the Darul Islam Rebellion in Indonesia', *Journal of Southeast Asian Studies* 14, 1, 1983, 109–33; R. J. May, 'Ethnic Sepa-

ratism in Southeast Asia', *Pacific Viewpoint* 31, 2, 1990, 28–59: pp. 28–43; Bilveer Singh, *East Timor, Indonesia and the World: Myths and Realities*, Singapore: Singapore Institute of International Affairs, 1995.

83. Ibid., p. 178.
84. Ibid., p. 173.
85. Ibid., pp. 174–6.
86. Lim, *Peasants and Their Agricultural Economy*, p. 234.
87. Ibid., pp. 112–13.
88. Ibid., p. 213.
89. Kahin, *Nationalism and Revolution*, pp. 18–19, 42.
90. Ibid., p. 18.
91. Clifford Geertz, *Agricultural Involution: The Process of Ecological Change in Indonesia*, Berkeley, Los Angeles, & London: University of California Press, 1963, p. 89.
92. Ibid., p. 97.
93. J. H. Boeke, *Structure of the Netherlands Indian Economy*, New York: Institute of Pacific Relations, 1942, p. 26.
94. Benjamin White, '"Agricultural Involution" and its Critics: Twenty Years After Clifford Geertz', Institute of Social Studies Working Paper Series 6, The Hague: Institute of Social Studies, 1983; Joel S. Kahn, 'Indonesia After the Demise of Involution: Critique of a Debate', *Critique of Anthropology* 5, 1, 1985, 69–96; Alec Gordon, 'Economic History versus "Agricultural Involution": Towards a Usable Past for Southeast Asia', in Peter Limqueco, ed., *Partisan Scholarship: Essays in Honour of Renato Constantino*, Manila & Wollongong: JCA Publishers, 1989, pp. 131–51; G. R. Knight, 'Capitalism and Commodity production in Java', in Hamza Alavi, P. L. Burns, G. R. Knight, P. B. Mayer, and Doug McEachern, *Capitalism and Colonial Production*, London & Sydney: Croom Helm, 1982, pp. 119–58.
95. Knight, 'Capitalism and Commodity production in Java', p. 120.
96. Ibid.
97. Svein Aas, 'The Relevance of Chayanov's Macro Theory to the Case of Java', in E. J. Hobsbawm *et al.*, eds, *Peasants in History: Essays in Honour of Daniel Thorner*, Calcutta: Oxford University Press, 1980, pp. 221–48: p. 238.
98. R. E. Elson, 'Sugard Factory Workers and the Emergence of "Free Labour" in Nineteenth-Century Java', *Modern Asian Studies* 20, 1, 1986, 139–74: p. 145. See also Elson, 'The Cultivation System and Agricultural Involution', Centre of Southeast Asian Studies Working Papers No. 14, Melbourne: Monash University, p. 29.
99. Ibid., p. 159.
100. Aas, 'The Relevance of Chayanov', pp. 238–9.
101. Elson, 'The Cultivation System', p. 24.
102. Jennifer Alexander & Paul Alexander, 'Shared Poverty as Ideology: Agrarian Relationships in Colonial Java', *Man* 17, 1982, 597–619.
103. Jeff Kingston, 'Agricultural Involution Among Lampung's Javanese?', *Southeast Asian Studies* 27, 4, 1990, 485–507.
104. Kahin, *Nationalism and Revolution*, p. 42.
105. Ravindra K. Jain, *South Indians on the Plantation Frontier in Malaya*,

186 *Notes*

New Haven & London: Yale University Press, 1970, p. 295.
106. J. A. Barnes, 'Foreword,' in Jain, *South Indians*, p. viii.
107. Kahun, *Nationalism and Revolution*, p. 93.
108. Clifford Geertz, *The Social History of an Indonesian Town,* Cambridge, MA: MIT Press, 1965, pp. 127ff.
109. W. F. Wertheim, 'From Aliran Toward Class Struggle in the Countryside of Java,' *Pacific Viewpoint* 10, 2, 1969, 1–17.
110. Ibid., p. 4.
111. Ibid., p. 6.
112. Ibid., p. 10.
113. Martin Rudner, 'Malayan Labor in Transition: Labor Policy and Trade Unionism, 1955–1963', *Modern Asian Studies* 7, 1, 1973, 21–45.
114. James C. Scott, *The Moral Economy of the Peasant: Rebellion and Subsistence in Southeast Asia*, New Haven & London: Yale University Press, 1976, pp. 57–8.
115. Kahin, *Nationalism and Revolution*, pp. 16, 18.
116. Scott, *Moral Economy*, p. 63.
117. Martin J. Murray, *The Development of Capitalism in Indochina (1870–1940)*, Berkeley, Los Angeles & London: University of California Press, 1980, p. 272.
118. Ibid., p. 276.
119. Ibid., p. 311.

Chapter 5

1. Hamid Algadri, *C. Snouck Hurgronje: Politik Belanda Terhadap Islam dan Keturunan Arab*, Jakarta: Penerbit Sinar Harapan, 1984, p. 31.
2. Robert van Niel, *The Emergence of the Modern Indonesian Elite*, The Hague: W. van Hoeve, 1970, p. 56.
3. Ibid., pp. 62–3.
4. Ibid., p. 65.
5. George M. Kahin, *Nationalism and Revolution in Indonesia*, Ithaca: Cornell University Press, 1952, pp. 65–6.
6. van Niel, *The Emergence*, pp. 88–90; Kahin, *Nationalism and Revolution*, p. 67.
7. van Niel, *The Emergence*, p. 94.
8. Ibid., p. 96.
9. Ibid., p. 117.
10. *Sarekat-Islam Congres (le Nationaal Congres)*, 17–24 Juni 1916 te Bandoeng, Behoort bij de Geheime Missive van den Wd. Adviseur voor Inlandsche Zaken dd. 29 September 1916 no. 226, Batavia: Landsdrukkerij, 1916, pp. 32, 36.
11. *Sarekat-Islam Congres (2e Nationaal Congres)*, 20–27 October 1917 te Batavia, Behoort bij de Geheime Missive van den Regeeringscommissaris voor Inlandsche en Arabische Zaken van 23 Augustus 1918 no. 416, Batavia: Landsdrukkerij, 1919, pp. 2–4.
12. Ibid., p. 13.
13. *Neratja*, no. 80, 25th October, 1917.
14. *Sarekat-Islam Congres (2e Nationaal Congres)*, p. 5.

15. De Roode, *Het Vrije Woord*, 10th November, 1917.
16. van Niel, *The Emergence*, p. 142.
17. Ibid., p. 152.
18. Ibid., pp. 152–3.
19. *Overzicht van de Gestie der Centraal Sarekat Islam in het jaar 1921*, Weltevreden: Landsdrukkerij, 1922, p. 11.
20. Kahin, *Nationalism and Revolution*, p. 77.
21. Ruth T. McVey, *The Rise of Indonesian Communism*, Ithaca: Cornell University Press, 1965, pp. 14–15.
22. Ibid., p. 15.
23. Adolf Baars, 'Het S.I-Congres te Bandung,' *Het Vrije Woord*, 25th June, 1916.
24. Kahin, *Nationalism and Revolution*, p. 87.
25. Ibid., p. 90.
26. Union of Indonesian National Political Associations (Permufakatan Perhimpunan Politik Kebangsaan Indonesia)
27. Ibid.
28. Ibid., pp. 92–3.
29. Ibid., p. 96.
30. Ibid., pp. 96–7.
31. Radin Soenarno, 'Malay Nationalism, 1896–1941,' *Journal of Southeast Asian History* 1, 1, 1960, 1–28: p. 6.
32. For a critical evaluation of Al-Hadi's thought, see Shaharuddin Maaruf, *Malay Ideas on Development: From Feudal Lord to Capitalist*, Singapore: Times Books International, 1988, chapter 4.
33. William R. Roff, *The Origins of Malay Nationalism*, New Haven & London: Yale University Press, 1967, p. 87.
34. Mahmoud el-Jounousij, 'Editorial,' *Seruan Azhar* 1, October, 1925. Cited in Roff, *The Origins*, p. 89.
35. Roff, *The Origins*, p. 89.
36. Soenarno, 'Malay Nationalism,' pp. 10–11.
37. Ibid., p. 11.
38. Ibid., p. 18.
39. Ibid., pp. 22–8.
40. Ibid., p. 23.
41. Ibid.
42. Ibid., pp. 23–4.
43. Ibid., p. 24.
44. Ibid.
45. Ibid., p. 26.
46. Kahin, *Nationalism and Revolution*, p. 103.
47. Ibid., p. 133.
48. Cheah Boon Kheng, *Red Star Over Malaya: Resistance and Social Conflict During and After the Japanese Occupation of Malaya, 1941–46*, Singapore: Singapore University Press, 1983, p. 29.
49. Kahin, *Nationalism and Revolution*, p. 104.
50. On the development of communism in Malaya see C. F. Young 'Origins and Development of the Malayan Communist Movement, 1919–1930', *Modern Asian Studies* 25, 4, 1991, 625–48.

51. Soenarno, 'Malay Nationalism,' p. 20.
52. Cheah, *Red Star*, pp. 50–1.
53. Kahin, *Nationalism and Revolution*, p. 106.
54. Ibid., p. 121.
55. Cheah, *Red Star*, p. 115.
56. Angus Mcintyre, 'The "Greater Indonesia" Idea of Nationalism in Malaya and Indonesia' *Modern Asian Studies* 7, 1, 1973, 75–83: p. 82.
57. Soenarno, 'Malay Nationalism,' p. 22.
58. M. C. Ricklefs, *A History of Modern Indonesia, c. 1300 to the Present*, Basingstoke: Macmillan, 1981, p. 159.
59. Ratnam, *Communalism*, p. 11.
60. See Anthony Reid, 'Nineteenth Century Pan Islamism in Indonesia and Malaysia', *Journal of Asian Studies* 26, 2, 1967, 276–83.
61. Regarded as the foremost institution of higher learning in the Muslim world.
61. Mcintyre, 'The "Greater Indonesia" Idea,' p. 76.
63. Ibid., p. 81.
64. Ibid., p. 80.
65. Ibid., pp. 82–3.
66. Saifuddin Anshari, *The Jakarta Charter of June 1945: The Struggle for an Islamic Constitution in Indonesia*, Kuala Lumpur: Muslim Youth Movement of Malaysia, 1979, p. 13.
67. Sukarno, *The Birth of Panca Sila: An Outline of the Five Principles of the Indonesian State*, Jakarta: The Ministry of Information, 1958, pp. 28–9.
68. Ibid., p. 29.
69. Ibid., p. 30.
70. Ratnam, *Communalism*, p. 20.
71. Ibid., p. 21.
72. Ibid., p. 22.
73. Ibid., p. 22.
74. Mohamed Noordin Sopiee, 'The Advocacy of Malaysia before 1961', *Modern Asian Studies* 7, 4, 1973, 717–32: p. 717.
75. *Straits Times*, 27 December 1955, cited in Sopiee, 'The Advocacy of Malaysia', p. 724.
76. Editorial, *Sunday Standard* 27 December 1955, cited in Sopiee, 'The Advocacy of Malaysia', p. 724.
77. *Malay Mail* 28 December 1955, cited in Sopiee, 'The Advocacy of Malaysia', p. 724.
78. S. Sjahrir, *Out of Exile*, New York: John Day, 1949, p. 112.
79. Cheah, *Red Star*, p. 121.
80. Ariffin Omar, *Bangsa Melayu: Malay Concepts of Democracy and Community 1945–1950*, Kuala Lumpur: Oxford University Press, 1993, ch. 6; Leslie Palmier, 'Indonesia's Rejection of Tradition', *Asian Affairs* 20, 2, 1989, 195–204.
81. Benedict R. O'G. Anderson, 'Old State, New Society: Indonesia's New Order in Comparative Historical Perspective', *Journal of Asian Studies* 42, 3, 1983, 477–96: p. 482.
82. Herbert Feith, *The Decline of Constitutional Democracy in Indonesia*, Ithaca: Cornell University Press, 1962, p. 44.

83. Christopher Chase-Dunn, *Global Formation: Structures of the World-Economy*, New York: Basil Blackwell, 1989, p. 113.
84. James V. Jesudason, *Ethnicity and the Economy: The State, Chinese Business, and Multinationals in Malaysia*, Singapore: Oxford University Press, 1989, pp. 56–60.
85. Pierre van der Eng. 'Marshall Aid as a Catalyst in the Decolonization of Indonesia, 1947–1949', *Journal of Southeast Asian Studies* 19, 2, 335–52.
86. Karl von Vorys, *Democracy Without Consensus: Communalism and Political Stability in Malaysia*, Princeton: Princeton University Press, 1975, p. 73.
87. Federation of Malaya, *Report of the Working Committee Appointed by a Conference of His Excellency, the Governor of the Malayan Union, Their Highnesses The Rulers of the Malay States and the Representatives of the United Malays National Organization*, Kuala Lumpur: Malayan Union Government Press, 1947.
88. Ibid., p. 23.
89. Charles Schumaker, 'The Formative Years of Malaysian Politics: The MCA and the Alliance,' unpublished manuscript cited in von Vorys, *Democracy Without Consensus*, p. 109.
90. von Vorys, *Democracy Without Consensus*, p. 111.
91. Minutes of the first National Convention held under the joint sponsorship of UMNO and MCA at Kuala Lumpur, August 23, 1953, cited in von Vorys, *Democracy Without Consensus*, pp. 112–13.
92. Karl Marx, *Manifesto of the Communist Party*, Peking: Foreign Languages Press, 1965, p. 35.
93. E. M. Wood, 'The Separation of the Economic and the Political in Capitalism,' *New Left Review* 127, 1981, 66–95: p. 89.
94. Haldun Gulalp, 'Capital Accumulation, Classes and the Relative Autonomy of the State,' *Science and Society* 51, 3, 1987, 287–313: p. 307.
95. K. J. Ratnam, *Communalism and the Political Process in Malaya*, Kuala Lumpur: University of Malaya Press, 1965, p. 22.
96. Ibid.
97. Ibid., p. 1.
98. Ibid., p. 160.
99. Ibid., p. 210.
100. By this time the Malayan Indian Congress had joined the Alliance.
101. Karl Marx, *The German Ideology*, New York: International Publishers, 1978, pp. 79–80.
102. For more details on the Indonesia struggle for independence see Kahin, *Nationalism and Revolution*; Anthony Reid, *The Indonesian National Revolution, 1945–1950*, Hawthorn, Victoria: Longman, 1974; C. Smit, *De Indonesische Quaestie*, Leiden: Brill, 1952; Alastair M. Taylor, *Indonesian Independence and the United Nations*, Ithaca: Cornell University Press, 1960.
103. Feith, *The Decline of Constitutional Democracy*, p. 9.
104. Kahin, *Nationalism and Revolution*, pp. 148–78.
105. Feith, *The Decline of Constitutional Democracy*, p. 10.
106. Ibid., pp. 10–11.
107. Ibid., p. 11.

190

Notes

108. Ibid., p. 12.
109. Ibid., pp. 12–13.
110. The BFO was the organization of federal states set up by the Dutch in the regions of Indonesia that they controlled during the revolution.
111. Ibid., pp. 13–14.
112. Ibid., p. 15.
113. Ibid.
114. W. F. Wertheim, *Indonesian Society in Transition: A Study of Social Change*, The Hague & Bundung: W. van Hoeve, Ltd., 1959, p. 321.
115. W. F. Wertheim, *Evolution and Revolution: The Rising Waves of Emancipation*, Harmondsworth, England: Penguin, 1974, p. 246.
116. For a discussion on the intellectual dependence of Indonesian nationalists on the West see Leslie Palmier, 'Indonesia's Rejection of Tradition', *Asian Affairs* 20, 2, 1989, 195–204.
117. Yoshihara Kunio, *The Rise of Ersatz Capitalism in Southeast Asia*, Singapore: Oxford University Press, 1988.
118. Edmund Terence Gomez, *Politics in Business: UMNO's Corporate Investments*, Kuala Lumpur: Forum, 1990, p. 29.
119. Edmund Terence Gomez, *Political Business: Corporate Involvement of Malaysian Political Parties*, Townsvile, Qld: Centre for Southeas Asian Studies, James Cook University of North Queensland, 1994, p. 39.
120. Jesudason, *Ethnicity and the Economy*, pp. 36–38.
121. Jomo, *A Question of Class*, pp. 266, 269.
122. Kunio, *The Rise of Ersatz Capitalism*, pp. 72–4.
123. Heng Pek Koon. 'The Chinese Business Elite of Malaysia', in Ruth McVey, Southeast Asian Capitalists, Ithaca: *Southeast Asian Capitalists*, Cornell University, 1992, p. 289.
124. Goh Cheng Teik, *The May Thirteenth Incident and Democracy in Malaysia*, Kuala Lumpur: Oxford University Press, 1971.
125. See Heng, *Chinese Politics in Malaysia*, for a review of the various election results since 1959.
126. Jesudason, *Ethnicity and the Economy*, ch. 5; Gomez, *Political Business*, pp. 39, 289–90.
127. Jesudason, *Ethinicity and the Economy*, p. 157.
128. For Feith, the revolution is the root of the weakness of the state vis-à-vis society. See Herb Feith, 'Constitutional Democracy: How Well Did it Function?', in David Bourchier & John Legge, eds, *Democracy in Indonesia: 1950s and 1990s*, Clayton, Victoria: Centre of Southeast Asian Studies, Monash University, 1994, pp. 16–25: p. 24.
129. Ulf Sundhaussen, 'Indonesia: Past and Present Encounters with Democracy', in Larry Diamond, Juan J. Linz & Seymour Martin Lipset, eds, *Volume 3, Democracy in Developing Countries: Asia*, Boulder: Lynne Rienner, 1989, pp. 423–74: p. 443.
130. Fachry Ali, 'The State and Types of Social Formation in Indonesia', in *Transnationalization of the State and Social Formation: The Indonesian Experience*, Working Papers of the United Nations University Asian Perspective Project (Southeast Asia), Quezon City, 1984, pp. 70–87: p. 74.
131. Robison, *Indonesia: The Rise of Capital*, pp. 11–12.

132. Yahya Muhaimin, 'Muslim Traders: The Stillborn Bourgeoisie', *Prisma* 49, 1990, 83–90.
133. Ibid., p. 21.
134. Ibid., pp. 21–2.
135. Ibid., p. 26.
136. J. A. C. Mackie, 'Anti-Chinese Outbreaks in Indonesia, 1969–68', in Mackie, ed., *The Chinese in Indonesia*, Hong Kong: Heinemann Educational Books, 1976, pp. 77–138.
137. W. F. Wertheim, *East-West Parallels: Sociological Approaches to Modern Asia*, The Hague: W. van Hoeve, 1964, pp. 76–7; The Siauw Giap, 'Group Conflict in a Plural Society', *Revue du Sudest Asiatique* no. 1, 1966, 1–31: p. 19.
138. Robison, *Indonesia: The Rise of Capital*, p. 29. See Charles A. Coppel, *Indonesian Chinese in Crisis*, Kuala Lumpur: Oxford University Press, 1983.
139. Mely G. Tan, 'The Ethnic Chinese in Indonesia: Issues and Implications', in Leo Suryadinata, ed., *Southeast Asian Chinese: The Socio-Cultural Dimension*, Singapore: Times Academic Press, 1995, pp. 13–27, pp. 16–17.
140. W. S. Chen, 'Masalah "Dominasi Ekonomi Indonesia oleh Golongan Tionghoa"' *Review of Indonesian and Malaysian Affairs* 21, 2, 1987, 82–93: p. 82.
141. Paul Rabe, 'Dutch Colonial Economic Policy toward the Etrhnic Chinese in Indonesia' *Journal of Southeast Asia Business* 8, 2, 1992, 41–57: pp. 55–6.
142. See Leo Suryadinata, *Pribumi Indonesians, the Chinese Minority and China*, Singapore: Heinemann Asia, 1986, ch. 6.
143. Statement of Imron Rosjadi, an NU parliamentarian. See *Ichtisar Parlemen*, 1957, 31, 293, cited in Ulf Sundhaussen, *The Road to Power: Indonesian Military Politics 1945–1967*, Kuala Lumpur: Oxford University Press, 1982, p. 124.
144. Sundhaussen, *Road to Power*, p. 125.
145. Anderson, 'Old State, New Society', pp. 482–3.
146. Donald K. Emmerson, 'The Bureaucracy in Context: Weakness in Strength', in Karl D. Jackson & Lucien W. Pye, eds, *Political Power and Communications in Indonesia*, Berkeley: University of California Press, 1978, pp. 82–136: p. 87.
147. Anderson, 'Old State, New Society', p. 483.
148. Y. A. Muhaimin, *Bisnis dan Politik: Kebijaksanaan Ekonomi Indonesia 1950–1980*, Jakarta: LP3ES, 1990, p. 1.
149. For more on corruption, kleptocracy and rent-seeking see S. Andreski, *Parasitism and Subversion: The Case of Latin America*, London: Weidenfeld & Nicolson, 1966; Andreski, 'Kleptocracy as a System of Government in Africa', in Arnold J. Heidenheimer, ed., *Political Corruption: Readings in Comparative Analysis*, New York: Reinhart & Winston, 1970, pp. 346–57; Syed Hussein Alatas, *The Problem of Corruption*, Singapore: Times Books International, 1986; Alatas, *Corruption: Its Nature, Causes and Functions*, Aldershot: Avebury, 1990; G. Ashoff, 'Rent-Seeking: A New Concept in the Economic Theory', *Economics* 40, 1989; D. Kuntjoro-Jakti, 'Pendekatan Politik Ekonomi (Political-Economy): Jembatan Di Antara Ilmu Ekonomi dan Ilmu Politik', *Jurnal Ilmu Politik* 8, 1990,

3–31; Syed Farid Alatas, 'The Post-Colonial State: Dual Functions in the Public Sphere', Department of Sociology Working Papers, No. 121, National University of Singapore, 1994.

Chapter 6

1. R. Robison, *Indonesia: The Rise of Capital*, Canberra: Asian Studies Association of Australia, 1986, p. 40.
2. R. Anspach, 'Indonesia,' in F. Golay, R. Anspach, R. Pfanner, and E. Ayal, eds, *Underdevelopment and Economic Nationalism in Southeast Asia*, Ithaca: Cornell University Press, 1969, pp. 111–201: pp. 171–9; Robison, *Indonesia*, pp. 44–5; J. Sutter, *Indonesianisasi: Politics in a Changing Economy, 1940–1955*, Ithaca: Department of Fareastern Studies, Cornell University, 1959, pp. 1017–35.
3. Robison, *Indonesia*, p. 45.
4. Ibid., p. 46.
5. Ibid., p. 47. Robison here refers to this means of capital accumulation as deriving from the 'patrimonial' aspect of Indonesian state power. Apart from using such an anachronistic term, it also draws attention away from the problem of kleptocracy at high levels of government. While corruption has been recognized as a problem, it has not become a field of study. More to the point, the phenomenon of corruption as a significant means of capital accumulation has not received due attention.
6. Robison, *Indonesia*, p. 48.
7. Ibid., p. 58.
8. H. Schmitt, 'Foreign Capital and Social Conflict in Indonesia,' *Economic Development and Cultural Change* 10, 3, 1962, 284–93: p. 289.
9. Robison, *Indonesia*, p. 61.
10. Herbert Feith, *The Decline of Constitutional Democracy In Indonesia*, Ithaca: Cornell University Press, 1962, p. 568.
11. Rex Mortimer, 'Class, Social Cleavage and Indonesian Communism,' *Indonesia* 8, 1969, 1–20: p. 8.
12. Ibid., p. 9.
13. Ibid., p. 12.
14. Ibid., p. 15.
15. Harold Crouch, *The Army and Politics in Indonesia*, Ithaca & London: Cornell University Press, 1978, pp. 29–30.
16. Ibid., p. 31.
17. Ibid., p. 33.
18. Robison, *Indonesia*, p. 62.
19. Herbert Feith, 'Dynamics of Guided Democracy,' in Ruth T. McVey, ed., *Indonesia*, New Haven: Southeast Asia Studies, Yale University, 1963, pp. 359–409: pp. 363–4.
20. Ibid., p. 373.
21. Jomo Kwame Sundaram, *A Question of Class: Capital, the State, and Uneven Development in Malaya*, Singapore: Oxford University Press, 1986, p. 221.
22. Ibid., P. J. Drake, *Financial Development in Malaysia and Singapore*, Canberra: Australian National University Press, 1969, p. 160.

23. Jomo, *A Question of Class*, p. 224.
24. Ibid., p. 223.
25. Ibid., p. 226.
26. J. H. Beaglehole, 'Malay Participation in Commerce and Industry: The Role of RIDA and MARA,' *Journal of Commonwealth Political Studies* 7, 3, 1969, 216–45: p. 221.
27. Jomo, *A Question of Class*, p. 248.
28. In 1963, the Federation of Malaya joined with the Borneo states of Sabah and Sarawak and with Singapore to become Malaysia. In 1965 Singapore was expelled from Malaysia over differences pertaining to the Alliance system of government, among other things.
29. Jomo, *A Question of Class*, p. 248.
30. The term *bumiputera* literally meaning 'prince of the earth' refers to indigenes or natives but also includes all those in Malaysia who are not of Malay stock, such as Arabs, but who are culturally Malays. It therefore excludes Chinese, Indians, Eurasians and Europeans. In Indonesia, the term with similar connotations is *pribumi*. For a discussion of these terms and their political and economic contexts, see Sharon Siddique & Leo Suryadinata, 'Bumiputera and Pribumi: Economic Nationalism (Indiginism) in Malaysia and Indonesia,' *Pacific Affairs* 54, 4, 1981–2, 663–87.
31. Kongress Ekonomi Bumiputera, *Kertas-kertas Kerja*, Kuala Lumpur: Jabatan Cetak Kerajaan, 1965, p. 105.
32. For figures on income inequality during this period see Ishak Shari & Rogayah M. Zain, 'Some Aspects of Income Inequality in Peninsular Malaysia 1957–70,' in H. T. Oshima & T. Mizoguchi, eds., *Income Distribution by Sector and Over Time in East and Southeast Asian Countries*, Manila: Council of Asian Manpower Studies, 1978; Donald R. Snodgrass, 'Trends and Patterns in Malaysian Income Distribution 1957–70,' in David Lim, ed., *Readings in Malaysian Economic Development*, Kuala Lumpur: Oxford University Press, 1975. For further discussions on income inequality see Parvez Hassan, 'Growth and Equity in East Asia,' *Finance and Development* June, 1978, 28–32; Geoffrey B. Hainsworth, 'Economic Growth and Poverty in Southeast Asia: Malaysia, Indonesia and the Philippines,' *Pacific Affairs*, 52, 1, 1979; Charles Hirschman, 'Economic Progress in Malaysia: How Widely Has It Been Shared?' *UMBC Review* 10, 1974, 35–44; Jomo Kwame Sundaram & Ishak Shari, 'Income Inequalities in Post-Colonial Peninsular Malaysia,' *Pacific Viewpoint* 23, 1, 1982, 67–76.
33. C. MacAndrews, 'The Politics of Planning: Malaysia and the New Third Malaysia Plan (1976–80),' *Asian Survey* 17, 3, 1977, 293–308: p. 295.
34. The left was not in party politics due to the CPM's involvement in guerrilla warfare before independence. Furthermore, the CPM had been considerably weakened through colonial repression, as discussed in Chapter 4.
35. G. S. Cheema, 'Malaysia's Development Strategy: The Dilemma of Redistribution With Growth,' *Studies in Comparative International Development* 13, 2, 1978, 40–55: p. 46.
36. Ibid.

37. For an analysis of the May 1969 events, see Goh Cheng Teik, *The May Thirteenth Incident and Democracy in Malaysia*, Kuala Lumpur: Oxford University Press, 1971.
38. S. H. Alatas, 'The Politics of Coalition in Malaysia,' *Current History* 63, 376, 1972, 271–7: p. 271.
39. Ibid.
40. Ibid., p. 273.
41. For more details on parliamentary representation see Herbert Feith, 'Dynamics of Guided Democracy,' p. 345.
42. Robison, *Indonesia*, p. 70.
43. K. Thomas & J. Panglaykim, *Indonesia – The Effects of Past Policies and President Suharto's Plans for the Future*, Melbourne: CEDA, 1973, pp. 56–9.
44. Robison, *Indonesia*, p. 75.
45. J. Panglaykim, *An Indonesian Experience: Its State Trading Corporations*, Jakarta: Fakultas Ekonomi, Universitas Indonesia, 1967, pp. 237–8.
46. Robison, *Indonesia*, p. 75.
47. L. Castles, 'The Fate of the Private Entrepeneur', in T. K. Tan, ed., *Sukarno's Guided Indonesia*, Brisbane: Jacaranda, 1967, pp. 73–88: p. 85.
48. Robison, *Indonesia*, p. 81.
49. Ibid., pp. 85, 97.
50. Ibid., p. 76. See pp. 76–9 for more on the reasons for the state's failure to establish capitalism.
51. Castles, 'The Fate of the Private Entrepreneur,' p. 77.
52. Robison, *Indonesia*, p. 78.
53. Herbert Feith, 'The Politics of Economic Decline,' in T. K. Tan, ed., *Sukarno's Guided Indonesia*, pp. 46–57: p. 54.
54. Donald Hindley, 'Alirans and the Fall of the Old Order,' *Indonesia* 9, 1970, 23–66: p. 33.
55. Ibid., p. 34. For other versions see W. F. Wertheim, 'Whose Plot? – New Light on the 1965 Events', *Journal of Contemporary Asia* 9, 2, 1979, 196–215; Coen Holtzappel, 'The 30 September Movement: A Political Movement or an Intelligence Operation?' *Journal of Contemporary Asia* 9, 2, 1979, 216–40; Harold Crouch, 'Another Look at the Indonesian "Coup"', *Indonesia* 15, 1973 1–20; Donald Hindley, 'Political Power and the October 1965 Coup in Indonesia', *Journal of Asian Studies* 26, 2, 1967, 237–50; Guy J. Pauker, 'The GESTAPU Affair of 1965: Reflections on the Politics of Instability in Indonesia', *Southeast Asia* 1, 1971, 43–56; Nugroho Notosusanto & Ismail Saleh, *Tragedi Nasional: Percobaan Kup G30S/PKI di Indonesia*, Jakarta: Intermasa, 1993; Arswendo Atmowiloto, *Pengkhianatan G30S/PKI*, Jakarta: Sinar Harapan, 1994; D. S. Moeljanto & Taufiq Ismail, *Prahara Budaya: Kilas-Balik Ofensif Lekra/PKI Dkk*, Bandung: Mizan, 1995.
    For an official account see Sekretariat Negara Republik Indonesia, *Gerakan 30 September: Pemberontakan Partai Komunis Indonesia – Latarbelakang, Aksi, dan Penumpasannya*, Jakarta, 1994.
56. Ibid., p. 36.
57. Ibid., p. 37.
58. Ibid., p. 53.

59. Onghokham, 'Elite dan Monopoli dalam Perspektif Sejarah', *Prisma* 14, 2, 1985, 3–13: p. 13.
60. Government of Malaysia, *The Second Malaysia Plan, 1971–1975*, Kuala Lumpur: Government Printer, 1971, p. 4.
61. Ibid.
62. Government of Malaysia, *Mid-term Review of the Second Malaysia Plan*, Kuala Lumpur: Government Printer, 1973, p. 81.
63. S. H. Alatas, *The Second Malaysia Plan 1971–1975: A Critique*, Occasional Paper No. 15, Singapore: Institute of Southeast Asian Studies, 1972, p. 9.
64. Jesudason, *Ethnicity and the Economy*, pp. 147ff; Jomo, *A Question of Class*, pp. 269–70.
65. Heng Pek Koon, 'The Chinese Business Elite of Malaysia', in Ruth McVey, *Southeast Asian Capitalists*, Ithaca: Southeast Asian Program, Cornell University, 1992, pp. 127–44.
66. Lim Mah Hui & Douglas V. Porpora, 'Capitalism and Democracy in Malaysia,' *Southeast Asian Journal of Social Science* 16, 1, 1988, 92–106: 105.
67. Judith Nagata, *The Reflowering of Malaysian Islam: Modern Religious Radicals and Their Roots*, Vancouver: University of British Columbia Press, 1984, p. 230.
68. Ibid.
69. Shamsul Amri Baharuddin, 'A Revival in the Study of Islam in Malaysia,' *Man* 18, 2, 1983, 399–404: p. 401.
70. John Higley, Ursula Hoffman-Lange, Charles Kadushin & Gwen Moore, 'Elite Integrations in Stable Democracies: A Reconsideration', *European Sociological Review* 7, 1, 1991, 35–53.
71. R. A. Dahl, *Who Governs?* New Haven: Yale University Press, 1961; N. W. Polsby, *Community Power and Political Theory*, New Haven: Yale University Press, 1980.
72. C. Wright Mills, *The Power Elite*, New York: Oxford University Press, 1956.
73. Ralph Miliband, *The State in Capitalist Society*, New York: Basic, 1969; G. William Domhoff, *Who Rules America Now? A View for the Eighties*, Englewood Cliffs: Prentice-Hall, 1983.
74. Higley *et al.*, 'Elite Integration', p. 35.
75. A. Lijphart, 'Consociational Democracy', *World Politics* 21, 1969, 207–25; L. G. Field & J. Higley, *Elites and Non-Elites: The Possibilities and Their Side Effects*, Andover, MA: Warner Modular Publications, 1973; L. G. Field & J. Higley, *Elitism*, Boston: Routledge & Kegan Paul, 1980; L. G. Field & J. Higley, 'National Elites and Political Stability', in G. Moore, ed., *Research in Politics and Society: Studies of the Structure of National Elite Groups (vol. 1)*, Greenwich, CT: JAI Press, 1985, pp. 1–44; J. Higley & Michael G. Burton, 'The Elite Variable in Democratic Transitions and Breakdowns', *American Sociological Review* 54, 1, 1989, 17–32; R. D. Putnam, *The Comparative Study of Political Elites*, Englewood Cliffs: Prentice-Hall, 1976.
76. Michael G. Burton & J. Higley, 'Elite Settlements', *American Sociological Review* 1, 2, 1987, 295–307.

77. Herbert Feith, *The Decline of Constitutional Democracy in Indonesia*, Ithaca: Cornell University Press, 1962, pp. 24–5. For a shortened version see Feith, 'Dynamics of Guided Democracy', in Ruth T. McVey, ed., *Indonesia*, New Haven: Southeast Asia Studies, Yale University, 1967, pp. 309–409.

78. Hans O. Schmitt, 'Post-Colonial Politics: A Suggested Interpretation of the Indonesia Experience, 1950–1958', *Australian Journal of Politics and History* 9, 2, 1963, 176–83: p. 181.

79. George M. Kahin, 'Indonesia', in Kahin, ed., *Major Governments of Asia*, Ithaca: Cornell University Press, 1963, pp. 535–700: p. 629.

80. Goh Cheng Teik, 'Why Indonesia's Attempt at Democracy in the Mid-1950s failed', *Modern Asian Studies* 6, 2, 1972, 225–44: p. 241.

81. Herb Feith, 'Constitutional Democracy: How Well Did it Function?', in David Bourchier & John Legge, eds, *Democracy in Indonesia: 1950s and 1990s*, Clayton, Victoria: Centre of Southeast Asian Studies, Monash University, 1994, pp. 16–25: p. 22.

82. Goh, 'Indonesia's Attempt at Democracy', pp. 242–4.

83. Feith, 'Constitutional Democracy', pp. 23–4.

84. Michael Leifer, *Dilemmas of Statehood in Southeast Asia*, Singapore: Asia Pacific Press, 1972, p. 89; Edi Quiko, 'The Rise and Fall of Sukarno: A Brief Analysis of Indonesia's Political Development, 1949–1965', *Asian Profile* 5, 5, 1977, 463–74: p. 464; Alfian, *Politik, Kebudayaan dan Manusia Indonesia*, Jakarta: LP3ES, 1980, p. 139; Richard Robison, 'Indonesia: Tensions in State and Regime', in Kevin Hewison, Richard Robison, Gary Rodan, ed., *Southeast Asia in the 1990s: Authoritarianism, Democracy and Capitalism*, St. Leonard, NSW: Allen & Unwin, 1993, pp. 41–74: p. 43; Donald Hindley, 'Alirans and the Fall of the Old Order', *Indonesia* 9, 1970, 23–65;

85. David Brown, *The State and Ethnic Politics in Southeast Asia*, London: Routledge, 1994, p. 121.

86. Brown, *The State and Ethnic Politics*, p. 122.

87. Brown, *The State and Ethnic Politics*, pp. 122–3.

88. J. Eliseo Rocamora, *Nationalism in Search of Ideology: The Indonesian Nationalist Party, 1946–1965*, Quezon City: Philippine Centre for Advanced Studies, University of the Philippines, 1975, p. 236.

89. Roeslan Abdulgani, *Nationalism, Revolution and Guided Democracy in Indonesia: Four Lectures by Roeslan Abdulgani*, Clayton: Centre of Southeast Asian Studies, Monash University, 1973, p. 44.

90. Jamie Mackie, 'Inevitable or Avoidable: Interpretations of the Collapse of Parliamentary Democracy', in David Bourchier & John Legge, eds., *Democracy in Indonesia: 1950s and 1990s*, Clayton, Victoria: Centre of Southeast Asian Studies, Monash University, 1994, pp. 26–38: p. 30.

91. J. D. Legge, *Indonesia*, Englewood Cliffs: Prentice-Hall, 1965, pp. 143–4.

92. Ernst Utrecht, 'Army and Opposition in Indonesia', *Journal of Contemporary Asia* 9, 2, 1979, 175–86.

93. N. G. Schulte Nordholt, 'State-Citizen Relations in Suharto's Indonesia: Kawula-Gusti', CASP 16, Comparative Asian Studies Programme (CASP), Erasmus University, 1987, p. 32.

94. Bilveer Singh, *Dwifungsi ABRI: The Dual Function of the Indonesian Armed Forces*, Singapore: Singapore Institute of International Affairs, 1995, pp. 39–40.
95. Marvin L. Rogers, 'Depoliticization of Indonesia's Political Parties: Attaining Military Stability', *Armed Forces and Society* 14, 2, 1988, 247–72: p. 250.
96. Rogers, 'Depoliticization', p. 251.
97. For an account of the development and actualization of the *dwifungsi* principle from the liberal democracy to the New Order period see Bilveer Singh, *Dwifungsi ABRI*, pp. 69–95.
98. Chandra Muzaffar, *Freedom in Fetters: An Analysis of the State of Democracy in Malaysia*, Penang: Aliran, 1986, p. 322.
99. *Straits Times*, 14 May 1969.
100. Goh, *May Thirteenth*, p. 28–9.
101. *Straits Times*, 31 May 1969.
102. Tunku Abdul Rahman Putra Al-Haj, *May 13: Before and After*, Kuala Lumpur: Utusan Melayu Press, 1969, p. 140; Goh, *May Thirteenth*, p. 30; *Utusan Melayu*, 6 & 7 June 1969.
103. *Utusan Zaman*, 20 July 1969.
104. See Syed Hussein Alatas, 'The Politics of Coalition in Malaysia'.
105. Goh, *May Thirteenth*, p. 27.
106. Zakaria Haji Ahmad, 'Malaysia', in Zakaria Haji Ahmad & Harold Crouch, eds., *Military-Civilian Relations in Southeast Asia*, Singapore: Oxford University Press, 1985, pp. 118–35: p. 122.
107. Chin Kim Wah, *The Defense of Malaysia and Singapore: The Transformation of a Security System 1957–1971*, Cambridge: Cambridge University Press, 1983, p. 24.
108. Zakaria, 'Malaysia', p. 123.
109. Zakaria, 'Malaysia', pp. 119, 121.

Chapter 7

1. See Chapter 1, pp. 35–44.
2. For more on these methods see Victoria Bonnell, 'The Uses of Theory, Concepts and Comparison in Historical Sociology', *Comparative Studies in Society and History* 22, 2, 1980, 156–73; Theda Skocpol & Margaret Somers, 'The Uses of Comparative History in Macrosocial Inquiry', *Comparative Studies in Society and History* 22, 2, 1980, 174–97; Dietrich Rueschemeyer, 'Different Methods – Contradictory Results? Research on Development and Democracy', *International Journal of Comparative Sociology* 32, 1–2, 1991, 9–38.
3. Christopher Chase-Dunn, *Global Formation: Structures of the World Economy*, Cambridge, MA: Basil Blackwell, 1989, pp. 123–30.
4. Guillermo O'Donnell, 'Reflections on the Patterns of Change in the Bureaucratic–Authoritarian State,' *Latin American Research Review* 13, 3–38, 1978; O'Donnell, 'Tensions in the Bureaucratic–Authoritarian State and the Question of Democracy,' in David Collier, ed., *The New Authoritarianism in Latin America*, Princeton: Princeton University Press, 1979, pp. 285–318.

5. Clive Y. Thomas, *The Rise of the Authoritarian State in Peripheral Societies*, New York & London: Monthly Review Press, 1984.

6. Richard Robison, 'Democratisation: The Middle Class Moves into Politics, *Inside Indonesia* October 1989, pp. 12–13.

7. J. Soedjati Djiwandono, 'Indonesia in 1988: Progress in Democratic Experiment?' *Indonesian Quarterly* 17, 4, 1989, 335–49: p. 335.

8. Max Lane, 'On the Verge of a Return to Mass Politics', *Inside Indonesia* June 1992, pp. 6–8.

9. Anders Uhlin, 'Transnational Democratic Diffusion and Indonesian Democracy Discourses', *Third World Quarterly* 14, 3, 1993, 517–44.

10. Riwanto Tirtosudarmo, 'Indonesia 1991: Quest for Democracy in a Turbulent Year', *Southeast Asian Affairs* 1992, 123–39: 128–9. For other groups, NGOs and activists see Uhlin, 'Transnational Democratic Diffusion'.

11. R. Eep Saefulloh Fatah, 'Dwi Fungsi ABRI dan Demokratisasi: Retrospeksi dan Prospeksi Peranan Politik Militerdi Masa Orde Baru', *Cendekia Muda* 1, 1, 1993: p. 16.

12. 'Postscriptum', *Suara Pembaruan*, 3 January 1990, p. 3. See also Ian Chalmers' comment on this in 'Indonesia 1990: Democratization and Social Forces', *Southeast Asian Affairs* 1991, 107–21.

13. 'ABRI in the 90s takes a political back seat: Ma'ruf', *Jakarta Post*, 17 February 1995.

14. J. Soedjati Djiwandono, 'Democratic Experiment in Indonesia: Between Achievements and Expectations', *Indonesian Quarterly* 15, 4, 1987, 661–9: p. 667.

15. Syed Farid Alatas, 'Keterbukaan Media di Indonesia', *Negarawan* October–November 1995.

16. For a chronology of this and related events see *Gatra* August 3, 1996, pp. 23, 27.

17. *Straits Times* September 20, 1996.

18. Ibid.

19. Ibid.

20. Al Chaidar, 'Prospek Pembangunan Politik Indonesia: Involusi Politik', *Cendekia Muda* 1, 1, 1993, 44–55: p. 55.

21. James V. Jesudason, 'Statist Democracy and the Limits to Civil Society in Malaysia', *Journal of Commonwealth and Comparative Politics* 33, 3, 1995, 335–56; William Case, 'Semi-Democracy in Malaysia: Withstanding the Pressures for Regime Change', *Pacific Affairs* 66, 2, 1993, 183–205.

22. S. Sothi Rachagan, *Law and the Electrocal Process in Malaysia*, Kuala Lumpur: University of Malaya Press, 1993, chap. 3.

23. Johan Saravanamuttu, 'Authoritarian Statism and Strategies for Democratisation: Malaysia in the 1980s', in Peter Limqueco, ed., *Partisan Scholarship: Essays in Honour of Renato Constantino*, Manila & Wollongong, JCA Publishers, 1989, pp. 233–51.

24. Zainur Zakaria, 'The 1994 Constitutional Amendments: The End of Judicial Independence', *Aliran Monthly* 14, 5, 1994, 10–11.

25. R. William Liddle, 'Can All Good Things Go Together? Democracy, Growth, and Unity in post-Suharto Indonesia', in David Bourchier & John Legge, eds, *Democracy in Indonesia: 1950s and 1990s*, Monash Papers on Southeast

Asia No. 31. Melbourne: Centre of Southeast Asian Studies, Monash University, 1994, pp. 287–301: p. 290.

26. Liddle, 'Can All Good Things Go Together?' p. 291.

27. Harold Crouch, 'Democratic Prospects in Indonesia', in David Bourchier & John Legge, eds, *Democracy in Indonesia: 1950s and 1990s*, Monash Papers on Southeast Asia No. 31. Melbourne: Centre of Southeast Asian Studies, Monash University, 1994, pp. 115–27: 121–2.

28. Harold Crouch, *Patrimonialism and Military Rule in Indonesia*, World Politics 31, 4, 1979, 571–87: pp. 576–7.

29. Ibid., p. 579.

30. Crouch, 'Democratic Prospects in Indonesia', p. 122.

31. Ibid.

32. H. Feith, 'Suharto's Search for a Format', *Australia's Neighbours* 56–57, 1968; B. R. O'G. Anderson, 'The Last Days of Indonesia's Suharto?' *Southeast Asia Chronicle* 63, 1978; H. Crouch, *The Army and Politics in Indonesia*, Ithaca: Cornell University Press, 1978.

33. Crouch, 'Democratic prospects in Indonesia', p. 120.

34. Paul Jacob, 'Hartono fires a salvo to back Suharto's election', *Straits Times* 21 April 1996.

35. Michael R. J. Vatikiotis, *Indonesian Politics Under Suharto: Order, Development and Pressure for Change*, London: Routledge, 1993, p. 203.

36. Philip J. Eldridge, *Non-Government Organizations and Democratic Participation in Indonesia*, Kuala Lumpur: Oxford University Press, 1995, p. 219.

37. Andra L. Corrothers & Estie W. Suryatna, 'Review of the NGO Sector in Indonesia and Evolution of the Asia Pacific Regional Community Concept among Indonesian NGOs', in Tadashi Yamamoto, ed., *Emerging Civil Society in the Asia Pacific Community: Nongovernmental Underpinnings of the Emerging Asia Pacific Regional Community*, Singapore: Institute of Southeast Asian Studies, 1995, pp. 121–41: p. 127.

38. Lim Teck Ghee, 'Nongovernmental Organizations in Malaysia and Regional Networking', in Tadashi Yamamoto, ed., *Emerging Civil Society in the Asia Pacific Community: Nongovernmental Underpinnings of the Emerging Asia Pacific Regional Community*, Singapore: Institute of Southeast Asian Studies, 1995, pp. 165–81: pp. 166–7.

39. 'KL govt acts to curb increase in NGOs', *Straits Times* February 4, 1995.

40. David Martin Jones, 'Asia's Rising Middle Class', *The National Interest* 38, 1994–5, 46–50: p. 47.

41. John Girling, 'Development and Democracy in Southeast Asia', *Pacific Review* 1, 4, 1988, 332–40: p. 336.

Bibliography

Aas, Svein. 'The Relevance of Chayanov's Macro Theory to the Case of Java', in E.J. Hobsbawm *et al.*, eds, *Peasants in History: Essays in Honour of Daniel Thorner*, Calcutta: Oxford University Press, 1980, pp. 221–8.

Abdulgani, Roeslan. *Nationalism, Revolution and Guided Democracy in Indonesia: Four Lectures by Roeslan Abdulgani*, Clayton: Centre of Southeast Asian Studies, Monash University, 1973.

Abrahamian, Ervand, 'Oriental Despotism: The Case of Qajar Iran,' *International Journal of Middle East Studies* 5, 1974, 3–31.

Adas, Michael. 'From Avoidance to Confrontation: Peasant Protest in Precolonial and Colonial Southeast Asia,' *Comparative Studies in Society and History* 23, 2, 1981, 217–47.

Akat, Asaf Savas. 'Proposal for a Radical Reinterpretation of the Asiatic Versus the European Social Formation', in Anouar Abdel Malek, ed., *The Civilization Project: The Visions of the Orient*, Mexico City: El Colegio de Mexico, 1981, pp. 69–79.

Akhmadi, Heri. 'Military-Bureaucratic Political Machinery in Indonesia,' *New Asian Visions* 5, 1, 1988, 64–73.

Alatas, Syed Farid. 'Notes on Various Theories Regarding the Islamization of the Malay Archipelago', *Muslim World* 75, 3–4, 1985, 162–75.

Alatas, Syed Farid. 'Theoretical Perspectives on the Role of State Elites in Southeast Asian Development', *Contemporary Southeast Asia* 14, 4, 1993, 368–95.

Alatas, Syed Farid. 'The Post Colonial State: Dual Functions in the Public Sphere', Department of Sociology Working Papers, No. 121, National University of Singapore, 1994.

Alatas, Syed Farid. 'Keterbukaan Media di Indonesia', *Negarawan* October–November 1995.

Alatas, Syed Hussein. 'The Politics of Coalition in Malaysia', *Current History* 63, 376, 1972, 271–7.

Alatas, Syed Hussein. *The Second Malaysia Plan 1971–1975: A Critique*, Occasional Paper No. 15, Singapore: Institute of Southeast Asian Studies, 1972.

Alatas, Syed Hussein. *The Myth of the Lazy Native*, London: Frank Cass, 1977.

Alatas, Syed Hussein. *The Problem of Corruption: Its Nature, Causes and Functions*, Aldershot: Averby, 1990.

Al-Attas, Syed M. Naguib. *Preliminary Statement on a General Theory of the Islamization of the Malay–Indonesian Archipelago*, Kuala Lumpur: Dewan Bahasa dan Pustaka, 1969.

Al-Attas, Syed M. Naguib. *Islam dalam Serjarah dan Kebudayaan Melayu*, Kuala Lumpur: Penerbit University Kebangsaan Malaysia, 1972.

Alavi, Hamza. 'Peasants and Revolution', *The Socialist Register*, London, Merlin, 1965, pp. 241–77.

Alavi, Hamza. 'The State in Post-Colonial Societies: Pakistan and Bangladesh', *New Left Review* 74, 1972, 59–81. .

Alavi, Hamza. 'India and the Colonial Mode of Production', *Economic and Political Weekly* 10, 33–5 (special issue), 1975, 1235–62.

Alavi, Hamza. 'State and Classes Under Peripheral Capitalism', in Hamza Alavi & Teodor Shanin, eds., *Introduction to the Sociology of Developing Societies*, London: Macmillan Educational Ltd., 1982, pp. 289–307.

Alexander, Jennifer & Paul Alexander. 'Shared Poverty as Ideology: Agrarian Relationships in Colonial Java', *Man* 17, 1982, 597–619.

Alfian. *Politik, Kebudayaan dan Manusia Indonesia*, Jakarta: LP3ES, 1980.

Alfian, *Masalah dan Prospek Pembangunan Politik di Indonesia: Kumpulan Karangan*, Jakarta: Gramedia, 1990.

Ali, Fachry. 'The State and Types of Social Formation in Indonesia', in *Transnationalization of the State and Social Formation: The Indonesian Experience*, Working Papers of the United Nations University Asian Perspective Project (Southeast Asia), Quezon City, 1984, pp. 70–87.

Allen, G. C. & A. G. Donnithorne. *Western Enterprise in Indonesia and Malaya: A Study in Economic Development*, New York: The Macmillan Company.

Almond, Gabriel A. 'Comparative Political Systems', *Journal of Politics* 18, 1956, 391–409.

Almond, Gabriel A. 'Introduction: A Functional Approach to Comparative Politics', in Almond & James S. Coleman, eds, *The Politics of Developing Areas*, Princeton University Press, 1960, pp. 3–64.

Almond, Gabriel A. 'Development Approach to Political Systems', *World Politics* 17, 1965, 183–214.

Almond, Gabriel A. & G. Bingham Powell, Jr., *Comparative Politics: A Developmental Approach*, Boston: Little Brown, 1966.

Amin, S. M. *Indonesia di Bawah Rezim Demokrasi Terpimpin*, Jakarta: Bulan Bintang, 1967.

Amin, Samir. *Unequal Development: An Essay on the Social Formations of Peripheral Capitalism*, Sussex: Harvester Press, 1976.

Amirahmadi, Hooshang. 'The Non-Capitalist Way of Development,' *Review of Radical Political Economics* 19, 1, 1987, 22–46.

Anderson, B. R. O'G. 'The Last Days of Indonesia's Suharto?' *Southeast Asia Chronicle* 63, 1978.

Anderson, Benedict R. O'G. 'Old State, New Society: Indonesia's New Order in Comparative Historical Perspective', *Journal of Asian Studies* 42, 3, 1983, 477–96.

Anderson, Benedict & Audrey Kahin, eds., *Interpreting Indonesian Politics: Thirteen Contributions to the Debate*, Ithaca, NY: Cornell Modern Indonesia Project, Southeast Asia Program, Cornell University, 1982.

Andreski, S. *Parasitism and Subversion: The Case of Latin America*, London: Weidenfeld & Nicolson, 1966.

Andreski, S. 'Kleptocracy as a System of Government in Africa', in Arnold J. Heidenheimer, ed., *Political Corruption: Readings in Comparative Analysis*, New York: Reinhart Winston, 1970, pp. 346–57.

Anshari, Saifuddin. *The Jakarta Charter of June 1945: The Struggle for an Islamic Constitution in Indonesia*, Kuala Lumpur: Muslim Youth Movement of Malaysia, 1979

Anspach, R. 'Indonesia', in F. Golay, R. Anspach, R. Pfanner, and E. Ayal, eds, *Underdevelopment and Economic Nationalism in Southeast Asia*, Ithaca: Cornell University Press, 1969, pp. 111–201.

Appelbaum, Richard P. & Jeffry Henderson, eds, *States and Development in the Asian Pacific Rim*, Newbury Park: Sage, 1992.

Apter, David E. *The Politics of Modernization*, Chicago: University of Chicago Press, 1965.

Apter, David E. & Charles Andrain, 'Comparative Government: Developing New Nations,' *Journal of Politics* 30, 2, 1968, 372–416.

Ariffin Omar. *Bangsa Melayu: Malay Concepts of Democracy and Community 1945–1950*, Kuala Lumpur: Oxford University Press, 1993.

Aron, Raymond. *Democracy and Totalitarianism*, London: Weidenfeld & Nicholson, 1968.

Asad, Talal & Harold Wolpe, 'Concepts of Modes of Production,' *Economy and Society* 5, 4, 1976, 470–506.

Ashoff, G. 'Rent-Seeking: A New Concept in the Economic Theory', *Economics* 40, 1989.

Atmowiloto, Arswendo. *Pengkhianatan G30S/PKI*, Jakarta: Sinar Harapan, 1994.

Bakker, J. I. 'Class Relations in Java in the Nineteenth Century: A Weberian Perspective', *Canadian Journal of Development Studies* 8, 1, 1987, 137–56.

Bakker, J. I. 'Patrimonialism, Involution, and the Agrarian Question in Java: A Weberian Analysis of class Relations and Service Labour', in John Gledhill, Barbara Bender, and Mogens Trolle Larsen, eds, *State and Society: The Emergence and Development of Social Hierarchy and Political Centralization*, London: Unwin Hyman, 1988, pp. 279–99.

Barbu, Zevedie. *Democracy and Dictatorship: Their Psychology and Patterns of Life*, London: Routledge & Kegan Paul, 1956.

Barnes, J. A. 'Foreword,' in Ravindra K. Jain, *South Indians on the Plantation Frontier in Malaya*, New Haven & London: Yale University Press, 1970.

Beaglehole, J. H. 'Malay Participation in Commerce and Industry: The Role of RIDA and MARA,' *Journal of Commonwealth Political Studies* 7, 3, 1969, 216–45.

Bedlington, S. S. *Malaysia and Singapore: The Building of New States*, Ithaca: Cornell University Press, 1978.

Benda, Harry J. 'The Structure of Southeast Asian History,' in Benda, *Continuity and Change in Southeast Asia: Collected Journal Articles of Harry J. Benda*, New Haven: Yale University Southeast Asia Studies, 1972, pp. 121–53.

Block, Fred. 'The Roles of the State in the Economy', in Neil J. Smelser & Richard Swedberg, eds, *The Handbook of Economic Sociology*, Princeton: Princeton University Press, 1994, pp. 691–710.

Blomstrom, Magnus & Bjorn Hettne. *Development Theory in Transition – The Dependency Debate and Beyond: Third World Responses*, London: Zed, 1985, p. 20.

Blumberger, J. Th. *De Communistische Beweging in Nederlandsch-Indie*, Haarlem: Tjeen Willink, 1935.

Boeke, J. H. *Structure of the Netherlands Indian Economy*, New York: Institute of Pacific Relations, 1942.

Boeke, J. H. *The Structure of Netherlands Indian Economy*, New York: Institute of Pacific Relations, 1946.

Boeke. *Economics and Economic Policy of Dual Societies: As Exemplified by*

Bibliography 203

Indonesia, New York: Institute of Pacific Relations, 1953.

Bollen, Kenneth. 'World System Position, Dependency, and Democracy: The Cross-National Evidence', *American Sociological Review* 48, 4, 1983, 468–79.

Bollen, Kenneth A. & Robert W. Jackman. 'Economic and Noneconomic Determinants of Political Democracy in the 1960s', *Research in Political Sociology* 1, 1985, 27–48.

Bonnell, Victoria. 'The Uses of Theory, Concepts, Comparison in Historical Sociology', *Comparative Studies in Society and History* 22, 2, 1980, 156–73.

Bornschier, Volker & Peter Heintz, eds, *Compendium of Data for World-System Analysis: A Sourcebook of Data Based on the Study of MNCs, Economic Policy and National Development*, Zurich: Soziologisches Institut de Universitat Zurich, n.d.

Bornschier, Volker, Christopher Chase-Dunn, & Richard Rubinson. 'Cross-National Evidence of the Effects of Foreign Investment and Aid on Economic Growth and Inequality: A Survey of Findings and a Reanalysis' *American Journal of Sociology* 84, 3, 1978, 651–83.

Boron, Atilio. 'New Forms of Capitalist State in Latin America: An Exploration', *Race and Class* 20, 3, 1979, 263–76.

Bosch, M. 'Rol van de Staat in Indonesies Industrialisaties: Huidige Industriepolitiek Vol Tegenstrijdigheden,' *Indonesia Feiten en Meningen* 11, 5, 1986, 24–30.

Bottomore, Tom. *Dictionary of Marxist Thought*, Cambridge, MA: Harvard University Press, 1983.

Bronson, Bennet. 'Exchange at the Upstream and Downstream Ends: Notes Towards a Functional Model of the Coastal State in Southeast Asia', in Karl L. Hutterer, ed., *Economic Exchange and Social Interaction in Southeast Asia: Perspectives from Prehistory, History, and Ethnography*, Ann Arbor: University of Michigan Center for South and Southeast Asian Studies, 1978, pp. 39–52.

Brown, David. *The State and Ethnic Politics in Southeast Asia*. London: Routledge, 1994.

Brown, Richard H. & William T. Lin, eds., *Modernization in East Asia: Political, Economic and Social Perspectives*, Westport, CT: Praeger, 1992.

Budiardjo, Miriam. *Dasar-Dasar Ilmu Politik*, Jakarta: Gramedia, 1992.

Budiman, Arief. 'The Emergence of the Bureaucratic Capitalist State in Indonesia,' in Lim Teck Ghee, ed., *Reflections on Development in Southeast Asia*, Singapore: Institute of Southeast Asian Studies, 1988, pp. 110–28.

Bukharin, N. *Imperialism and World-Economy*, London: Merlin, 1972.

Bulkin, Farchan. 'Negara, Masyarakat dan Ekonomi', *Prisma* 8, 1984, 3–17.

Burger, D. H. 'Structuurveranderingen in de Javaanse Samenleving,' *Indonesie* 2&3, 1949/49 & 1949/50, 381–98 & 1–18, 101–23, 225–50, 347–50, 381–9, 5123–34.

Burns, P. L. 'Capitalism and the Malay States', in Hamza Alavi, P. L. Burns, G. R. Knight, P. B. Mayer, and Doug McEachern, *Capitalism and Colonial Production*, London & Sydney: Croom Helm, 1982, pp. 159–78.

Burton, Michael G. & J. Higley. 'Elite Settlements', *American Sociological Review* 1, 2, 1987, 295–307.

Butwell, Richard. *Southeast Asia: A Political Introduction*, New York: Praeger, 1975.

Canak, William L. 'The Peripheral State Debate: State Capitalist and Bureau-cratic – Authoritarian Regimes in Latin America', *Latin American Research Review* 19, 1, 1984, 3–36.

Cariño, L. V. *Bureaucratic Corruption in Asia: Causes, Consequences and Controls*, Quezon City: JMC Press & Manila: College of Public Adminis-tration, University of the Philippines, 1986.

Case, William. 'Semi-Democracy in Malaysia: Withstanding the Pressures for Regime Change', *Pacific Affairs* 66, 2, 1993, 183–205.

Castles, L. 'The Fate of the Private Entrepeneur', in T. K. Tan, ed., *Sukarno's Guided Indonesia*, Brisbane: Jacaranda, 1967, pp. 73–88.

Chai Hon-Chan. *The Development of British Malaya, 1986–1909*, Kuala Lumpur: Oxford University Press, 1964.

Chaidar, Al. 'Prospek Pembangunan Politik Indonesia: Involusi Politik' *Cendekia Muda* 1, 1, 1993, 44–55.

Chalmers, Ian. 'Indonesia 1990: Democratization and Social Forces', *Southeast Asian Affairs* 1991, 107–21.

Chan Heng Chee, 'Democracy: Evolution and Implementation – An Asian Perspective', in Robert Bartley, Chan Heng Chee, Samuel P. Huntington and Shijuro Ogata, *Democracy and Capitalism: Asian and American Per-spectives*, Singapore: Institute of Southeast Asian Studies, 1993, pp. 1–26.

Chandra Muzaffar, *Freedom in Fetters: An Analysis of the State of Democ-racy in Malaysia*, Penang: Aliran, 1984.

Chase-Dunn, Christopher. 'The Effects of International Economic Dependence on Development and Equality: A Cross-National Study', *American Socio-logical Review* 40, 6, 1975, 720–38.

Chase-Dunn, Christopher. *Global Formation: Structures of the World-Economy*, New York: Basil Blackwell, 1989.

Cheah Boon Kheng. *Red Star Over Malaya: Resistance and Social Conflict During and After the Japanese Occupation of Malaya, 1941–46*, Singapore University Press. 1983.

Cheema, G. S. 'Malaysia's Development Srategy: The Dilemma of Redistri-bution With Growth,' *Studies in Comparative International Development* 13, 2, 1978, 40–55.

Chen, W. S. 'Masalah "Dominasi Ekonomi Indonesia oleh Golongan Tionghoa"', *Review of Indonesian and Malaysian Affairs* 21, 2, 1987, 82–93.

Chin Kim Wah. *The Defense of Malaysia and Singapore: The Transformation of a Security System 1957–1971*, Cambridge: Cambridge University Press, 1983.

Chua Beng Huat. 'Looking for Democratization in Post-Soeharto Indonesia', *Contemporary Southeast Asia* 15, 2, 1993, 131–60.

Chua, Beng-Huat. *Communitarian Ideology and Democracy in Singapore*, London: Routledge, 1995.

Coppel, Charles A. *Indonesian Chinese in Crisis*, Kuala Lumpur: Oxford University Press, 1983.

Corrothers, Andra L. & Estie W. Suryatna. 'Review of the NGO Sector in Indonesia and Evolution of the Asia Pacific Regional Community Concept among Indonesian NGOs', in Tadashi Yamamoto, ed., *Emerging Civil Soci-ety in the Asia Pacific Community: Nongovernmental Underpinnings of the Emerging Asia Pacific Regional Community*, Singapore: Institute of South-east Asian Studies, 1995, pp. 121–41.

Cotton, James. 'From Authoritarianism to Democracy in South Korea', *Political Studies* 37, 1989, 244–59.

Cotton, James. 'The Limits to Liberalization in Industrializing Asia: Three Views of the State', *Pacific Affairs* 64, 3, 1991, 311–27.

Cotton, James. 'The State in the Asian NICs', *Asian Perspective* 18, 1, 1994, 39–56.

Cowan, C.D. *Nineteeth-Century Malaya: The Origins of British Political Control*, London: Oxford University Press, 1961.

Creppell, Ingrid. 'Democracy and Literacy: The Role of Culture in Political Life', *European Journal of Sociology* 30, 1989, 22–47.

Crouch, Harold. 'Another Look at the Indonesian "Coup"', *Indonesia* 15, 1973, 1–20.

Crouch, Harold. *The Army and Politics in Indonesia*, Ithaca: Cornell University Press 1978.

Crouch, Harold. *Patrimonialism and Military Rule in Indonesia, World Politics* 31, 4, 1979, 571–87.

Crouch, Harold. 'Authoritarian Trends, the UMNO Split and the Limits to State Power,' in Joel Kahn & Francis Loh, eds, *Fragmented Vision: Culture and Politics in Contemporary Malaysia*, Sydney: Allen & Unwin, 1992, pp. 21–43.

Crouch, Harold. 'Malaysia: Neither Authoritarian Nor Democratic,' in Kevin Hewison, Richard Robison, & Garry Rodan, eds, *Southeast Asia in the 1990s: Authoritarianism, Democracy and Capitalism*, St Leonard, NSW: Allen & Unwin, 1993, pp. 135–57.

Crouch, Harold. 'Democratic Prospects in Indonesia', in David Bourchier & John Legge, eds, *Democracy in Indonesia: 1950s and 1990s*, Monash Papers on Southeast Asia no. 31. Melbourne: Centre of Southeast Asian Studies, Monash University, 1994, pp. 115–27.

Cutright, Phillip. 'National Political Development: Measurement and Analysis,' *American Sociological Review* 28, 2, 1963, 253–64.

Dahl, Robert A. *A Preface to Democratic Theory*, Chicago: University of Chicago Press, 1956.

Dahl, R. A. *Who Governs?* New Haven: Yale University Press, 1961.

Darling, Frank C. *The Westernization of Asia: A Comparative Political Analysis*, Boston: G. K. Hall & Co. & Cambridge: Schenkman Publishing Co., 1979.

Department of Information, Republic of Indonesia. *The Process and Progress of Pancasila Democracy*, Jakarta: 1991/1992.

Deutsch, Karl W. 'Social Mobilization and Political Development', *American Political Science Review* 55, 3, 1961, 473–514.

Deyo, Frederic C. ed., *The Political Economy of the New Asian Industrialism*, Ithaca: Cornell University Press, 1987.

Dhakidae, Daniel. 'Partai Politik dan Sistem Kepartaian di Indonesia', *Prisma* 10, 12, 1981, 3–23.

van Dijk, C. 'The Indonesian General Elections 1971–92,' *Indonesia Circle* 58, 1992, 48–66.

Djiwandono, J. Soedjati. 'Democratic Experiment in Indonesia: Between Achievements and Expectations', *Indonesia Quarterly* 15, 4, 1987, 661–9.

Djiwandono, J. Soedjati. 'Indonesia in 1988: Progress in Democratic Experiment?', *Indonesian Quarterly* 17, 4, 1989, 335–49.

Doh Chull Shin, 'On the Third Wave of Democratization: A Synthesis and Evaluation of Recent Theory and Research', *World Politics* 47, 1994, 135–70.

Domhoff, William G. *Who Rules America Now? A View for the Eighties*, Englewood Cliffs: Prentice-Hall, 1983.

Drake, P. J. *Financial Development in Malaysia and Singapore*, Canberra: Australian National University Press, 1969. Editorial, *Sunday Standard* 27 December 1955.

Ekiert, Grzegorz. 'Democratization Processes in East Central Europe: A Theoretical Reconsideration', *British Journal of Political Science* 21, 3, 1991, 285–313.

Eldridge, Philip J. *Non-Government Organizations and Democratic Participation in Indonesia*, Kuala Lumpur: Oxford University Press, 1995.

Elson, R. E. 'The Cultivation System and Agricultural Involution', Centre of Southeast Asian Studies Working Papers No. 14, Melbourne: Monash University, 1978.

Elson, R. E. 'Sugar Factory Workers and the Emergence of "Free Labour" in Nineteenth-Century Java', *Modern Asian Studies* 20, 1, 1986, 139–74.

Elson, R. E. *Village Java under the Cultivation System 1830–1870*, Asian Studies Association of Australia Publication Series #25, 1994.

Emerson, Rupert. *Malaysia: A Study in Direct and Indirect Rule*, New York: The Macmillan Company, 1937.

Emerson, Rupert. *Representative Government in Southeast Asia*, Cambridge MA: Harvard University Press, 1955.

Emerson, Rupert. *From Empire to Nation: The Rise of Self-Assertion of Asian and African Peoples*, Cambridge, MA: Harvard University Press, 1960.

Emmerson, Donald K. *Indonesia's Elite: Political Culture and Cultural Politics*, Ithaca: Cornell University Press, 1976.

Emmerson, Donald K. 'The Bureaucracy in Context: Weakness in Strength', in Karl D Jackson & Lucien W. Pye, eds, *Political Power and Communications in Indonesia*, Berkeley: University of California Press, 1978, pp. 82–136.

van der Eng, Pierre. 'Marshall Aids as a Catalyst in the Decolonization of Indonesia, 1947–1949', *Journal of Southeast Asian Studies* 19, 2, 335–52.

Engels, Friedrich. *The Peasant War in Germany*, Chicago: University of Chicago Press, 1967.

Ethier, Diane. ed. *Democratic Transition and Consolidation in Southern Europe, Latin America and Southeast Asia*, Basingstoke: Macmillan, 1990.

Ethier, Diane. 'Democratic Consolidation in Southern Europe, Latin America and Southeast Asia: Comparative Perspectives', *Journal of developing Societies* 7, 1991, 195–217.

Etzioni-Halevy, Eva. 'Democratic–elite Theory: Stabilization versus Breakdown of Democracy', *European Journal of Sociology* 31, 2, 1990, 317–50.

Evans, Peter B., Dietrich Rueschemeyer & Theda Skocpol, eds. *Bringing the State Back In*, Cambridge: Cambridge University Press, 1985.

Fasseur, C. 'Some Remarks on the Cultivation System in Java', *Acta Historiae Neerlandicae* 10, 1976, 143–62.

Fasseur. 'Purse or Principle: Dutch Colonial Policy in the 1860s and the Decline of the Cultivation System', *Modern Asian Studies* 25, 1, 1991, 33–52.

Fatah, R. Eep Saefullah. 'Dwi Fungsi ABRI dan Demokratisasi: Retrospeksi dan Prospeksi Peranan Politik Militer di Masa Orde Baru,' *Cendekia Muda* 1, 1, 1993, 5–20.

Fatimah Halim, 'Capital, Labour and the State: The West Malaysian Case,' *Journal of Contemporary Asia* 12, 3, 1982, 259–80.

Fatimah Halim. 'The State in West Malaysia,' *Race and Class* 24, 1, 1982, 33–45.

Federation of Malaya, *Report of the Working Committee Appointed by a Conference of His Excellency, the Governor of the Malayan Union, Their Highnesses The Rulers of the Malay States and the Representative of the United Malays National Organization*, Kuala Lumpur: Malayan Union Government Press, 1947.

Feith, Herbert. *The Decline of Constitutional Democracy in Indonesia*, Ithaca: Cornell University Press, 1962.

Feith, Herbert. 'Dynamics of Guided Democracy', in Ruth T. McVey, ed., *Indonesia*, New Haven: Southeast Asian Studies, Yale University, 1963, pp. 359–409.

Feith, Herbert. 'The Politics of Economic Decline', in T. K. Tan, ed., *Sukarno's Guided Indonesia*, Brisbane: Jacaranda, 1967, pp. 46–57.

Feith, Herbert. 'Suharto's Search for a Format', *Australia's Neighbors* 56–7, 1968.

Feith, Herbert. Constitutional Democracy: How Well Did it Function?, in David Bourchier & John Legge, eds, *Democracy in Indonesia: 1950s and 1990s*, Clayton, Victoria: Center of Southeast Asian Studies, Monash University, 1994.

Field, L. G. & J. Higley. *Elites and Non-Elites: The Possibilities and Their Side Effects*, Andover, MA: Warner Modular Publications, 1973.

Field, L. G. & J. Higley. *Elitism*, Boston: Routledge & Kegan Paul, 1980.

Field, L. G. & J. Higley. 'National Elites and Political Stability', in G. Moore, ed., *Research in Politics and Society: Studies of the Structure of National Elite Groups (vol. 1)*, Greenwich, CT: JAI Press, 1985, pp. 1–44.

Forster-Carter, Aidan. 'The Modes of Production Controversy,' *New Left Review* no. 107, 1978.

Frank, A. G. *Capitalism and Underdevelopment in Latin America*, New York: Monthly Review Press, 1967.

Friedman, Edward. ed. *The Politics of Democratization: Generalising East Asian Experiences*, Boulder: Westview, 1994.

Furnivall, J. S. *Colonial Policy and Practice: A Comparative Study of Burma and Netherlands India*, New York: New York University, 1956.

Gaffar, Afan. *Javanese Voters: A Case Study of Election Under a Hegemonic Party System*, Yogyakarta: Gadjah Mada University Press, 1992.

Geertz, Clifford. *Agricultural Involution: The Process of Ecological Change in Indonesia*, Berkeley, Los Angeles, & London: University of California Press, 1963.

Geertz, Clifford. *The Social History of an Indonesian Town*, Cambridge, MA: MIT Press, 1965.

Girling, John L. S. *The Bureaucratic Polity in Modernizing Societies: Similarities, Differences, and Prospects in the ASEAN Region*, Singapore: Institute of Southeast Asian Studies, 1986.

Girling, John. 'Development and Democracy in Southeast Asia', *Pacific Review* 1, 4, 1988, 320–40.

Glassburner, Bruce. 'Political Economy and the Soeharto Regime,' *Bulletin of Indonesian Economic Studies* 14, 3, 1978, 24–51.

208	*Bibliography*

Goh Cheng Teik, *The May Thirteenth Incident and Democracy in Malaysia*, Kuala Lumpur: Oxford University Press, 1971.
Goh Cheng Teik. 'Why Indonesia's Attempt at Democracy in the Mid-1950s failed', *Modern Asian Studies* 6, 2, 1972, 225–44.
Gomez, Edmund Terence. *Politics in Business: UMNO's Corporate Invest-ments*, Kuala Lumpur: Forum, 1990.
Gomez, Edmund Terence. *Political Business: Corporate Involvement of Ma-laysian Political Parties*, Townsvile, Qld: Centre for Southeast Asian Studies, James Cook University of North Queensland, 1994.
Gordon, Alec. 'Economic History versus "Agricultural Involution": Towards a Usable Past for Southeast Asia', in Peter Limqueco, ed., *Partisan Scholar-ship: Essays in Honour of Renato Constantino*, Manila & Wollongong: JCA Publishers, 1989, pp. 131–51.
Gordon, Alec. 'Imaginary Histories and the real Thing: A Critique of Ander-son and Benda on the "Autonomous State" in Indonesia', *Journal of Con-temporary Asia* 23, 4, 1993, 444–65.
Government of Malaysia. *The Second Malaysian Plan, 1971–1975*, Kuala Lumpur: Government Printer, 1971.
Government of Malaysia. *Mid-term Review of the Second Malaysian Plan*, Kuala Lumpur: Government Printer, 1973.
Grinter, Lawrence E. 'The Social Psychology of Political Development', *Southeast Asian Spectrum* 2, 1, 1973, 1–10.
Gulalp, Haldun. 'Capital Accumulation, Classes and the Relative Autonomy of the State,' *Science and Society* 51, 3, 1987, 287–313.
Gullick, J. M. *Indigenous Political Systems of Western Malaya*, London: The Athlone Press, 1958.
Gunawan, B. 'Political Mobilization in Indonesia: Nationalists Against Com-munists', *Modern Asian Studies* 7, 4, 1973, 707–15.
Gusfield, R Joseph. 'Tradition and Modernity: Misplaced Polarities in the Study of Social Change', *American Journal of Sociology* 72, 4, 1967, 351–62.
Hadiz, Vedi R. 'Politik, Budaya, dan Perubahan Sosial: Sebuah Rekonstruksi dan Kritik Terhadap Pemikiran Ben Anderson', *Prisma* 18, 2, 1989, 29–49.
Hagen, Everett E. *On the Theory of Social Change*, Homewood, IL: The Dorsey Press, 1962.
Hainsworth, Geoffrey B. 'Economic Growth and Poverty in Southeast Asia: Malaysia, Indonesia, and the Philippines,' *Pacific Affairs*, 52, 1, 1979.
Halim Salleh. 'State Capitalism in Malaysian Agriculture', *Journal of Con-temporary Asia* 21, 3, 1991, 327–43.
Hall, R. Kenneth. *Maritime Trade and State Development in Early Southeast Asia*, Honolulu: University of Hawaii Press, 1985.
Hamid Algadri C. *Snouck Hurgronje: Politik Belanda Terhadap Islam dan Keturunan Arab*, Jakarta: Penerbit Sinar Harapan, 1984.
Hamzah, A. *Korupsi dalam Pengelolaan Proyek Pembangunan*, Jakarta: Penerbit Akademika Pressindo, 1985.
Hamzah, A. *Korupsi di Indonesia: Masalah dan Pemecahannya*, Jakarta: Gramedia, 1991.
Hassan, Parvez. 'Growth and Equity in East Asia' *Finance and Development* June, 1978, 28–32.
Heng Pek Koon, *Chinese Politics in Malaysia: A History of the Malaysian*

Chinese Association, Singapore: Oxford University Press, 1988.

Heng Pek Koon. 'The Chinese Business Elite of Malaysia', in Ruth McVey, *Southeast Asian Capitalists*, Ithaca: Cornell University, 1992.

Hess, Robert D. 'The Socialization of Attitudes toward Political Authority,' *International Social Science Journal* 15, 1963, 542–59.

Higley, John & Michael G. Burton. 'The Elite Variable in Democratic Transitions and Breakdowns', *American Sociological Review* 54, 1, 1989, 17–32.

Higley, John, Ursula Hoffman-Lange, Charles Kadushin & Gwen Moore. 'Elite Integrations in Stable Democracies: A Reconsideration', *European Sociological Review* 7, 1, 1991, 35–53.

Hindess, Barry & Paul Q. Hirst, *Pre-Capitalist Modes of Production*, London & Boston: Routledge & Kegan Paul, 1975.

Hindley, Donald. 'Alirans and the Fall of the Old Order,' *Indonesia* 9, 1970, 23–66.

Hirschman, Charles. 'Economic Progress in Malaysia: How Widely Has It Been Shared?' *UMBC Review* 10, 1974, 35–44.

Holtzappel, Coen. 'The 30 September Movement; A Political Movement or an Intelligence Operation?' *Journal of Contemporary Asia* 9, 2, 1979, 216–40;

Hoselitz, Bert *et al. Theories of Economic Growth*, Glencoe, IL: Free Press, 1960.

Hua Wu Yin, *Class and Communalism in Malaysia: Politics in a Dependent State*, London: Zed Books, 1983.

Huntington, Samuel P. *Political Order in Changing Societies*, New Haven: Yale University Press, 1968.

Huntington, Samuel P. 'Will More Countries Become Democratic', *Political Science Quarterly* 99, 2, 1984, 193–218.

Huntington, Samuel P. *The Third Wave: Democratization in the Late Twentieth Century*, Norman: University of Oklahoma Press, 1991.

Huntington, Samuel P. 'Democracy's Third Wave', *Journal of Democracy* 2, 2, 1991, 12–34.

Huntington, Samuel P. 'How Countries Democratize', *Political Science Quarterly* 106, 4, 1991–2. 579–616.

Ingleson, J. *In Search of Justice: Workers and Unions in Colonial Java*, Singapore: Oxford University Press, 1986.

Ishak Shari & Rogayah M. Zain. 'Some Aspects of Income Inequality in Peninsular Malaysia 1957–70,' in H. T. Oshima & T. Mizoguchi, eds., *Income Distribution of Sector and Over Time in East and Southeast Asian Countries*, Manila: Council of Asian Manpower Studies, 1978.

Jackman, Robert W. 'On the Relation of Economic Development to Democratic Performance,' *American Journal of Political Science* 17, 3, 1973, 611–21.

Jackson, Karl. 'Bureaucratic Polity: A Theoretical Framework for the Analysis of Power and Communications in Indonesia', in Karl D. Jackson & Lucian W. Pye, eds, *Political Power and Communication in Indonesia*, Berkeley: University of California Press, 1978, pp. 82–136.

Jain, Ravindra K. *South Indians on the Plantation Frontier in Malaya*, New Haven & London: Yale University Press, 1970.

Jayasuriya, Kanishka. 'Political Economy of Democratisation in East Asia', *Asian Perspective* 18, 2, 1994, 141–80.

Jeshurun, Chandran. 'The British Foreign Office and the Siamese Malay States, 1890–97' *Modern Asian Studies* 5, 1971, 143–59.

Jeshurun, Chandran. 'Government Responses to Armed Insurgency in Malaysia, 1857–82', in Jeshurun ed., *Governments and Rebellions in Southeast Asia*, Singapore: Institute of Southeast Asian Studies, 1985, pp. 134–65.

Jesudason, James V. *Ethnicity and the Economy: The State, Chinese Business, and Multinationals in Malaysia*, Singapore: Oxford University Press, 1989.

Jesudason, James V. 'The Limits to Civil Society and Democracy in Malaysia.' Paper presented at a conference on Transition to Democracy, organized by the Friederich–Naumann Stiftung, Phuket 28 May – 1 June 1993.

Jesudason, James V. 'Statist Democracy and the Limits to Civil Society in Malaysia', *Journal of Commonwealth and Comparative Politics* 33, 3, 1995, 335–56.

Johansen, Robert C. 'Military Policies and the State System as Impediments to Democracy,' *Political Studies* 40, special issue, 1992, 99–115.

Jomo Kwame Sundaram, *A Question of Class: Capital, the State, and Uneven Development in Malaya*, Singapore: Oxford University Press, 1986.

Jomo Kwame Sundaram & Ishak Shari. 'Income Inequalities in Post-Colonial Peninsular Malaysia', *Pacific Viewpoint* 23, 1, 1982, 67–76.

Jones, David Martin. 'Asia's Rising Middle Class', *The National Interest* 38, 1994–5, 46–50.

Kahin, George M. *Nationalism and Revolution in Indonesia*, Ithaca: Cornell University Press, 1952.

Kahin, George M. 'Indonesia', in Kahin ed., *Major Governments of Asia*, Ithaca: Cornell University Press, 1963, pp. 535–700.

Kahn, Joel S. 'Indonesia After the Demise of Involution: Critique of a Debate', *Critique of Anthropology* 5, 1, 1985, 69–96.

Kamaruddin M. Said, 'Mogok dan Konflik Industri di Malaysia: Sautu Pembicaraan Awal', *Jurnal Antropologi dan Sosiologi* 7, 1979, 75–108.

Kartjono, 'Demokratisasi di Tingkat "Grassroots": Peranan Lembaga Swadaya Masyarakat,' *Prisma* 17, 6, 1988, 28–40.

Kartodirdjo, Sartono. *Protestant Movements in Rural Java: A Study of Agrarian Unrest in the Nineteenth and Early Twentieth Centuries*, Singapore: Oxford University Press, 1973.

de Kat Angelino, A. D. A. *Colonial Policy Vol 2: The Dutch East Indies*, Chicago: University of Chicago Press, 1931.

Kershaw, Roger. 'Difficult Synthesis: Recent Trends in Malay Political Sociology and History', *Southeast Asian Journal of Social Science* 16, 1, 1988, 134–58.

Kingston, Jeff. 'Agricultural Involution Among Lampung's Javanese?', *Southeast Asian Studies* 27, 4, 1990, 485–507.

Knight, G. R. 'Capitalism and Commodity Production in Java', in Hamza Alavi, P. L. Burns, G. R. Knight, P. B. Mayer, and Doug McEachern, *Capitalism and Colonial Production*, London & Sydney: Croom Helm, 1982, pp. 119–58.

Kongress Ekonomi Bumiputera. *Kertas-kertas Kerja*, Kuala Lumpur: Jabatan Cetak Kerajaan, 1965.

van der Kroef, Justus. 'Separatist Movements in Indonesia', *Southeast Asian Spectrum* 4, 4, 1976, 9–19.

Kunio, Yoshihara. *The Rise of Ersatz Capitalism in Southeast Asia*, Singapore: Oxford University Press, 1988.

Kuntjoro-Jakti, Dorodjatun. 'Pendekatan Politik Ekonomi (Politcal-Economy): Jembatan Di Antara Ilmu Ekonomi dan Ilmu Politik", *Journal Ilmu Politik* 8, 1990, 3–13.

Laclau, Ernesto. 'Feudalism and Capitalism in Latin America,' *New Left Review* no. 67, 1971, 19–38.

Lane, Max. '"Openness", Political Discontent and Succession in Indonesia: Political Developments in Indonesia 1989–91', Australia–Asia Papers no. 56, Centre for the Study of Australia–Asia Relations, Division of Asian and International Studies, Griffith University, Nathan, Qld, 1991.

Laothamatas, Anek. *Business Associations and the New political Economy of Thailand: From Bureaucratic Polity to Liberal Corporatism*, Boulder: Westview, 1992.

Lawson, Stephanie. 'Conceptual Issues in the Comparative Study of Regime Change and Democratization', *Comparative Politics* 25, 2, 1993, 183–205.

Legge, J. D. *Indonesia*, Englewood Cliffs: Prentice-Hall, 1965.

Leifer, Michael. *Dilemmas of Statehood in Southeast Asia*, Singapore: Asia Pacific Press, 1972, p. 89.

Lenin, V. I. 'The Development of Capitalism in Russia,' in Lenin, *Collected Works, Vol. 3*, Moscow: Progress Publishers, 1972.

Lenin, V. I. *Imperialism, the Highest Stage of Capitalism*, Peking: Foreign Language Press, 1975.

van Leur, J. C. *Indonesian Trade and Society*, The Hague: W. Van Hoeve, 1955.

Leys, Colin. 'The "Overdeveloped" Post-Colonial State: A Re-Evaluation', *Review of African Political Economy* 5, 1976, 40–8.

Liddle, R. William. 'Models of Indonesian Politics', Paper presented to the Department of Politics Seminar, Monash University, 1977.

Liddle, R. William. 'The Politics of *Ekonomi Pancasila*: Some Reflections on a Recent Debate', *Bulletin of Indonesian Economic Studies* 18, 1, 1982, 96–101.

Liddle, R. William. 'Indonesia in 1987: The New Order at the Height of its Power,' *Asian Survey* 28, 2, 1988, 180–91.

Liddle, R. William. 'Can All Good Things Go Together? Democracy, Growth, and Unity in post-Suharto Indonesia', in David Bourchier & John Legge, eds, *Democracy in Indonesia: 1950s and 1990s*, Monash Papers on Southeast Asia No. 31. Melbourne: Centre of Southeast Asian Studies, Monash University, 1994, pp. 287–301.

Lijphart, Arend. 'Consociational Democracy', *World Politics* 21, 2, 1969, 207–25.

Lim Chong-Yah. *Economic Development of Modern Malaya*, Kuala Lumpur: Oxford University Press, 1967.

Lim Mah Hui, 'Contradictions in the Development of Malay Capital: State, Accumulation and Legitimation,' in John G. Taylor & Andrew Turton, eds, *Sociology of Developing Societies: Southeast Asia*, Houndmills: Macmillan, 1988, pp. 19–32.

Lim Mah Hui & Douglas V. Porpora. 'Capitalism and Democracy in Malaysia', *Southeast Asian Journal* of Social Science 16, 1, 1988, 92–106.

Lim Mah Hui & William Canak, 'The Political Economy of State Policies in Malaysia,' *Journal of Contemporary Asia* 11, 2, 1981, 208–24.

Lim Teck Ghee. *Origins of a Colonial Economy: Land and Agriculture in Perak, 1874–1897*, Penang: Penerbit Universiti Sains Malaysia, 1976.

Lim Teck Ghee. 'Nongovernmental Organizations in Malaysia and Regional Networking', in Tadashi Yamamoto, ed., *Emerging Civil Society in the Asia Pacific Community: Nongovernmental Underpinnings of the Emerging Asia Pacific Regional Community*, Singapore: Institute of Southeast Asian Studies, 1995, pp. 165–81.

Lipset, S. M. 'Some Social Requisites of Democracy: Economic Development and Political Legitimacy', *American Political Science Review* 53, 1, 1959, 69–105.

Lipset, S. M. 'The Social Requisites of Democracy Revisited: 1993 Presidential Address', *American Sociological Review* 59, 1, 1994, 1–22.

Lipset, S. M., Kyong-Ryung Seong & John Charles Torres, 'A Comparative Analysis of the Social Requisites of Democracy', *International Social Science Journal* 136, 1993, 155–178.

Loong Wong, 'The State and Organised Labour in West Malaysia, 1967–1980', *Journal of Contemporary Asia* 23, 2, 1993, 214–37.

Lucas-Ruffignas, Anne E. *The Contemporary Peasantry in Mexico: A Class Analysis*, New York: Praeger, 1985.

Luckham, Robin. 'Militarism: Force, Class and International Conflict', *IDS Bulletin* 9, 1, 1978, 19–32.

MacAndrews, C. 'The Politics of Planning: Malaysia and the New Third Malaysia Plan (1976–80),' *Asian Survey* 17, 3, 1977, 293–308.

MacDougall, John A. 'Patterns of Military Control in the Indonesian Higher Central Bureaucracy,' *Indonesia* 33, 1982, 89–121.

Macintyre, Andrew. *Business and Politics in Indonesia*, Sydney: Allen & Unwin, 1990.

Mackie, J. A. C. 'Anti-Chinese Outbreaks in Indonesia, 1968–69', in Mackie ed., *The Chinese in Indonesia*, Hong Kong: Heinemann Educational Books, 1976.

Mackie, Jamie. 'Inevitable or Avoidable: Interpretations of the Collapse of Parliamentary Democracy', in David Bourchier & John Legge, eds., *Democracy in Indonesia: 1950s and 1990s*, Clayton, Victoria: Centre of Southeast Asian Studies, Monash University, 1994, pp. 26–38.

Magenda, Burhan D. 'Ethnicity and State-Building in Indonesia: the Cultural Base of the New Order', in Remo Guidieri, Francesco Pellizi & Stanley J. Tambiah, eds, *Ethnicities and Nations: Process of Interethnic Relations in Latin America, Southeast Asia, and the Pacific*, Houston: Rothko Chapel, 1988, pp. 345–61.

Mahasin, Aswab. 'State, People, and Problems of Legitimacy', *Prisma: The Indonesian Indicator*, 34, 1984, 3–12.

Mahmoud el-Jounousij. 'Editorial,' *Seruan Azhar* 1, October, 1925. Malay Mail 28 December 1955.

Mao Tse-Tung. 'Report on an Investigation of the Peasant Movement in Hunan', in Mao *Selected Works, Vol. 1*, Peking: Foreign Languages Press, 1967.

Mao Tse-Tung. 'A Report of the Front Committee to the Central Committee of the Party,' in Stuart Schram, *The Political Thought of Mao Tse-Tung*, New York: Praeger, 1976.

Martin J. Murray. *The Development of Capitalism in Indochina (1870–1940)*, Berkeley, Los Angeles & London: University of California Press, 1980.

Marx, Karl. *The Eighteenth Brumaire of Louis Bonaparte*, New York: International Publishers, 1963.

Marx, Karl. *Pre-Capitalist Economic Formations*, E. J. Hobsbawm, trans., London: Lawrence & Wishart, 1964.

Marx, Karl. *Manifesto of the Communist Party*, Peking: Foreign Languages Press, 1965.

Marx, Karl. *Capital, Vol. 3*, London: Lawrence & Wishart, 1970, p. 791.

Marx, Karl. *Contribution to the Critique of Political Economy*, Moscow: Progress Publishers, 1970.

Marx, Karl. *The German Ideology*, New York: International Publishers, 1970.

Marx, Karl. *The Class Struggle in France, 1848–1850*, Moscow: Progress Publishers, 1972.

Marx, Karl. 'India', in Karl Marx & Frederick Engels, *On Colonialism*, Moscow: Progress Publishers, 1974, pp. 77–80.

Marx, Karl. 'The Class Struggles in France,' pt. 2, in Karl Marx & Frederick Engels, *Collected Works: Volume 10, Marx & Engels, 1849–1851*, Moscow: Progress Publishers, 1978, pp. 45–145.

Mashuri, 'Pancasila Democracy', *Indonesian Quarterly* 5, 4, 1977, 32–43.

Mauzy, Diane K. 'Malaysia in 1987: Decline of the "Malay Way"' *Asian Survey* 28, 2, 1988, 213–22.

Maxwell, William E. 'Labour and Custom of the Malays with Reference to the Tenure of Land', *Journal of the Straits Branch, Royal Asiatic Society* 13, 1884, 75–220.

Maxwell, William E. 'The Law Relating to Slavery Among the Malays', *Journal of the Straits Branch, Royal Asiatic Society* 19, 1890, 247–96.

May, R. J. 'Ethnic Separatism in Southeast Asia,' *Pacific Viewpoint* 31, 2, 1990, pp. 28–43.

Mcintyre, Angus. 'The "Greater Indonesia" Idea of Nationalism in Malaya and Indonesia' *Modern Asian Studies* 7, 1, 1973, 75–83.

McVey, Ruth T. *The Rise of Indonesian Communism*, Ithaca: Cornell University Press, 1965.

Means, Gordon P. *Malaysian Politics*, London: Hodder & Stoughton, 1976.

Michels, Robert. *Political Parties*, New York: Free Press, 1962.

Miliband, Ralph. 'Marx and the State,' *Socialist Register*, London: Merlin Press, 1965.

Miliband, Ralph. *The State in Capitalist Society*, New York: Basic, 1969.

Mills, C. Wright. *The Power Elite*, New York: Oxford University Press, 1956.

Milne, R. S. & D. K. Mauzy, *Politics and Government in Malaysia*, Singapore: Federal Publications, 1977.

Milner, A. C. 'Islam and Malay Kingship', *Journal of the Royal Asiatic Society of Great Britain and Ireland* 1, 1981, 46–70.

Milner, A. C. 'Islam and the Muslim State', in M. B. Hokker, ed., *Islam in Southeast Asia*, Leiden: Brill, 1983, pp. 23–49.

Minutes of the first National Convention held under the joint sponsorship of UMNO and MCA at Kuala Lumpur, August 23, 1953.

Moeljanto, D. S. & Taufiq Ismail, *Prahara Budaya: Kilas-Balik Ofensif Lekra/ PKI Dkk*, Bandung: Mizan, 1995.

Moertono, Soemarsaid. *State and Statecraft in Old Java: A Study of the Late Mataram Period, 16th to 19th Century,* Ithaca: Modern Indonesia Project, Southeast Asia Program, Department of Asian Studies, Cornell University, 1968.

Mohamad Abdad Mohamad Zain, 'Ekonomi Politik Kabinet: Satu Peralihan Kelas di Kalangan Elit Kuasa dan Hala Himpunan Lebihan di Malaysia Kini,' *Kajian Malaysia* 7, 1/2, 1989, 38–57.

Mohamed Noordin Sopiee. 'The Advocacy of Malaysia before 1961', *Modern Asian Studies* 7, 4, 1973, 717–32.

Mohamed Noordin Sopiee. 'The Penang Secession Movement, 1948–1951', *Journal of Southeast Asian Studies* 4, 1, 1973, 52–71.

Moore, Barrington Jr. *Social Origins of Dictatorship and Democracy,* Boston: Beacon Press, 1966.

Mortimer, Rex. 'Class, Social Cleavage and Indonesian Communism,' *Indonesia* 8, 1969, 1–20.

Mosca, Gaetano. *The Ruling Class,* New York: McGraw-Hill, 1939.

Muhaimin, Yahya. *Bisnis dan Politik: Kebijaksanaan Ekonomi Indonesia 1950–1980,* Jakarta: LP3ES, 1990.

Muller, Georg P. (with the collaboration of Volker Bornschier), *Comparative World Data: A Statistical Handbook for the Social Sciences,* Baltimore & London: The Johns Hopkins University Press, 1988, pp. 240, 304.

Nagata, Judith. *The Reflowering of Malaysian Islam: Modern Religious Scandals and Their Roots,* Vancouver: University of British Columbia Press, 1984.

Nathan, K. S. 'Malaysia in 1988: The Politics of Survival', *Asian Survey* 29, 2, 1989, 129–39.

Neubauer, Deane. 'Some Conditions of Democracy', *American Political Science Review* 61, 4, 1967, 1002–9.

van Niel, Robert. *The Emergence of the Modern Indonesian Elite,* The Hague: W. van Hoeve, 1970.

Nor Azizan Idris, 'Nepotisme dalam Politik Malaysia,' *Ilmu Masyarakat* 20, 1991, 16–43.

Nordholt, N. G. Schulte. 'State–Citizen Relations in Suharto's Indonesia: Kawula-Gusti', *CASP 16,* Comparative Asian Studies Programme (CASP), Eramus University, 1987.

Notosusanto, Nugroho & Ismail Saleh. *Tragedi Nasional: Percobaan Kup G30S/PKI di Indonesia,* Jakarta: Intermasa, 1993.

NSTP, *Elections in Malaysia: Facts and Figures,* Kuala Lumpur: NSTP Research and Informations Services, 1994.

O'Donnell, Guillermo. 'Reflections on the Patterns of Change in the Bureaucratic–Authoritarian State', *Latin American Research Review* 13, 1, 1978, 3–38.

O'Donnell, Guillermo. *Modernization and Bureaucratic Authoritarianism,* 2nd edn., Berkeley: University of California, Institute of International Studies, 1979.

O'Donnell, Guillermo. 'Tensions in the Bureaucratic–Authoritarian State and the Question of Democracy', in David Collier, ed., *The New Authoritarianism in Latin America,* Princeton: Princeton University Press, 1979, pp. 285–318.

O'Donnell, Guillermo. 'Delegative Democracy', *Journal of Democracy* 5, 1, 1994, 55–69.

O'Donnell, G. & P. C. Schmitter. *Transitions from Authoritarian Rule: Tentative Conclusions About Uncertain Democracies*, Baltimore: Johns Hopkins University Press, 1986.

Onghokham. 'Elite dan Monopoli dalam Perspektif Sejarah', *Prisma* 14, 2, 1985, 3–13.

Onis, Ziya. 'The Logic of the Developmental State', *Comparative Politics* 24, 1, 1991, 109–26.

Organski, A. F. K. *The Stages of Political Development*, New York: Alfred A. Knopf, 1965.

Overzicht van de Gestie der Centraal Sarekat Islam in het jaar 1921, Weltevreden: Landsdrukkerij, 1922.

Paige, Jeffrey M. *Agrarian Revolution: Social Movements and Export Agriculture In The Underdeveloped World*, New York: The Free Press, 1975.

Palmier, Leslie. 'Indonesia's Rejection of Tradition', *Asian Affairs* 20, 2, 1989.

Panglaykim, J. *An Indonesian Experience: Its State Trading Corporations*, Jakarta: Fakultas Ekonomi, Universitas Indonesia, 1967.

Pareto, Vilfredo. *The Mind and Society*, 4 vols., New York: Harcourt Brace Jovanovich, 1935.

Parmer, J. Norman. 'Chinese Estate Workers' Strikes in Malaya in March 1937,' in C. D. Cowan, ed., *The Economic Development of Southeast Asia: Studies in Economic History and Political Economy*, London: George Allen & Unwin, 1964, pp. 154–73.

Pauker, Guy J. 'The GESTAPU Affair of 1965: Reflections on the Politics of Instability in Indonesia', *Southeast Asia* 1, 1971, 43–56.

Petras, James. 'State Capitalism and the Third World', *Development and Change* 8, 1, 1977, 1–17.

Petras, James. 'The "Peripheral State": Continuity and Change in the International Division of Labour', *Journal of Contemporary Asia* 12, 4, 1982, 415–31.

Petras, James. 'State, Regime and the Democratization Muddle', *Journal of Contemporary Asia* 19, 1, 1989, 26–33.

Pigeaud, Th. G. Th. *Java in the Fourteenth Century: A Study in Cultural History*, 5 vols, The Hague: Martinus Nighoff 1960–3.

Poggi, Gianfranco. *The Development of the Modern State: A Sociological Introduction*, Stanford, CA: Stanford University Press, 1978.

Polsby, N. W. *Community Power and Political Theory*, New Haven: Yale University Press, 1980.

Portes, A. & J. Walton. *Labor, Class and the International System*, Orlando: Academic Press, 1981.

Poulantzas, Nicos. 'Capitalism and the State,' *New Left Review* 58, 1969.

Prewitt, K. & A. Stone, *The Ruling Elites: Elite Theory, Power, and American Democracy*, New York: Harper & Row, 1973.

Putnam, R. D. *The Comparative Study of Political Elites*, Englewood Cliffs: Prentice-Hall 1976.

Pye, Lucian. *Guerilla Communism in Malaya: Its Social and Political Meaning*, Princeton: Princeton University Press, 1956.

Pye, Lucian. 'The Politics of Southeast Asia,' in Gabriel A. Almond & James S. Coleman, eds, The *Politics of Developing Areas*, Princeton: Princeton University Press, 1960, pp. 65–152.

Bibliography

Pye, Lucian. *Politics, Personality, and Nation Building*, New Haven: Yale University Press, 1962.

Quiko, Edi. 'The Rise and Fall of Sukarno: A Brief Analysis of Indonesia's Political Development, 1949–1965', *Asian Profile* 5, 5, 1977, 463–74.

Rabe, Paul. 'Dutch Colonial Economic Policy toward the Ethnic Chinese in Indonesia' *Journal of Southeast Asia Business* 8, 2, 1992, 41–57.

Rabushka, Alvin A. & Kenneth A. Shepsle, *Politics in Plural Societies: A Theory of Democratic Instability*, Columbus, OH: Merril, 1972.

Rachagan, S. Sothi. *Law and the Electoral Process in Malaysia*, Kuala Lumpur: University of Malaya Press, 1993.

Radin Soenarno, 'Malay Nationalism, 1896–1941,' *Journal of Southeast Asian History* 1, 1, 1960. 1–28.

Ratnam, K. J. *Communalism and the Political Process in Malaya*, Kuala Lumpur: University of Malaya Press, 1965.

Reeve, David. 'Sukarnoism and Indonesia's "Functional Group" State – Part One: Developing "Indonesian Democracy",' *Review of Indonesian and Malaysian Affairs* 12, 2, 1978, 43–94.

Reeve, David. 'Sukarnoism and Indonesia's "Functional Group" State – Part Two: Implementing "Indonesian Democracy",' *Review of Indonesian and Malaysian Affairs* 13, 1, 1979, 52–115.

Reid, Anthony. 'Nineteenth Century Pan Islamism in Indonesia and Malaysia', *Journal of Asian Studies* 26, 2, 1967, 276–83.

Reid, Anthony. *The Indonesian National Revolution, 1945–1950*, Hawthorn, Victoria: Longman, 1974.

Ricklefs, M. C. *A History of Modern Indonesia, c. 1300 to the Present*, Bloomington, IN: Indiana University Press, 1981.

Riggs, Fred. *Thailand: The Modernization of a Bureaucratic Polity*, Honolulu: East-West Center Press, 1960.

Robison, Richard. 'Towards a Class Analysis of the Indonesian Military Bureaucratic State,' *Indonesia* 25, 1978, 17–39.

Robison, Richard. 'Culture, Politics, and Economy in the Political History of the New Order,' *Indonesia* 31, 1981, 1–29.

Robison, Richard. *Indonesia: The Rise of Capital*, Sydney: Allen and Unwin, 1986.

Robison, Richard. 'Authoritarian States, Capital-Owning Classes, and the Politics of Newly Industrializing Countries: The Case of Indonesia', *World Politics* 41, 1, 1988, 52–74.

Robison, Richard. 'Indonesia: Tensions in State and Regime', in Kevin Hewison, Richard Robison, Gary Rodan eds, *Southeast Asia in the 1990s: Authoritarianism, Democracy and Capitalism*, St. Leonard, NSW: Allen & Unwin, 1993, pp. 41–74.

Rocamora, J. Eliseo. *Nationalism in Search of Ideology: The Indonesian Nationalist Party, 1946–1965*, Quezon City: Philippine Centre for Advanced Studies, University of the Philippines, 1975.

Roff, William R. *The Origins of Malay Nationalism*, New Haven & London: Yale University Press, 1967.

Rogers, Marvin L. 'Depoliticization of Indonesia's Political Parties: Attaining Military Stability', *Armed Forces and Society* 14, 2, 1988, 247–72.

Rosjadi, Imron. *Ichtisar Parlemen*, 1957, 31, 293.

Rostow, Walter W. *The Stages of Economic Growth: A Non-Communist Manifesto*, Cambridge: Cambridge University Press, 1961.

Rouffaer, G. P. 'Vorstenlanden', *Adatrechtbundel* 34, 81, serie D, The Hague: K. Instituut voor de Taal-, Land-, en Volkenkunde van Nederlandsch-Indies, 1931.

Rubinson, Richard. 'Dependence, Government Revenue, and Economic Growth, 1955–1970', *Studies in Comparative International Development* 12, 2, 1977, 3–28.

Rudner, Martin. 'Malayan Labor in Transition: Labor Policy and Trade Unionism, 1955–1963', *Modern Asian Studies* 7, 1, 1973, 21–45.

Rueschemeyer, Dietrich. 'Different Methods – Contradictory Results? Research on Development and Democracy', *International Journal of Comparative Sociology* 32, 1–2, 1991, 9–38.

Sadka, Emily. *The Protected Malay States, 1895–1974*, Kuala Lumpur: University of Malaya Press, 1968.

Sadli, M. 'Some Remarks on Prof. Boeke's Theory of Dualistic Economies', *Ekonomi dan Kewangan Indonesia* 10, 6, 1957, 363–84.

Santoso, Amir. 'Democracy and Parliament: Future Agenda,' *Indonesian Quarterly* 20, 1, 1992, 84–93.

Saravanamuttu, Johan 'The State, Authoritarianism and Industrialization: Reflections on the Malaysian Case,' *Kajian Malaysia* 5, 2, 1987, 43–75.

Saravanamuttu, Johan. 'Authoritarian Statism and Strategies for Democratisation: Malaysia in the 1980s', in Peter Limqueco, ed., *Partisan Scholarship: Essays in Honour of Renato Constantino*, Manila & Wollongong: JCA Publishers, 1989, pp. 233–51.

Saravanamuttu, Johan. 'The State and Democratisation: Reflections on the Malaysian Case.' Paper presented at the Joint Annual Convention of the British International Studies Association and the International Studies Association, London, 28 March – 1 April 1989.

Sarekat-Islam Congres (1e National Congres), 17–24 Juni 1916 te Bandoeng, Behoor bij de Gehime Missive van den Wd. Adviseur voor Inlandsche Zaken dd. 29 September 1916 no 226, Batavia: Landsdrukkerij, 1916.

Sarekat-Islam Congres (2e National Congres), 20–27 October 1917 te Batavia, Behoort bij de Geheime Missive van den Regeeringscommissaris voor Inlandsche en Arabische Zakan van 23 Augustus 1918 no. 416, Batavia: Landsdrukkerij, 1919.

Saul, John. 'The State in Post-Colonial Societies: Tanzania', in Saul, *The State and Revolution in Eastern Africa*, New York & London: Monthly Review Press, 1979, pp. 167–99.

Schmitt, H. 'Foreign Capital and Social Conflict in Indonesia,' *Economic Development and Cultural Change* 10, 3, 1962, 284–93.

Schmitt, Hans O. 'Post-Colonial Politics: A Suggested Interpretation of the Indonesian Experience, 1950–1958', *Australian Journal of Politics and History* 9, 2, 1963, 176–83.

Schumaker, Charles. 'The Formative Years of Malaysian Politics: The MCA and the Alliance,' unpublished manuscript.

Shahril Talib. *After Its Own Image: The Trengganu Experience, 1881–1941*, Kuala Lumpur: Oxford University Press, 1984.

Skocpol, Theda. *States and Social Revolution: A Comparative Analysis of France, Russia, and China*, Cambridge: Cambridge University Press, 1979.

Skocpol, Theda. 'What Makes Peasants Revolutionary', *Comparative Politics* 14, 3, 1982, 351–75.

Skocpol, Theda & Margaret Somers. 'The Uses of Comparative History in Macrosocial Inquiry', *Comparative Studies in Society and History* 22, 2, 1980, 174–97.

Scott, James, C. *The Moral Economy of the Peasant: Rebellion and Subsistence in Southeast Asia*, New Haven & London: Yale University Press, 1976.

Scott, James C. 'Hegemony and the Peasantry', *Politics and Society* 7, 3, 1977, 267–96.

Scott, James C. *Weapons of the Weak: Everyday Forms of Peasant Resistance*, New Haven: Yale University Press, 1986.

Scott, James C. & Benedict J. Tria Kerkvliet, eds, *Everyday Forms of Peasant Resistance in Southeast Asia*, London: Frank Cass, 1986.

Shaharuddin Maaruf. *Malay Ideas on Development: From Feudal Lord to Capitalist*, Singapore: Times Book International, 1988.

Shamsul Amri Bahruddin. 'A Revival in the Study of Islam in Malaysia,' *Man* 18, 2, 1983, 339–404.

Siddique, Sharon & Leo Suryadinata. 'Bumiputera and Pribumi: Economic Nationalism (Indiginism) in Malaysia and Indonesia,' *Pacific Affairs* 54, 4, 1981–2, 663–87.

de Silva, S. B. D. *The Political Economy of Undevelopment*, London: Routledge & Kegan Paul, 1982.

Singh, Bilveer. *Dwifungsi ABRI: The Dual Function of the Indonesian Armed Forces*, Singapore: Singapore Institute of International Affairs, 1995.

Singh, Bilveer. *East Timor, Indonesia and the World: Myths and Realities,* Singapore: Singapore Institute of International Affairs, 1995.

Sekretariat Negara Republik Indonesia, *Gerakan 30 September: Pemberontakan Partai Komunis Indonesia – Latarbelakang, Aksi, dan Penumpasannya*, Jakarta, 1994.

Smelser, Neil J. *Comparative Methods in the Social Sciences*, Englewood Cliffs, New Jersey: Prentice-Hall, 1976.

Smit, C. *De Indonesische Quaestie*, Leiden: Brill, 1952.

Snodgrass, Donald R. 'Trends and Patterns in Malaysian Income Distribution 1957–70', in David Lim, ed., *Readings in Malaysian Economic Development*, Kuala Lumpur: Oxford University Press, 1975.

Soebadi, S. 'Kartosuwiryo and the Darul Islam Rebellion in Indonesia', *Journal of Southeast Asian Studies* 14, 1, 1983, 109–33.

Stephens, John D. 'Democratic Transition and Breakdown in Western Europe, 1870–1939: A Test of the Moore Thesis', *American Journal of Sociology* 94, 5, 1989, 1019–77.

Steylen, Fridus. 'Bureaukratie Verlamt Emancipatie,' *Indonesia Feiten en Meningen* 11, 5, 1986, 20–1.

Stromquist, Shelton. 'The Communist Uprisings of 1926–1927 in Indonesia: A Reinterpretation', *Journal of Southeast Asian History*, 8, 2, 1967, 189–200.

Sukarno, *The Birth of Panca Sila: An Outline of the Five Principles of the Indonesian State*, Jakarta: The Ministry of Information, 1958.

Sundhaussen, Ulf. 'The Military: Structure, Procedures, and Effects on Indonesian Society,' in Karl D. Jackson & Lucian W. Pye, eds, *Political Power and Communications in Indonesia*, Berkeley, Los Angeles, & London: University of California Press, 1978, pp. 45–81.

Sundhaussen, Ulf. 'Indonesia: Past and Present Encounters with Democracy,' in Larry Diamond, Juan J. Linz, and Seymour Martin Lipset, eds, *Volume 3, Democracy in Developing Countries: Asia,* Boulder, CO: Lynne Rienner Publishers; London: Adamantine Press, Ltd., 1989 *Countries,* pp. 423–74.

Suryadinata, Leo. *Pribumi Indonesians, the Chinese Minority and China,* Singapore: Heinemann Asia, 1986.

Sutter, J. *Indonesianisasi: Politics in A Changing Economy, 1940–1955,* Ithaca: Department of Fareastern Studies, Cornell University, 1959, pp. 1017–35.

Swettenham, Frank. *British Malaya: An Account of the Origin and Progress of British Influence in British Malaya,* London: Allen & Unwin, 1948.

Tan Ban Teik. 'The Janggut Rebellion of 1915 in Kelantan: A Reinterpretation,' in Cheah Boon Kheng, ed., *Tokoh-tokoh Tempatan,* Pulau Pinang: Universiti Sains Malaysia, 1982, pp. 97–113.

Tan Chee Leng, 'Indonesia in 1992: Anticipating Another Soeharto Term', *Southeast Asian Affairs* 1993, 147–60.

Tan, Mely G. 'The Ethnic Chinese in Indonesia: Issues and Implications', in Leo Suryadinata, ed., *Southeast Asian Chinese: The Socio-Cultural Dimension,* Singapore: Times Academic Press, 1995, pp. 13–27.

Tan, Simon. 'The Rise of State Authoritarianism in Malaysia', *Bulletin of Concerned Asian Scholars* 22, 3, 1990, 32–42.

Taopan, M. *Demokrasi Pancasila: Analisa Konsepsional Aplikatif,* np: Sinar Grafika, 1989.

Taylor. *Indonesian Independence and the United Nations,* Ithaca: Cornell University Press, 1960.

Taylor, Charles & Michael C. Hudson. *World Handbook of Political and Social Indicators,* 2nd edn., New Haven, CT: Yale University Press, 1972.

The Siauw Giap. 'The Samin Movement in Java: Complementary Remarks', *Revue du Sud-est Asiatique* 1, 1961, 63–78.

The Siauw Giap. 'Group Conflict in a Plural Society', *Revue du Sud-est Asiatique* no. 1, 1966, 1–31.

The Siauw Giap. 'The Samin and Samat Movements in Java: Two examples of Peasant Resistance', *Revue du Sud-est Asiatique* 1, 1968, 107–14.

Thio, Eunice. 'Britain's Search for Security in North Malaya,' *Journal of Southeast Asian History* 10, 2, 1969, 279–303.

Thomas, Clive Y. 'The "Non-Capitalist Path" as Theory and Practice of Decolonisation and Socialist Transformation,' *Latin American Perspectives* 5, 2, 1978, 10–28.

Thomas, Clive Y. *The Rise of the Authoritarian State in Peripheral Societies,* New York & London: Monthly Review Press, 1984.

Thomas, K. & J. Panglaykim. *Indonesia – The Effects of Past Policies and President Suharto's Plans for the Future,* Melbourne: CEDA, 1973.

Thompson, Virginia. *Labour Problems in Southeast Asia,* New Haven: Yale University Press, 1947.

Tichelman, F. *The Social Evolution of Indonesia: The Asiatic Mode of Production and its Legacy,* The Hague: Martinus Nijhoff, 1980.

Timberlake, Michael & Kirk R. Williams, 'Dependence, Political Exclusion, and Government Repression: Some Cross-National Evidence,' *American Sociological Review* 49, 1, 1984, 141–6.

Tirtosudarmo, Riwanto. 'Indonesia 1991: Quest for Democracy in a Turbulent Year', *Southeast Asian Affairs* 1992, 123–39.

220   *Bibliography*

Tokei, Ferenc. 'Le Mode de Production Asiatique dans l'Oeuvre de K. Marx et F. Engels,' *La Pensée* no. 114, 1964, 7–32.

Tornquist, Olle. *Struggle for Democracy – A New Option in Indonesia?*, Uppsala: The AKUT series no. 33, University of Uppsala, 1984.

Tornquist, Olle. 'Rent Capitalism, State, and Democracy: A Theoretical Proposition,' in Arief Budiman, ed., *State and Civil Society in Indonesia*, Clayton, Vic.: Centre of Southeast Asian Studies, Monash University, 1990, pp. 29–49.

Tregonning, K. G. 'The Failure of Economic Development and Political Democracy in Southeast Asia', *Asian Studies* 5, 2, 1967, 323–31.

Tunku Abdul Rahman Putra Al-Haj. *May 13: Before and After*, Kuala Lumpur: Utusan Melaya Press, 1969.

Turner, Bryan S. *Marx and the End of Orientalism*, London: George Allen & Unwin, 1978.

Uhlin, Anders. 'Transnational Democratic Diffusion and Indonesian Democracy Discourses', *Third World Quarterly* 14, 3, 1993, 517–44.

Uhlin, Anders. 'Indonesian Democracy Discourse in a Global Context: The Transnational Diffusion of Democratic Ideas', Working Paper no. 83, Centre of Southeast Asian Studies, Monash University, Clayton, Vic., 1993.

Utrecht, Ernst. 'Army and Opposition in Indonesia', *Journal of Contemporary Asia* 9, 2, 1979.

Vandenbosch, Amry. *The Dutch East Indies: Its Government, Problems, and Politics*, Berkeley & Los Angeles: University of California Press, 1941.

Vatikiotis, Michael R. J. *Indonesian Politics Under Suharto: Order, Development and Pressure for Change*, London: Routledge, 1993.

van der Veen, Hans. 'Staats Obstakel voor Industrialisering,' *Indonesia Feiten en Meningen* 11, 5, 1986, 8–9.

van der Veen, Hans. 'Militarisering en Bureaukratisering Versterken Totalitair Karakter Indonesische Natie,' *Indonesia Feiten en Meningen* 11, 5, 1986, 16–18.

Vollenhoven, C. van. *Javaansch Adatrecht*, Leiden: E. J. Brill, 1923.

von Vorys, Karl. *Democracy Without Consensus: Communalism and Political Stability in Malaysia*, Princeton: Princeton University Press, 1975.

Wade, Robert. *Governing the Market: Economic Theory and the Role of Government in East Asian Industrialization*, Princeton: Princeton University Press, 1990.

Wahid, Abdurrahman & Dorodjatun Kuntjoro-Jaki. 'Government Responses to Armed Communist and Separatist Movements in Indonesia: Islamic and Military Perspectives,' in Jeshurun ed., *Governments and Rebellions in Southeast Asia*, Singapore: Institute of Southeast Asian Studies, 1985, pp. 166–79.

Weber, Max. *Economy and Society: An Outline of Interpretive Sociology*, Guenther Roth & Claus Wittich, eds, Berkeley, Los Angeles, & London: University of California Press, 1978.

Weffort, Francisco C. 'What is a "New Democracy"', *International Social Science Journal* 136, 1993, 245–56.

Wertheim, W. F. *Indonesian Society in Transition: A Study of Social Change*, The Hague & Bandung: W. Van Hoeve, 1959.

Wertheim, W. F. *East-West Parallels: Sociological Approaches to Modern Asia*, The Hague: W. van Hoeve, 1964, pp. 76–7.

Wertheim, W. F. 'From Aliran Toward Class Struggle in the Countryside of Java', *Pacific Viewpoint* 10, 2, 1969, 1–17.

Wertheim, W. F. *Evolution and Revolution: The Rising Waves of Emancipation*, Harmondsworth: Penguin 1974.

Wertheim, W. F. 'Whose Plot? – New Light on the 1965 Events', *Journal of Contemporary Asia* 9, 2, 1979, 196–215.

White, Benjamin. 'Agricultural Involution and its Critics: Twenty Years After Clifford Geertz', Institute of Social Studies Working Paper Series 6, The Hague: Institute of Social Studies, 1983.

Wolf, Eric. R. *Peasant Wars of the Twentieth Century*, New York: Harper & Row, 1969.

Wolf, Eric R. *Europe and the People Without History*, Berkeley, Los Angeles, & London: University of California Press, 1982.

Wong, David. *Land Tenure and Land Dealings in the Malay States*, Singapore: Singapore University Press, 1975.

Wood, E. M. 'The Separation of the Economic and the Political in Capitalism', *New Left Review* 127, 1981, 66–95.

Yahya Muhaimin. 'Muslim Traders: The Stillborn Bourgeoisie', Prisma 49, 1990. 83–90.

Young, C. F. 'Origins and Development of the Malayan Communist Movement, 1919–1930', *Modern Asian Studies* 25, 4, 1991.

Zakaria Haji Ahmad. 'Malaysia', in Zakaria Haji Ahmad & Harold Crouch, eds., *Military–Civilian Relations in Southeast Asia*, Singapore: Oxford University Press, 1985, pp. 118–35.

Zakaria Haji Ahmad. 'Malaysia: Quasi Democracy in a Divided Society,' in Larry Diamond, Juan J. Linz, and Seymour Martin Lipset, eds, *Volume 3, Democracy in Developing Countries: Asia*, Boulder, CO: Lynne Rienner Publishers; London: Adamantine Press, Ltd., 1989, pp. 347–81.

Zainur Zakaria, 'The 1994 Constitutional Amendments: The End of Judicial Independence', *Aliran Monthly* 14, 5, 1994, 10–11.

Zhao Ding-xin & John A. Hall, 'State Power and Patterns of Late Development: Resolving the Crisis of the Sociology of Development', *Sociology* 28, 1, 1994, 211–29.

Ziemann W. & M. Lanzendorfer, 'The State in Peripheral Societies', in Ralph Miliband & John Saville, eds, *The Socialist Register*, London: Merlin Press, 1977, pp. 143–77.

Newspapers and magazines
Dewan Masyarakat
Gatra
Het Vrije Woord
Inside Indonesia
Jakarta Post
Neratja
Seruan Azhar
Straits Times
Suara Pembaruan
Utusan Melayu

Index

Aas, S., 86
abangan (commoners, Java), 88
Abas, M. S., 4, 159
Abduh, M., 99
Abdulgani, R., 146–7
ABIM (Malaysian Muslim Youth
    Movement), 143–4
Abrahamian, E., 51
ABRI (Indonesia), 161
Aceh, 45, 161
Adas, M., 82
Africa, 153
Agrarian Law (Netherlands Indies,
    1870), 57
agriculture
    in Malaya, 59
    in Netherlands Indies, 57
Aidit, 139
AJI (Independence Alliance of
    Journalists, Indonesia), 156, 159
Alavi, H., 15, 34–8, 64–6, 71, 153
Alexander, J. and P., 87
Alfian, 159
Al-Hadi, Syed Sheikh Ahmad, 99
aliran, 88–9, 146
All-Indonesian National Economic
    Congress (Kensi), 130
Almond, G. A., 25
Ambonese Union (Sarekat Ambon), 107
Amin, S., 53, 63
Anderson, B. R. O., 111
Anshary, I., 145
Apter, D. E., 26
Aquino, C. (Philippine President), 8, 11
Aron, R., 2
Asiatic mode of production, 51–3
Aung San Suu Kyi (Burmese leader), 13
authoritarian state
    and bourgeoisie, weak, 24
    defined, 2
    elite class, conflict among, 154
    stability of, 16
authoritarianism, 15–16
    and bureaucracy, 33–4
    cultural theories of, 19–21
    and economic dependency, 32–3
    in Malaysia, 159–60
    psychological approach to, 19

and strength of state, 154
Avengers of the Country (Pembela
    Tanah Air, Peta), 105, 110

Baars, A., 97
Badan Panyelidik Usaha Persiapan
    Kemerdekaan (Indonesia), 105
Baharuddin, S. A., 143
Bakker, J. I., 51, 52
Bangladesh, 35, 36
Banjarmasin, 45
Bank Negara Indonesia (National Bank
    of Indonesia), 128
Bank of Indonesia, 128
Bank Industri Negara (National
    Industrial Bank, Indonesia), 128
Barisan Nasional (BN, Malaysia), 120
bengkok (salary-fields), 48, 52
Benteng programme (Indonesia), 128–9,
    138
Berdikari programme (Indonesia), 138
Bijenkomst voor Federaal Overleg
    (Federal Consultative Assembly,
    Indonesia), 117
BN (Barisan Nasional, Malaysia), 120
Boeke, J. H., 61, 65, 66, 76, 85–6
Bollen, K. A., 29, 160
Bonaparte, Napoleon, 27, 118
Borneo, 45, 109
Bornschier, V., 29
bourgeoisie, 23–4
    in core-periphery relations, 33
    and mass movements, 73
    in post-colonial state, 36–7
British Malaya
    economy of, 58–9, 85
    government of, 23
    income sources and mass movements,
        73
    labour unions in, 77–8
    mobilization of peasants in, 72–3
    nationalism in: contrasts with
        Netherlands Indies, 101–3; forms
        of, 106–9; and Japanese
        occupation, 103–6; leadership in,
        101–2; and Malayan Union
        scheme, 112–13; organizations,
        99–100